Converse with One Earthly

Converse with One Earthly

Beyond Magic, Half
Answer, Match Leftright

Jeannie Chen;
Cheng Hsiu Chen

Library of Congress Control Number:		2017913408
ISBN:	Hardcover	978-1-5434-4820-7
	Softcover	978-1-5434-4821-4
	eBook	978-1-5434-4822-1

Print information available on the last page.

Rev. date: 08/30/2017

To order additional copies of this book, contact:
Xlibris
1-888-795-4274
www.Xlibris.com
Orders@Xlibris.com
713110

CONTENTS

CHAPTER ONE

The Book Title and Etcetera

In the title, one can mean a high spirit or a general spirit within a person. A reader of this book who strives to reach spirituality and Tao is one unique and special individual. All spirits are from God and no gender difference; therefore, it is one. After one become two, or yin and yang, or women and men, it is no longer one. Uniting yin and yang within either a male or a female will return him or her back to one to be later united with God after physical death.

All spirits are capable of creating magic whether they know it or not, but a person should look beyond the magical power and focus on spiritual merits, particularly the five merits mentioned in our last book and this. Divination from high spirits or God provides only half of the answer for all questions asked. The other half of the answer lies within the principle reasoning of people. Left and right indicate yang and yin, man and woman, or Democratic and Republican. Their differences need to be reconciled to put back to become a person, one family, or one nation.

In this book, we use the term *high spirits* to include *God* and to broaden the scope to those who do not or not totally believe in God and to enable the teaching of this material in public school, which cannot involve religious teaching. High spirits means the noble or exalted spirits who have successfully learned and practiced Tao on earth. They can be dead or alive physically, and they can be famous saints or inconspicuous in history.

Many unsung heroes exist in almost every country's history. Their spirits, though less famous, may not be lower than those publicly exalted and famous. Though many high spirits possess power conferred by God, not all high spirits wish to use such power. Although capable of achieving God's will and helping Tao, the use of such power has its risk and reward; overuse can risk the soundness of one's own spirituality, and underuse can cause dissatisfaction. The reward is the satisfaction of a mission accomplished. Frequently, they use such power to alleviate secular pain and suffering, as Jesus Christ once did on earth.

Many tales of the gods and goddesses using such power to rescue imminently endangered ships on the sea were recorded in many cultures. Such magical lifesaving events usually happened after people on the ship prayed to a deity they believed in. High spirits' power can also be used to answer believers' questions as we wrote in our last book. God often delegates gods and goddesses to do things for him or her. As we discussed before, God can be a male or a female, or even one of each.

We used the phrase *high spirits* instead of *holy spirits* to avoid limiting our scope to only Christianity, which uses father, son, and Holy Spirit as trinity. When we say *high spirits*, they may indicate any one or many of the following from the East or the West: Buddha, Confucius, Jesus Christ, or successful disciples in various religions with high spirituality. History of both the East and the West documented their exceptional deeds on earth. Though high spirits mostly mean those who are deceased, but they need not be.

Practicing spirituality to a great level, some living people have high spirits too; nonetheless, they are rare. Most people on earth are subjected to the examination the spiritual world imposes. As we discussed in our previous book, any person with good spiritual practice might erode their heart at the last moment of life and be condemned. Every moment of a person's life counts, even the last one. Good spiritual practitioners know it well and watch out every second of their life.

We chose the phrase *high spirits* instead of simply *spirits* for a good reason. Just like different people can have different levels of spirituality, spirits can be high or low spirited depending on their deeds and mentality on earth. Similar to mean people, mean spirits perversely love to sabotage others for no apparent reason, or simply to seek pleasure in watching others suffer. These low-level spirits can cause accident or mishap at the moment of any carelessness by a human.

Some movies and musicals use *high spirits* in their titles to refer to ghosts. The high spirits referred to in our book are the spirits who feel joyful and prided as defined in many dictionaries. Low and mean spirits usually do not have these feelings. Like those people who seek revenge often do not feel joy after retaliation, the mean spirits feel a short moment of ecstasy from watching the pain of the hated. Most ignoble spirits have no real joy.

We chose the word *earthly* to emphasize the practicality of conversing with a high spirit, to hope our voices are heard throughout the earth, and to convey the unselfish facet of pure love in our spirits. All authors have good encounters with such conversation; many readers testified their similar encounter too as shown in chapter 2. We cannot emphasize enough that errors and mistakes occur from time to time, but for the most part the resulting answers were consistent, highly accurate, and practical for the spiritual good of the inquirer.

Though the author names on this book are different from our last, the composition of authors has not changed much. All the books are the result of cooperative efforts of many authors and high spirits. Deciding whose name on which book is up to high spirits or God, not the authors. Any author can choose a pen name to be approved. Plus, the authors are merely the originators of ideas, which must ultimately be approved by high spirits or God before being published, one paragraph at a time, painfully.

The authors sincerely hope that our perspectives and ideas be propagated to all citizens on earth. Citizens make up each country, not governments or social elites. Governments ought to be of the people, by the people, and for the people in the truest sense of a true democracy as we discussed in our last book. We will elaborate further on how a true democracy can replace representative democracy in chapter 13.

With the authors' pure love, we wrote this and the last books. One of the major attributes of high spirits is Ren or pure love. The highest love is the unselfish love toward total strangers. We do not need to know you in person because we have known you as a spiritual person like us. Pure love from one spirit to another is without bound and unselfish. We wrote the books to try to do our best to wake up all spirits on earth. Some may call it foolish, but sometimes people being too smart cannot love others purely and unselfishly.

Some readers reflected to us that our previous book was condescending, and we agree to a certain extent though we never meant it. The post office box in our first book is no longer valid. We switched all communication with readers to conversewith20001@gmail.com. With the approval of God or high spirits, we disclose here one of the easiest ways of consulting God: yes or no, with just two objects with both positive and negative sides each.

Two objects have four possible combinations. One positive and one negative mean yes; two positives or two negatives means no. Consultation with only two objects is easy enough that anybody can do it. One only needs to think hard on the kind of questions to ask and formulate all inquiries to elicit a yes or no answer. Using one object with positive and negative sides can work too, but it may be riskier than two objects. The error rate might increase.

The same as in the last book, every paragraph of this book has to be checked and passed in divination. Some mediocre answers exist in the thirty-two words in divination; a mediocre answer means not good and not bad. Usually we do not perform a deed when a mediocre answer appears in a divination unless there is no alternative or we extremely wish to do it. Doing it will likely result in waste of time with little or no help to the practice of Tao. Though monetary gain may result, such as a clinical trial that pays a lot of money, it is not worth the effort.

A minimally good range means this paragraph will be at least beneficial to some readers. If a paragraph does not reach the minimum, we have to find out why from the divination answer. A mediocre answer usually means this paragraph does not have any serious wrong; it just needs to be polished or clarified, to adjust the tone, to correct redundancy, or to do others. A bad answer often means some word or concept is seriously wrong or mistaken.

If a paragraph does not pass a divination, we try to figure out what may be wrong and fix it; then, another divination is done. If several attempts at the scanning level have not succeeded, going into the sentence level and doing divination one sentence at a time become necessary. After one or few sentences are pinpointed via divination, those sentences are checked in detail to determine what may be wrong.

Some authors have better senses than others about whether a paragraph will pass a divination or not. Most people are better at detecting grammatical error at some moment than others, like when one is very sleepy or just waken up. The same thing happens with trying to find what exactly is wrong with a paragraph. Some authors are sharp enough to pinpoint a few words out of a whole paragraph right away; while others have to go down to the sentence level frequently.

This laborious process could not be avoided. Pressured by deadline, we once were thinking about doing divination one chapter or one section at a time. But even one page at a time was denied in divination, and even citations need to pass divination. This process of quality check on every paragraph takes us around two months to complete. Most of us are exhausted, but we are happy to do it for each reader.

Differences between This Book and the Last

Our last book asked readers to read from the first chapter to the last in strict order to increase stamina and resilience of completely finishing one task at a time diligently and carefully. In this book, however, readers are welcome to read based on needs and preferences. Scan the beginning of this book where a list of all chapter titles appears to decide. People who feel that they have no sufficient faith in spirituality should read testimonies in chapter 2 first to boost faith.

Readers who wish to know the ultimate purpose of our writings can first read the last chapter on Datong World. Knowing the end, the beginning is likely easier to read and justify, especially from the fifth to ninth chapters. Some chapters we suggest to read first are the second, fourth, tenth, eleventh, twelfth, and sixteenth chapters. The twelfth chapter is probably the most difficult chapter. Reading chapter 4 several times before reading chapter 12 may help.

In addition, in this book we reference a lot back to our first book, but our previous book can be read after finishing reading this. This book is more organized than our last, and some people may not fully understand our points at some places when reading our last book alone. The differences in authors' spiritual maturity may have contributed to the disparity between the two books.

The writings of our two books are roughly five years apart, the spiritual maturity level can be expected to change in this timeframe for most spiritual practitioners, especially when they follow divination results. The lessons from the above guide us toward the right way or Tao. Less than 5 percent of the world's population is walking on Tao now; even we the authors are not sure whether we are close.

Deviation from Tao is like a lost sheep walking away from a shepherd to a place with little protection. A careless accident is rarely a pure one; it is often due to the deprivation of the umbrella from the shepherd. Walking on Tao may provide 70 percent of coverage; the rest depends on how well the spiritual practitioner progresses toward Tao. One who seeks only comfort and protection and not advancement is likely to rust.

More than two-thirds of this book was written in the final month before submitting the book's manuscript; less than one-third was written five to six months prior. Though we spend a lot of effort to try to finish this book on schedule based on directives from divinations, we feel that the qualities of our later two-thirds of writing were better than those of the earlier one-third.

A book differs from a person in that one is dead and the other alive. The need to be consistent with oneself is one of the five merits discussed in chapter 7. A person needs to attempt to achieve consistency on all fronts, but a book does not need to. The inconsistency within this book demonstrates the consistency of authors to reveal all truth, including our stages of spiritual growth.

An outline of this book is provided after the last chapter. Textbooks in schools and colleges should have similar outlines appended to help the study. The writing of outlines has not received enough attention in school that most students still write one paragraph before outlining. Writing paragraphs sequentially should only occur when one does not have a clear sight of what to write, and have only vague and general ideas. Outlining should be done at least 95 percent of the time.

Writing without an outline should be soon after followed by an outline-writing on what has been written to integrate into the main text. A vague or general idea can happen especially when the mind does not know exactly what to write but the spirit does. Largely untapped source of truth, most spirits can surprise the minds with the extensive depth the spirits can touch. Several authors were stunned at the depth of our own writing too from time to time, especially in the last month of our writing.

The detailed outlines at the book end do not always match the main text. You are encouraged to check carefully before using it as a study guide. The best way is to establish your own outlines with the option of starting from our outlines and modifying it while reading. One's own outline is less difficult to memorize than one from the authors.

In the outlines, the number of paragraphs within a chapter is shown in the parentheses following the title of the chapter. The number in parentheses at the end of each sectional title means the same. At the end of each topic sentence, a number following a capitalized X indicates the number of paragraphs for that topic sentence. One line of topic sentence may include several topic sentences, which may not be possible if syntax rule is followed strictly.

The outlines also have some commonly used abbreviations and symbols to shorten the length of the topic sentences. For example, education is shortened as *edu*, and management to *mgmt*. Simple mathematical symbols such as equal sign =, greater than sign >, and less than sign < are used with the same meanings. Readers are advised to use as many symbols as possible in their own outlines, just be sure that they will be understood later. We reduce our use of symbols to accommodate the common sense of most readers.

In the outlines, prepositions are also omitted when meanings are clear. Verb, noun, adjective, and adverb may be interchanged if the meanings remain unaffected. A past or future tense word may be replaced with a present tense. Not each outline sentence encompasses all that is written in the corresponding paragraphs. This is another reason why readers are encouraged to create their own outlines.

We the authors still have a long way to go before actually walking on Tao, but we do our best to encourage each other on this difficult and uncertain journey. Any feedback from readers would also contribute to our spiritual growth, whether positive or negative. If you would like to contribute or have any question from our last book or this, you can write to us via email.

CHAPTER TWO

Testimonies of Readers and Others

Many readers have given us their feedback pertaining to the accuracy of divination. Here, we only publish some that are worthy of notice. Bear in mind that no matter how accurate consultations with high spirits or God are, some errors might always exist. Either high spirits purposely mix them into the accurate ones to test the person, or the errors are caused by mistakes of self.

Testimonies on Health and Food

The first testimony is on the use of vinegar to physical health. A lady in Wisconsin wrote that a few weeks prior to their visit to her sister a divination indicated that she should not buy a bottle of vinegar then as she was about to. She had some early signs of arthritis, but she did not know why she was advised not to buy vinegar at the time. After they arrived at her sister's home, a book introducing the health benefits of vinegar was lying on their couch.

Her sister borrowed the book from a library earlier that day. She picked it up and read the prologue. Besides mentioning many potential benefits of vinegar, the prologue indicated that vinegar was not good for people with rheumatoid arthritis, which her mother had a serious case of before passing away few years prior. She mentioned the prologue and warned her sister about the potential danger of causing arthritis with vinegar.

Another testimony is from a man living in Florida. Growing up in Asia, he ate a lot of rice. A few years ago, he consulted God on whether a diet of mostly noodle or of mostly rice was better for his health, and God indicated that most noodle and flour products would be good. He faithfully followed God's instruction without knowing the reason. Recently, he discovered from an encyclopedia that all rice contain small amounts of arsenic. He realized that might be the main reason for the result of divination. Another possible reason was that flour products are better suited to his physical condition.

A third testimony is about addiction to sweet food. A woman in New York liked to eat sweet food such as cake, donut, candy, toffee, soda, pie, croissant, turnover, muffin, chocolate, cookie, and cinnamon roll. Some grocery stores sell nearly expired sweet leftovers at a huge discount. She craved those delicious and inexpensive sweets, but divination indicated that soda was not good for her. She later refrained from even buying it from time to time. Her divination might seem redundant to many health-conscious people, but divination likely saved her from a lot of diseases caused by sweets.

God indicated that the high fructose corn syrup was the main reason of staying away from soda; later, she recalled that such syrup was reported extensively on a television program as the culprit for teenage obesity. Each time she desired some particular nearly expired food displayed at the back of a store, she would consult high spirits on each individual item. Except red velvet cake, other cakes were not advised most of the time. It was probably due to their high sugar content and low nutrient value.

She indicated that cake, pie, donut, muffin, and chocolate were the most often denied items, yet she favored them the most. Though extremely reluctant, she put them back on the shelf because she felt her own belly overly grown from time to time too. Though not to the point of being obese, she knew heart diseases and diabetes can be caused by too much body fat. She understood God's restrictions were for her own good, so she obeyed.

Another kind of food she liked was eight-piece fried chicken. Occasionally, when hot chicken was not on sale, she bought refrigerated and nearly expired chicken. Several times, she did not encounter any problem after eating them. Last time, she got diarrhea from cold chicken from a reputable grocery store chain. Later she thought maybe God tried to teach her a lesson that all nearly expired food must be consulted before purchase.

She was wrong. God indicated that the reason for her getting diarrhea was excessive frequency of buying fried chicken and her overly indulged desire for tasty food, which hurt her spirituality. Though fried chicken was tasty and somewhat nutritious, God indicated that twice a month would be sufficient for health. It was not due to the excessive fat of fried chicken either, as some fats were needed by the body.

Another testimony about food is from a man in Missouri who expressed gratitude for not eating too many strawberries due to divination. He liked strawberries since childhood, but for some reason, divination had been denying many requests to buy. Though baffled by the answers, he resisted the desire to buy them many times. Lately, news on a pesticide study shed light on the reason: strawberry was listed as the fruit with the most pesticide residue among all fruits. (Ref 1, Ref 2)

Testimonies on Addictions

One reader was courageous enough to share the secret of pornographic addiction. His addiction to pornography began at childhood. He thanked God for keeping him in check with a religious family and busy school years. Realizing his Achilles' heel, he voluntarily asked God as to the timing of each intercourse. One time, he violated his own words. Within one hour, he was stopped by two different police officers in two cities for a broken headlight while none had happened for the previous couple of months. He repented and realized how quickly God could come upon him.

One of the testimonies above about excessive food desire hurting a spirit is akin to this testimony about excessive sexual desire; excessive desire hurts spirituality like a hot knife cutting into butter. Food and sex are essential for grown adults, but overly indulged desires relax the mind too much to the point of near corruption. Immoderate desires for money, power, fame, food, sex, and happiness draw the mind toward materialism and tip the balance between a person's spiritual side and material side.

A mind tipping either toward the spirit or toward the body would cloud its judgment. Leaning too much toward the spirit, a mind tends to lose touch with the reality or creates too much fanciful thinking. Leaning too much toward the body, a mind tends to get addicted easily or embarks on overly dangerous activities. Similar to walking on a balance beam, a mind must balance between the spirit and the body. Further discussion of this topic is in chapter 10 on balance of merits.

This testimony reminds us of several magical stories during World War II. One of them happened in China that a well-known goddess of China shielded a believer from being seen by a group of Japanese soldiers. Being accused of spying the previous day, that believer was in plain sight of the soldiers walking by.

Another happened to be a medic who was religious and served in the United States Marines during World War II. Decades after the war, the Japanese soldiers reported that every time they tried to shoot that medic when he was rescuing a fellow marine, their machine gun jammed for no reason whatsoever. It happened several times, only with that medic.

We want to stress once again that divination is not error free. Most errors are correctable with common sense. Do not be discouraged if you encounter some errors, especially those easily spotted. Also, many blessings from high spirits hide behind the scenes that we often do not even see them, such as a major accident totally avoided or its severity greatly reduced. Nothing in this world is truly free, except maybe blessings from high spirits or God. The faith and conformity to divination speak volumes to high spirits to confer such blessings.

Testimonies on Magical Events

One of the authors served in military and told other authors about a magical event his military buddy encountered. He shared a room with two other servicemen on base. The room was built very securely and locked at night when they slept. One morning, his buddy Joe showed him eight words on his left hand that magically appeared during the previous night. Joe said that he had a strange dream in which he kneeled down to accept something from someone, both of which were invisible to him.

Though invisible, Joe sensed the existence of the spirit and the authority it represented. The something received seemed to be a mission of some sort, but Joe had no idea what kind of mission that was. Joe asked the author and the third roommate whether they pulled a plank on him, but they denied any involvement.

The first two words meant engagement before a marriage; the second two words meant drumming up. The third two words meant election or electing someone, the same as electing a government official or representative; the fourth two words meant being bestowed a girlfriend. One strange thing to the very last word was that it was not found in any dictionary at all.

The author and another roommate explained to Joe that it was impossible to pull a prank like that because of the way those words appeared. To pull a prank, one could obtain a paper with the typed words and not yet dried ink. Pressing the paper on the hand for a few seconds would transfer the ink onto the palm. The words should have appeared as a mirror image due to the inversion process. Nevertheless, the eight words were not a mirror image.

In addition, the last word had never been seen before, though the word could be read with two sides with the left-hand side meaning moon and the right-hand side meaning friend. *Moon* is often used to describe females due to its *yin* property, so the last word could mean *girlfriend*. Wishing to pull a prank on Joe, a person would have to create an iron cast of the word first due to its rarity; it would likely be too much trouble for a prank.

Joe was not a superstitious person, but the words had him baffled without a scientific explanation. Afterward, Joe tried to erase the words and found that they were easily erasable. The ink used to print the words seemed to be quite ordinary. Unable to find any explanation, Joe soon put the incident in the back of his mind.

After that event, Joe had pretty ordinary days for the remainder of his service. That author kept contact with Joe after their services. One day, the author met Joe and had coffee together. Joe showed the author a piece of paper from a temple. Joe said that he never intended to go to any temple, but one day his coworkers at the restaurant he worked at gathered together and planned a trip to a temple at the top of a mountain. He was reluctant but finally agreed to go along.

When Joe and his coworkers arrived, all his coworkers wanted to ask for a piece of advice from a box which automatically drops a small ball containing the advice. Joe followed others to get a piece of advice for fun. The most amazing part was the corresponding meanings between the piece of advising paper and the eight words on his hand years earlier. A poem with four sentences was written on the advising paper.

The first sentence of the poem started out saying that it was nearly impossible to dodge the responsibility arrived at hand, no matter how reluctant you are to perform the task. The second sentence stated that you would sing, drink, and wander around for some time to come. The third sentence said that the news would be near between the year of chicken and dog. The fourth sentence stated that the marriage will be for the rest of your life.

Joe told the author that he was confused about the relationship between a duty and mission with girlfriend and marriage. He was also stunned by the matching meanings between what was on his hand and what was on that piece of paper. The two events were years apart. Joe is still single today.

The authors have no explanation either, except to say that we are as amazed at the incidents as Joe is. Just like what we wrote in our last book, where a family sent a fax to their house and magically stopped the wildfire from being spread to their house, the house owner could not explain it either. A lot of events happened to individuals who had no scientific explanation whatsoever.

Complacent Hurts

If not so directed specially in a divination, any prior divination result cannot be carried over to a similar event in the future. Failing to ask again when a similar event arises may result in heartache and monetary loss.

One of the authors did clinical trials at times. Once, he found a clinical trial at a distance of close to one hundred miles away. Though it would take some gas money to get there, he figured that the compensation for the screening alone would probably be enough to cover it if he failed the screening. Negligently, he failed to ask for the approval of the project. His later request to travel there, though approved, did not represent the approval of participating in that clinical trial.

After one day of travel and arriving at the doctor's office at Ventura, California, he felt strange about the procedure of that clinic. The staff at the clinic asked him to sign an agreement to pay if the insurance failed to. Normally, a clinical trial office does not ask test subjects to sign a promise to pay. Most clinical trials ask people to sign an agreement or contract of ten to thirty pages. It usually lists the purpose of a clinical trial, the potential risks, the amount of compensation, and other related information.

Unaware of the existence of any potential fake clinical trial, the author signed it. To his surprise, he did not qualify for the clinical trial after the blood work came back. A few months afterward, he found a bill from that doctor's office in the mail asking $800 for the two visits and the lab work. Dismayed, he filed a complaint with the Better Business Bureau, but the doctor did not respond to BBB after one month. Later, he also filed a complaint with the medical board.

After the Better Business Bureau put his complaint to rest, the author filed the case as potential fraud to con any unsuspecting innocent people also at BBB. A few days after such filing, he received a phone call from the female physician at that clinical trial to request a reversal of the fraud filing at BBB. In return, she would withdraw the $800 charge and mail a check to compensate for the gas money. Such a check was never received by that author. The physician also claimed that she was unaware of the $800 billing, but her staff had told the author that the female doctor always handled all her billing.

For that author, this incident created some headaches, which could likely have been avoided if he simply asked for approval before deciding to embark on the long journey. Past divination results cannot be carelessly applied to future events or purchase of food or material. Whether a result can be carried over to all future incidents needs to be clearly asked using the yes or no question. The headaches of the author amounted to more than the loss of gas money. Complacency can hurt like hell.

As we disclosed in our last book, some of the authors live in their cars at times. Such a living arrangement was not always approved when asked in a divination. Timing and condition may be some of the considerations by high spirits. Though living in a car can save living expenses as a fringe benefit, no author ever had a serious financial problem to the point of being unable to afford a rental place.

Mind sharpening and discipline on excessive television watching were some of the major reasons. Other advantages include ease of moving around, change of environment to help the mind, and spending more time at public places but not at home. Of course, the major disadvantage is the inconvenience.

One time, one of the authors was living in a car parked at an affluent area with high walls around the house and was getting ready to spend the night there. A stream of water sprayed over the fence onto the car roof as soon as the engine stopped running. Right away, that author perceived that the house occupant was not happy about parking there overnight, though no sign was posted to prohibit such parking at that street. That author drove the car away immediately.

Another time, another author felt that someone was nearby and was touching her car when she was sleeping. Out of complacence near bedtime, she did not go out to check what went wrong. Soon afterward, she found that two of her tires needed air every two weeks or so. Initially, she thought those were probably caused by the old age of the tires, but later a tire shop pointed out two nails on her tires at the dead center of both tires. She finally realized that someone deliberately screwed the two nails in, likely to repel her from parking there overnight.

She was perplexed by the mean spirits of some homeowners. When living in cars, she disagreed that she was homeless; her car was her home. The truly homeless were those who do not even have a car to stay in. People go to the wilderness to camp out all the time or live in mobile homes regularly. Why do many homeowners disdain and repel the homeless, though she dislikes many of the smelly homeless as unsanitary and unhealthy too? The answer is probably no spiritual education at all in today's schools. Though giving out donations from time to time, most do not have Ren or pure love toward any stranger.

CHAPTER THREE

Rise and Wane of a Person or a Nation

Once upon a time, a great nation was born and exalted. Many people in that country believed in God and tried to be as righteous as they could be. Most of them were also very conservative about following God's teaching and instruction, though many other countries might misinterpret it as a very liberal country based on wrong impression from mass media at the time. The nonstop economic boom and military strength were sustained for decades and was praised as a miracle at the time.

Like any country or person who becomes affluent over time, many people in that country became greedy, especially those in the elite positions in both the public and private sectors. More and more people believed in the liberal viewpoints portrayed in the media than decades prior. As a result, less people believed in spirituality or God. Like many industrialized countries in the world, their educational system prohibited the teaching of spirituality in the school. As a warning, God struck its finance center with an unprecedented anger.

Similar to the reaction of a person facing an initial sign of downfall, that country reacted with self-justification that they did not think any fault of theirs was to blame. Economical slowing and other disasters struck again without warning, but most people in the country had not been aware of them as the beginning of a downfall. What contributes to most of the actual downfall of a person or country is most likely not the downfall itself, but whether one is aware of it from the early signs, and whether one is trying to take corrective actions.

The small rise and fall of a person or a country is common throughout its lifetime. The key to preventing the ultimate demise of a person or a country is first to realize the start of a downfall. Taking some appropriate actions to avert further decline is the second important step. More often than not, a person or country does not even perceive such coming of a downfall and does explain disasters away as simply "bad luck." The complacency of a self-applied blindfold causes no action at all or wrong actions after the initial incident.

Whether a person or a country is good or great cannot be superficially judged by others. Most people who are about to be executed cannot literally believe that his or her life was about to be ended. Such a false belief derives from the elementary education, which injects unreal fantasy that "everyone is mortal except me." We will touch further on this major educational pitfall in chapter 15 on reforms of education.

Even the wisest person in the world may misread the signs and symptoms of a coming downfall, so do not judge hastily. One must carefully consider many factors that may point to many different directions. Only when all the factors are sure to point to the same direction can one be certain about an impending downfall. Oftentimes, the spiritual world or God does not just drop one bomb as a reminder of a wrong direction or pending downfall; they put many road blocks along the way to help lost souls to find the way back, especially for those who believe.

Our concerns for the downfall of this nation were not from just one or several signs. The signs and symptoms were abundant to the point of being unmistakable even to most commoners. People sitting on the top of a government or company are more likely to miss such apparent indicators than the average Joe. Top officials often focus attention toward something concrete and immediately impacting, not on any long-term outlook. Mental modes differ between the top elites and the bottom dwellers. We will further discuss this dangerous split in chapters 13 and 14 on government and public company reforms.

CHAPTER FOUR

Spirituality as a Scientific Study

The human mind is like the moon, which reflects light to Earth based on its position. Spirit is like the sun, which burns to generate light and heat independently without any outside source. Revolving around the spirit, the mind shifts its position and shows different light shapes like the moon. The relationship between mind and spirit is more complicated than the analogy of the sun and the moon; their relations need to be carefully studied scientifically to fully understand them.

Most who work in a hospital know that a full moon coincides with high accident rates. Without conducting any scientific study, most scientists are quick to dismiss this phenomenon or any miracle and astrological accuracy as coincidence. Collectively, they only believe what they see and ignore what they feel. Many ancient heritages of such abstract nature were denied any chance of being studied scientifically. Such blind faith in pure science formulated many degenerative education and social mishaps.

Though psychologists know love exists, they have no idea where it comes from. Though the public school teaches children to be nice and courteous to each other, social scientists do not really know where respect originates from. Most athletes and coaches know the importance of confidence, but most of them do not how confidence can increase physical strength and stamina. Though justice systems have existed in every country since the dawn of mankind, few truly know the reason behind choosing justice.

Studying psychology without including spirituality misses more than half of the whole picture. Similar defects occur in astronomy, social studies, medicine, economics, and many other studies related to humanity. This is why astronomers cannot figure out where dark energy came from. This is why war on addiction achieves limited success. This is why economic contraction and expansion are nearly impossible to predict or regulate. Science cannot solve all human problems with less than half of the understanding of the whole picture.

Tackling only the seeable and observable, many social science disciplines miss the key points. Though human spirits cannot be seen or touched, their effects can be tangibly measured. For thousands of years, people acknowledged the existence of the mind, but the real study of the mind didn't commence until the late nineteenth century. Similarly abstract as the mind, spirituality can likewise be studied with some assumptions and right perspectives.

In our last book, we touched on how spirituality can be a discipline of scientific study. In fact, most scientific studies are not complete without the light shining from spirituality. Scientists have only recently started to realize the limited reach of science.

For example, scientists do not know dark energy, which accounts for nearly 70 percent of the energy in the universe. Even on Earth, sciences cannot explain some strange phenomena or some superhumans with unexplained physical limits. Simply pushing them into the basket of miracles or exceptions is not satisfactory.

Spirituality as a scientific study now would resolve many of the scientifically unexplained or abnormal existence. The first major field of including spiritual study is the differences among human spirits other than human physical bodies. In medicine, genetic difference can only partly explain why some people get cancer and why some do not. Spiritual strength is one major force behind the scenes to prevent it from developing into an illness.

Chi not only exists in martial arts but also in spirituality. In fact, spirituality is the precursor of chi. Some practitioners with high spiritual strength can levitate in the air or exceed expected physical limits like resisting extreme heat or cold. Scientists used infrared imaging to see the hand temperature of a Tai Chi master being raised by two degrees or lowered by six degrees, but they can only observe the tip of an iceberg without any knowledge of spirituality. (Ref 3)

The influence of spirituality is far deeper than controlling the temperature of hands. Spirituality is literally the basis of psychology and other social sciences. Not only confidence and personality are rooted in the spirit, creativity, artistic nature, emotion, energy, and immune system are embedded in the spirit. The concept of mind, body, and spirit was originated from the experiences of ancient spiritual practitioners. It is a waste of a huge part of human heritage not being encompassed by modern scientists.

Prerequisites for Science to Recognize Spirituality

To recognize spirituality as a scientific field, scientists need to agree on some common ground to expand the boundary of science. The narrow vision of the previous scientific generations was probably caused by the extremely fast upwelling of knowledge during the age of industrial revolution and technological advances.

Excessive faith in science, which it did not deserve, is comparable to a physically growing teenager who believes that he or she would grow physically forever based on the observation of past physical growth. Such narrow vision of believing that science will be capable of explaining everything in the universe and that science can conquer all things is itself unscientific.

Such a false belief in science as almighty oversteps the core principle of science, or affirming a theory on hard evidence. Without any evidence to support, the belief that science can explain all things and conquer all things in the universe is a fallacy, and possibly a fantasy. Discovering the fact that nearly 70 percent of energy, or dark energy, is invisible is likely only the tip of an iceberg that science in the current form cannot explain many natural phenomena in the universe.

All scientists must man up—or woman up, so to speak—to admit that science cannot resolve all unknowns in the universe. Such courage of admitting what one does not know conforms to the scientific spirit. Though the knowledge base of science will continue to expand, such expansion is likely to have a limit, like a growing teenager. The main constriction is the focus of science on only those visible and excluding all invisible or intangible. But psychology is invisible.

Easily seen, the problems of addictions such as alcohol and illegal drugs have been a plague for many people around the world for centuries, but science provides very limited salvation even when one is willing to go to rehab. Even rehab physicians probably cannot argue that rehab centers for addictions work fine and dandy. The success rate of rehab is so miserable that it is barely documented.

Even rehab centers cannot claim full success when sending a patient home due to the high relapse rate. These weak points in psychology, psychiatry, spirituality, and other social sciences require all scientists to review and look into the weakness of science as a whole. (Ref 4)

Also a scientific spirit, admitting a weakness or mistake exactly shows the strength within such a person. The courage to accept spirituality as one discipline of science compensates a previous such weakness. A large portion of knowledge in psychology is based on survey; by the same token, much can be gained by including the use of surveys along with scientific studies in the study of spirituality. Other tools used by psychologists can also be duplicated into the study of spirituality.

Another key area in which psychologists miss greatly is that of the subconscious, which is the must-pass gate to spirituality. Though true that a subconscious mind is largely unperceivable, its impacts are usually quite obvious besides addictions. Most mental illnesses, especially those that are severe, likely have their origins hidden within the subconscious mind. The important role of the subconscious cannot be ignored simply because it cannot readily be realized immediately like the conscious mind.

Not only potentially capable of curing most addictions and mental illnesses, research on the subconscious opens the door for literally touching one's own spirit by each individual. Knowledge is power; following such knowledge can be extremely powerful. Doing a task purely out of the subconscious, one feels like being in a trance, where a person may not feel being in total control of one's own body and mind but is fully aware what happens in the surroundings. In fact, a lot of human potential power is likely hidden in the subconscious.

Also related to humans, the assumption that maximizing profit and efficiency would be the best for all mankind requires careful scientific scrutiny. This assumption is based on an underlying agreement that humans are no different from machines. Yet fundamentally, most scientists would agree that humans differ from machine. This kind of fatal fundamental error in the reasons and principles happens largely due to the gross neglect of invisible parts within all humans by most scientific fields.

Not balanced with humanity, attempts to maximize profit or efficiency sometimes lead to disasters. The spectacle of the 1986 NASA *Challenger* disaster spelled not only the doom of the astronauts but also the magnified view of how a small mistake could lead to huge damage. If men were machines, this mistake would not have happened. Nuclear power may be abundant and cheap, but the disasters in Russia and Japan caused by human error and tsunami prove that any small miscalculation is enough to turn the tables around or upside down. No scientist should continue to believe the inadequacy of such wrong assumption about human nature.

Admitting what can be seen does not always encompass all phenomena not only greatly broadens the view of science but also explores what is deeply hidden, such as within the study of spirituality and the subconscious. Seeing a sofa, a scientist knows its shape, color, and texture, but a student of spiritual study would imagine the internal composition and structure to form such a sofa and draw a scratch to illustrate such potential. The student may or may not be totally correct without cutting the sofa open, but some internal stuff definitely exists to form the sofa. Both approaches are scientific but with different perspectives.

Not a fantasy or a daydream, the imaging of the internal world is established on the external exhibition of physical characteristics. In psychology, object permanence describes the cognitive stage of very young children who think an object has disappeared since it is hidden under a sheet of paper. Does any object have real permanence in the universe over one hundred billion years?

All materials we see today will become ashes when Earth is destroyed. Whether an object is permanent depends on the length of time being viewed. Only through such infinite viewpoint of one hundred billion years can a person imagine the existence of all the internal structures and context.

With an X-ray machine, a scientist can see the internal structure and content of a sofa, instead of mentally imagining it. Measurable, X-ray cannot be seen by naked eyes. No scientist would doubt the existence of X-ray, mental illnesses, or addictions; no scientist should doubt that a spirit resides within each human because no observable change is seen between a living person and a dead one.

In fact, the subconscious might not be so invisible after all. New brain cells were born in hippocampus within forty genetically identical mice, which developed disparity of their propensities to explore the surrounding environment. Some mice became more active than others, and their brain structures diverge. Each event in human life alters the brain structure by adding or deleting cells in the brain; such changed wiring and infrastructure likely substantially contribute to the formation of the subconscious. It is also likely the main reason why addictions are so difficult to get rid of; the newly organized brain has so dictated the person as such, even with no compelling chemical substances involved such as nicotine. (Ref 5, Ref 6)

Such altered brain wiring and structure can probably also be used to explain memory process and function. People who take a longer time to memorize a particular set of knowledge on a book likely do not have the ability to update their brain cells and wiring as fast as those who take shorter time period. One popular memory trick for an upcoming school examination is to recite to oneself loudly and attempt to recall again every ten minutes. The sound vibration from hearing one's own voice, the movement of one's own muscles, and the recall effort likely help to speed up the wiring and regenerating process of the brain.

Mind, Body, and Spirit Closely Connected and Learning from Each Other

Closely connected to each other like different layers of skin, mind, body, and spirit cannot be separated without being hurt while alive. Spirit is the deepest layer, followed by mind, then body. Modern medicine and psychology interpret mind as confined to only the brain in the cranium, which is a mistake which neglects a huge hidden part of the mind, the subconscious. Nerves spread throughout the body, and a mind follows the nerves to cover the body.

Think of a mind as an interconnected highway system throughout a body. Acupuncture works on the same principle as a coordinated mind. Likely, different parts of the body are capable of thinking as the brain is. A mind can travel with nerves, which are connected to the whole body. Without training, the mind is confined to cranial cavity and does not know how to travel throughout the body to inspire other body parts to think, especially with modern education likely erroneously teaching that only the brain can think.

Though a brain serves as the central computer, the computing ability could be shifted to other body parts through nerves. Most athletes and coaches are familiar with this fact that different parts of the body possess certain autonomy, the main reason why they train hard before starting a season of games. Muscle memories such as riding a bike or typing on a keyboard can last for a lifetime; many people who have serious dementia are scientifically proven to maintain muscle memory, or likely part of their subconscious.

Modern medical research equipment can scan the body and present an image showing a chi system. These connected solid water molecules, or chi, probably act also as mental highways throughout the body. The way different parts of the body think independently may also explain why some people can withstand freezing temperature for hours without losing much body heat. The connected chi system may do the trick by preventing heat loss from the whole body. This chi system is also likely the foundation of acupuncture.

Do not underestimate the ability of the spirit to think as the mind does. In fact, when mind, body, and spirit interconnect strongly, the spirit and the body think just like the mind does, and the body and the mind would possess spiritual power, which defies gravity and medical common sense. Many so-called medical miracles were likely nothing but spirit resuming to work on the body and mind, and maybe auxiliarly boosted by the high spirits the sick believed.

When mind, body, and spirit are too far apart, the mind and body likely do not have enough spiritual power to work properly like trees totally buried under a large pile of dirt and soon die out. Some people who do not believe in spirituality at all may die from unexpected illness or an accident suddenly, no matter how careful they are. The spiritual life had long died before the physical body did. The distance between mind and spirit is like the rails of a railroad track; either too wide or too narrow would derail it.

If a mind is too close to the spirit, it may become too unmaterialistic and lose touch with reality. Some tell of past experiences where psychedelic drugs helped to achieve enlightenment, but losing touch with one's own body too long can result in physical death as many cases of drug overdose show. An overly zealous religious practice may have a similar effect. Though a mind banks on the spirit to thrive, a mind is an independent entity from the spirit and should be set free at times coordinated with spirit and body. Too long tying down a vivacious monkey, which is often analogized to a mind, would rarely teach it anything meaningful.

An imprisoned monkey may never lose its characteristics of being jerky and jumpy. Animals such as monkeys may not be tamed; as spiritual beings, people's minds can be tamed through correct education. Modern education does not achieve success on this front because almost no subject matter in schools pertains to mind, body, and spirit.

Beyond the missing of spiritual teaching, pupils are drawn farther away from their own spirits by the atheistic assumption of science. Whether to believe in a deity or God is in the realm of religion, but believing in spirits of one's own and others' is not unscientific. The pure materialistic approach of schools in the West is really not much better than the atheistic education in Communist countries.

Letting a human's mind go totally unrestricted may never tame it without education. A strong wild horse likes to sprint in open fields, but it rests when exhausted. At the dawn of human history, people liked to venture into the no-man's land; the driving force was not necessarily food or extra space; rather, probably the wild side of some ancient minds. Armed with strong spirits, they traversed thousands of miles in oceans and frozen earth without any instrument and endured. (Ref 7)

The best way to tame a wild mind is probably to respect and exalt its governing spirit. The main characteristics of an untamed mind are being wild, extreme, easily outrageous, jumpy, and egoistic. The spirit's main propensities are peaceful, moderate, even tempered, consistent, and unselfish. Some animals have spiritual qualities too, but probably no other animal possesses the potential of knowing how to use the power of its own spirit like the human. In other words, the human brain may render humans one of the few animals wired to readily tap into their own spiritual power.

Many psychologists and psychiatrists have been scratching their heads and wondering why some remedies or medicines work for some and not others. Though genetics may be a part of the answer, the vital key to unlock is probably the disparity of spiritual strength and the internal distance between mind, body, and spirit. Without understanding spirituality, psychology and psychiatry will likely continue to be nearly clueless for centuries to come.

Each life passes a lot of obstacles to become reality. The only lives found in the solar system so far are on Earth, which works diligently to sustain lives on it. Modern satellite technology enlightens scientists on the complex interactions within Earth itself to feed lives. Such interactions between various parts of Earth along with complex interactions between different animals sustained human societies. The interaction among mind, body, and spirit is likely more complex than that of Earth.

From another viewpoint, their close relationship can be explained by a famous Confucian quote that when three people walk together, one of them must be the teacher. The three people alluded to were probably mind, body, and spirit. Often, mind has to learn from spirit or body to be less materialistic or more practical. Spirit learns from mind or body to be more logical or realistic. Body learns from spirit or mind to be more transparent or less complaint.

For example, a mind often does not understand or even accept the eventual decay of a physical body. Many females are afraid of getting old, at which time they lose most youthful beauty; their minds naively think that their bodies could be young forever. Mind is like a thin crust being pressed between two giants of spirit and body; mind is inherently narrow, or so-called narrow minded.

Mind is pure yin as it is totally dark, encased within the cranial cavity, with no windows and nowhere to go except thinking and controlling the movement of the physical body and five senses. Confined in a room with no window, a person cannot see or realize the eventual death of the connected physical body of the same association, like the strange feeling of a distant cousin. Likewise, mind does not realize that money is for the good of the body only, and nothing can be done with money to truly benefit the mind. Sugars pass the brain barrier to sustain the brain, and that is pretty much all.

Consequently, most minds want to make as much money as they can, even beyond the needs of the linked body. It frequently does not realize that money is useless when the physical body vanishes. Psychology has proven that mind is extremely fallible and unstable by itself alone.

Probably, mind is the major mover and shaker of the three; spirit and body are largely stationary and reactive. Nevertheless, mind has a restricted view from confinement that it knows little of the natural laws of body and spirit. Mind wants its body to stay young forever, but the physical body has no power to maintain youth. Spirit can do but doing so without a proper reason may violate its own spiritual law, or against Tao.

In a nutshell, mind is fundamentally flawed despite its intelligence and smartness. The defection does not lie in its reasoning ability but in its confined nature of being in a dark dungeon. In order to overcome its natural defects, mind needs to learn from spirit by opening itself up to connect to all in universe. In other words, mind needs to learn from spirit the qualities of three dimensional, versatility, abstractness, peacefulness, tranquility, and infinity to escape the darkness.

Knowledge is fine to be utilized in the physical world, but learning spiritual qualities elevates mind to live out of the box the same way as spirit and body. A huge gap exists between subconscious mind and mere knowledge. Smokers may know that smoking is unhealthy and that it may hasten death, but most of them do not learn it subconsciously enough to believe and do it. They see others die from lung and other cancers caused by smoking but do not believe that they will die from it; they continue to use tobacco.

Without spirit, brain and physical body soon rot to the bone, so spirit is the most important. One of the most common flaws of mind is its erroneous thinking that mind is the most import of the three. A mover and shaker needs support from others to lead; without the cooperation of spirit and body, mind cannot direct on its own, like a movie director without any crew. Humbleness in a mind with respect to its spirit and body means that the mind has learned the spiritual merit of appropriateness, or that a mind is not the number one among the three.

Being much taller than ants due to its position at the top of body, a mind often mistakes that it is more important than an ant. If people have their brains at the feet instead, they might not think as such. Height and size do not determine one's level of importance, spirit does. Without spirit, mind and body soon cease to exist, so the level of importance of an organism is decided by spirit. However, spirit is abstract and immaterial, so humans are no more important than ants, albeit humans rule the world to maintain Tao.

Differences between Spirit and Mind

Generally speaking, each mind and spirit has its own unique characteristics. The tangibility of body differs substantially from the intangible spirit and mind. Physical body has been studied for thousands of years, so here we focus on discussing the intangible spirit and mind. The two are both nonmaterial and invisible to naked eyes, though their manifestation can frequently be observed.

The general properties of spirit are abstractness, root for personality, preferring bland but no demise of vapid, liking to change but no inconsistency, embedded with Ren, appropriateness, righteousness, wisdom, and consistency, and tending to be quiet and peaceful but not inactive. Above properties are inheritances from Tao Heaven when spirits were separated from God. Precious as they truly are, few really care nowadays. Becoming the norm, vivid sight and sound are the most pursued.

New scientific experiments likely have indirectly proved that spirit is the root of personality. In the past, studies in psychology listed environment as one of many possible causes of sculpting personality; other potential influences are genes, parents, siblings, culture, and other biological factors such as height and weight. Being treated differently was also considered a key factor in the development of personality. (Ref 8, Ref 9)

The research on identical twin mice mentioned earlier in this chapter proves that identical twins can have very different personalities living in the same growing environment. The NPR article "How Can Identical Twins Turn out So Different?" reported that Dr. Eric Turkheimer did not find any evidence of environment as a factor for personality development. Twin siblings with identical parents and family environment started out similar, but their personalities diverged afterward.

Three months of a mouse's life roughly equate to ten human years. Genetic mutation was even less likely a possibility for humans. The huge personality difference between most siblings in most families is an undisputed fact, which results in the infighting of many brothers and sisters. If parents and environment for children's growth have even a slight bearing on influencing personality, the strong dissimilarity between most siblings would not have existed, not to mention the less likely influence of the mouse parents, which could not verbally communicate with offspring.

The theory of Turkheimer that tiny events in life or gene mutation could amplify to the point of impacting personality development is probably not totally right, though his hypothesis that small changes in behavior can lead to the resculpting of the brain is likely to be correct. Genetically speaking, the likelihood of gene mutation within the two-year lifespan of a mouse is very small. The feedback loops from parents and teachers of identical human twins are likely to stay roughly the same for both twins. They likely attended the same schools and had the same teachers. A plausible answer is the differences in the spirits of the twins.

No two spirits are exactly identical, even those of identical twins. The differences in identical twin personalities point to the separative spirits which manifest into personalities. Few identical twins do possess similar personalities and common traits. Such commonality may derive from the splitting of one spirit into two, especially one from a high spirit. Deducting from this line of reasoning, a high spirit who split into two to incarnate in different families can have very similar personalities, provided both of the split spirits are strong enough to modify their inherited personalities.

Such modification is possible through epigenome or manipulation of gene expression during growth. A high spirit who incarnates into a family can have two possible results. The first is that the inherited propensity overpowers the residing spirit to manifest ancestral resemblance. The residing spirit overpowering the inherited propensity is the second possibility.

Both results are not absolute; in fact, for most mediocre spirits, a mixture of both results is probably more likely than either of the two extremes above. The cases of Buddha and Jesus Christ likely belong to the second extreme result. The cases of drunkards, drug addicts, and Italian family gangs likely resemble the first extreme.

In psychology, many mental characteristics have been studied for over a century. Here we cover only what has not been extensively researched and some areas where wrong assumptions may lie. Earlier in this chapter, we discussed how the subconscious mind has indirectly been proven to exist through the light shed by identical twin mice experiment; such subconsciousness may be common within many animals.

A whale or a bird knows the path of return after traveling halfway around the world thousands of miles away, using their subconscious minds as they have limited capability from the conscious mind, which is determined by their smaller brain size compared to humans.

Memories of the animals probably cannot explain such miraculous behaviors even halfway; most humans cannot accomplish such a feat with their high brain capacity and intelligence. Another name for this subconsciousness is instinct or intuition, of which most other animals have more than humans, likely due to their smaller brain capacity. The basic instinct of most male humans, including teenagers, to turn heads toward attractive females is deeply embedded in the subconscious.

Similar to the impossibility of removing dead bodies from the top of Mount Everest or of drilling an oil well in Challenger Deep in the western Pacific Ocean, even specially manufactured equipment with modern technology can hardly do it. Compared to the deepest ocean and the tallest mountain, delving into the human subconscious may be even harder than the most advanced technology, which reside in the conscious level, would allow.

It, however, can be a fountain of spiritual wealth because the subconscious mind is the gatekeeper of spirit. All spiritual power has to be manifested through this extremely *narrow gate*, as Jesus Christ implicitly said in the New Testament. With lower spirit and intelligence, animals and plants have no capacity to learn Tao like humans do. They do not have the potential to understand Tao as humans do.

Such spiritual wealth is not as worthless as trash. A high spirit can literally turn a piece of iron into gold with the learned spirituality. Jesus certainly possessed this ability, but he did not do it as it was against his life goal of propagating Tao and spirituality. Furthermore, gold is only precious to mediocre people like the authors and most readers. Despite the authors' understanding of Tao, spiritual capabilities of ours have not even reached one-tenth of Jesus's; we cannot cure the sick or turn iron into gold.

The main function of meditation is to penetrate the barrier of the conscious mind to connect with the subconscious mind. A mind has three distinct compartments: conscious, subconscious, and unconscious. The unconscious governs the heart rate, breathing, digestion, reflex, and other automatic functions to sustain a life.

Please note that what we call *subconscious* is equivalent to the term *unconscious* used by Sigmund Freud and many psychologists today. We believe that *subconscious* is a better term to describe it than *unconscious*. The word *unconscious* with a prefix *un-* denotes something that is out of the reach of the conscious mind, but at least part of the time, even for mediocre people, the subconscious mind can be reached, like during meditation, when unintended words are spoken spontaneously, or during a severe depression. At such time, the submarine surfaces and all people can see it, including the self.

The main reason for the misnomer of *unconscious mind* was due to the erroneous assumption that the subconscious mind is completely hidden and cannot be made aware or controlled. The analogy of the ice below the surface of an iceberg was made by the father of psychology Sigmund Freud. One high priority of an uncompromising science is to ensure that right terms are correctly chosen to correspond with the reality.

A conscious mind is like the earth's surface facing the sun where all things can be easily seen; the nighttime is like a subconscious mind, which must be illuminated by the moon or artificial lighting to see things. Even with street lamps, roads are not as easily seen as during the daytime. With no serious effort to install street lamps into the subconscious mind, it is pitch-black. Conscious mind is yang like a positive pole, and subconscious mind is yin like a negative pole; we will further elaborate yin and yang in the chapter on Tao.

A healthy mind needs a good balance between its conscious and subconscious minds. Too much conscious mind can cause constant mental agitation and insomnia; nonstop daylight for many days scorches the earth's surface to over 170 degrees Fahrenheit. Excessive subconscious mind can create the weather of Seattle, Washington, where the nearly constant cloudy days cause many people to be depressed.

Unconscious mind is constantly active to try to keep a person alive. The central location of the unconscious mind is the *medulla oblongata* in hindbrain; its connected nerves for controlling breathing, heart rate, and vasomotor functions are also part of the unconscious mind. The feeling of sleepiness or hunger from the unconscious compels a person to sleep or to eat. The physical pathway of the unconscious mind is separated from that of the conscious and subconscious minds; otherwise, a person would be able to stop his or her own heartbeat at will.

A school examination or a basketball practice would probably tax the conscious mind more than the subconscious. A cup of coffee with an acquaintance not seen for years or an intimate moment with a wife or girlfriend is likely to tap more on the subconscious mind than the conscious. The percentage of mixture between the conscious and the subconscious may also be appropriated by the conscious mind, such as during meditation or other time of active mental inward watch and adjustment.

During a sound sleep with no dream, the subconscious and conscious minds are turned off, and the only one active is the unconscious. When subconscious mind worries about an unfinished business before sleeping, dreams may be triggered by unconscious and subconscious minds. People who can forgo worries subconsciously rarely dream; those who cannot may have dreams or insomnia.

A robust cooperation between all three minds constitutes good mental health. The loss of support from any one mind for an extended period of time can result in mental illness or death. The unconscious can cause a heart attack to stop heartbeat and breathing. Depression happens when the subconscious cannot be adjusted fast enough to mitigate worries for crises at the conscious level. An anxiety in the subconscious occurs when the conscious mind cannot satisfactorily resolve an external threat.

The general characteristics discussed above portray an approximate picture for spirit and mind. One specific characteristic that differs between mind and spirit is outwardness versus inwardness. Most minds tend to focus on what happens externally such as when using a computer. This outwardness can fend off a potential danger like a fire. On the other hand, most spirits tend to focus inward to balance minds and body to achieve a whole, healthy person.

The basic function of a mind to ward off external threats can wreak havoc on spiritual peace. Most spirits like as little disturbance from mind as possible. Examples of unnecessary intrusion of mind are trivial news, irrelevant conversation, false alarm, inappropriate attraction from the opposite sex, lingering futile thought, excessive concern for a family or a friend, inordinate pickiness from another person, useless regret, looking too far ahead for a future appointment, unwarranted sales phone call, and other pointless agitations.

A list of above bothersome fusses can fill a page very soon, especially for those who have insomnia. Insomnious people are encouraged to list all hidden agitations out on a piece of paper or two, or maybe ten. The more one writes them out, the more one will catch the cumbersome thoughts which were often put on by oneself like a truckload of luggage being transported onto an airplane; only one of them is useful to the insomnious person. No wonder airlines try to levy fees for extra luggage.

Above fussing thoughts often come from an old habitual way of thinking since childhood. Not just causing insomnia and loss of focus, they can be dangerous on the wheel. Similar to the distraction of texting, excessive intruding thoughts take attention away from driving. The ten pages inscribed may even save one's own life in the future if one also diligently cleans up one's own mental garbage based on the inscribed.

The inwardness of spirit helps to maintain balance of internal body functions, to balance minds, to prioritize tasks, to minimize external disturbance, to remind the mind about an upcoming appointment at a proper moment, to counterbalance outward attention, to focus available attention on the task at hand, to impart meaning to life via wisdom, righteousness, consistency, appropriateness, and Ren, and to multitask on balance.

If the spiritual balancer does not exist or becomes inactive, the outward mind soon is lost in this attractive and "exciting" world. In fact, the inaction or ineffectiveness of most spirits today leads to empty life meaning for most people. A mind without an active spirit can gradually become callous like the earth's surface facing away from the sun for days; it turns cold over time.

The major reason why terrorists could recruit many volunteers in suicide bombings is attributed to the high percentage of inactive spirits around the globe. On its own, a mind has no reference for right or wrong and cannot adequately judge a belief or person. The large-scale imbalance produces the almost chaotic state in the world today. The election of off-chart Donald Trump and other nearly crazy top officials in many countries yardsticks such serious imbalance between spirit and mind.

Active minds which do not keep in peace with their own spirits can impinge terrors like those terrorists. The terrorist belief violates the true spiritual belief of Muslims, which has the property of inwardness with no hatred or violence. Their anti-spirit beliefs are mostly empty flags to lure the discontent and the lost.

Another specific characteristic separating spirit from mind is three-dimensional versus one point. An abstract spirit is immaterial, so it can be infinite dimensions. The number zero has nothing inside; therefore, it has complete freedom comparable to an infinity, which often magically returns to zero. A bomb explosion destroys all things nearby and leaves no material in the vicinity. Zero symbolizes Tao and perfect spirituality, alluding to its infinite possibilities.

Through its infinite dimension, spirit can closely communicate with body. The tight connection includes each organ and every cell. Without this connection, the body can develop cancer. Though carcinogens do exist, the main cause of cancer is likely the local absence of spirit, which produces an anaerobic locale suitable for cancer growth.

Characteristically one single point, a mind goes forward or backward only linearly, which coincides with the linearity of time. Mind lives in a one-dimensional space if not connecting to spirit or body. Mind is inherently narrow by itself, hence termed *narrow minded.* Frequently, mind forgets to retract when warranted to do so; like an unstoppable train, it is bound to collide and cause major damage.

Writing till here, our computer shut down unexpectedly, and we lost a few written paragraphs. Our excessive concentration on the writing negligently negated our watch for frequent saving to the computer. This mistake cost us one and half hours to recover the lost data. Our linear minds are still fallible and prone to negligence, which we shall improve.

The third specific difference between spirit and mind is the abstract method of recording versus the physical etching on brain surface. If our deduction is correct, brains change structure all the time by adding or subtracting cells on brain surfaces. This can potentially be a research topic in a future spiritual study in which no scientific tool is excluded. Change of brain structure probably is particularly prominent among students, especially medical students.

Some people can memorize a reading instantly at the first pass; some require multiple readings. The difference is likely caused by the locations used for memory: the former is on spirit, and the latter is on brain. All the memory techniques thus have an additional meaning at the spiritual level.

A brain may have limited capacity for memory due to the limited surface area, but the capacity for spiritual memory is likely unlimited due to the abstract nature of the storage space. In addition, a spiritual memory is likely to be more precise than a mental one as the former is recorded electronically similar to a recording on a computer, but the latter may rely on cell modification or rewiring on brain configuration.

The fourth difference in specific characteristics is unbiased versus biased due to personality. Being abstract, a spirit has no bias through using no lens. Unlike a life with a start and an ending, a spirit has neither, so no prejudice accumulates. This unbiased spirit sees through things clearer than a biased mind. Only a person with an unbiased spirit can judge fairly on a lawsuit, even if it involves personal interest.

Being biased, a mind judges based on prejudice of a lifetime. Like adding a tinted lens before an observed, the tint twists the truthfulness of objects. The personality of President Trump acts as a colored lens for himself, so he is criticized for being untrue; it is merely his biased views passing through his own personality.

The color of spirit is none, but the color of mind depends on individuals, who can have as many colors as the number of people. House painters know well that the choices of colors are nearly infinite; just the number of white shades alone is at least twenty. Mixing any two colors in various proportions, one will produce a bunch of colors, similar to two parents who give birth to ten children with all different personalities.

On a cloudy day, would one wear a clear glasses or tinted glasses to do a job, to talk, or to walk, provided the person has twenty/twenty vision? Most people wear no glasses at all, so why do many people put on personal bias to see, to hear, to talk, and to perform? Excessive smartness in humans causes bias. Pride and prejudice often come hand in hand; pride propels people to do things based on their prejudice, but people seldom realize it.

In Buddhism, no mind monkey can escape from Buddha's hand. A very good personality is still not as good as no personality. No matter how good a mind is, it is never as good as no mind. Forgoing personality, a person can achieve enlightenment. Tribulation is meant to peel a person off from one's own personality, like the peeling of banana skin. Studying spirituality before psychology would clear confusion about differences in personality.

The diverse characteristics between mind and spirit can cause trouble between them. Though a mind is the mover and shaker among the three, a spirit can have a mind of its own if the mind deviates too much from Tao. Cancer is but one of many possible protests by a dissatisfied spirit. Once, an author traveled to Hawaii and was tripped by his own spirit.

While in Maui, he was almost robbed by a guy of the exact same age after he read the newspaper after the incident. This was likely not a coincidence. At that time, that author was very lost spiritually and mentally. It was a warning from his own spirit that things were going in the wrong direction than it should, albeit it took a few more years before that author started to wake up.

Another time was at a clinical trial. Few days after his doctor checked his electrocardiogram or ECG, he was baffled by his ECG failure at a clinical trial screening. Confirmed by divination, the reason was the meddling of his own spirit. His spirit was unhappy that he rushed that morning to take the appointment and interrupted his ongoing project.

The clashes between spirit and mind are the same as arguments between husband and wife, both of which are one yang and one yin. The fundamental disagreements between the two opposites often have no right or wrong answers, but mind is often the one at fault due to its inherent ignorance, not spirit, which has Tao hidden within. To spirit, money means next to nothing as long as there is enough; to mind, money means everything and is never enough.

The infighting often escapes mind's notice as most minds focus on the outside world; spirit's abstractness adds to the communicative difficulty between the two. A fight between yin and yang has no win-win or clear-cut answer unless both are willing to yield.

Mediocre spirits know everything, but they do not know the reason behind without thinking. High spirits know the reason behind because their minds are transparent from spiritual practices. The thinking process is not needed by high spirits, who know most reasons and principles. The minds of high spirits are trained to penetrate the subconscious level and directly into spirituality, which contains all the reasons and principles built inside since the beginning of time.

A mediocre spirit such as the authors' and most readers' needs to think carefully to understand the reason or principle behind a happening because we have not reached enlightenment, which is the condition where subconscious mind is transparent and can reason without the help of conscious mind. A low spirit such as a ghost in hell probably cannot even think, like a drunkard or a drug addict whose mind is mostly blocked at the conscious level, not to mention the subconscious or spiritual level.

On the other hand, mind can reason but does not know all things as spirit does. Confined in the cranial cavity, mind has a limited viewing angle to what is in front, to what is happening now, to what is memorized, and to what physically exists. If a reasoning result is not written down on paper or computer, the mind soon forgets the reason. Mind is the gate to spirituality, it can also block spirituality.

Spirits Often Fall Asleep

Most people cannot perceive their own spirits as they do their own bodies. Detaching from one's own spirit often occurs due to not believing in the existence of one's own spirit. For some religious people with strong faith, the content of teaching may not be critical enough to wake up their own spirits. Being mentally awake does not indicate being spiritually awake. We estimated that 80 to 90 percent of spirits today are not awake at all.

Higher than above assessment, high spirits or God adjusted our estimate upwardly to 95 to 98 percent of people who are spiritually asleep. Despite the sheer number and popularity, most religious schools around the globe are likely not doing a good job. After all, most saints who created religions no longer incarnate on earth, such as Jesus Christ, Buddha, Mohammad, Lao-Tzu, and Confucius. We wish they do incarnate someday as some of them promised to do. The leaders of a religion who teach spirituality do not necessarily possess spirituality.

Those religious lessons probably should not be blamed; even the majority of the authors were spiritually asleep just a few months ago. The writing of this book literally woke all of us up to the point of shedding tears of deep regret. Possessing the knowledge of spirituality may not be an absolute indicator of the presence of spirituality; in fact, it is more often not than is in today's world.

As elaborated in the last section on spirit and mind disparity, distracting thoughts suck available attention from upholding spirituality. Without guarding spirit regularly by minimal attention, the spiritual computer crashes and sleeps. Analogized to a mutually supportive role of two linked computers, the complete ignorance of one toward another soon puts it to sleep. An area in spirit constantly operates the unconscious mind to maintain heart rate and breathing, yet the area in mind to operate spirit is often missing or inactive. Let us call this spirit-operating area in a mind *critical mental area*.

The vital aspect for sustaining this area is to diverge some care inward. Over focus on outside tasks without any inward attention can cause negligence as the example of our failure to plug in demonstrated. Extravagant spotlight on a task in front is counterproductive and likely to cost more time or money to fix a careless neglect.

Our intense focus on the writing was to push for a deadline we set, but more time was spent to fix the neglect later. When walking on Tao solidly, the deadline can be extended; rushing or stressing out can cause mishaps that later cost more than the time saved. Do not despise such small neglect caused by total outward focus; the Chernobyl nuclear accident resulted in the death of thirty-one directly and in many more later through radiation.

Contrarily, not enough concentration can bring disaster as well. Aimlessly wandering thoughts can overshadow and unplug the critical mental area to cause a spiritual crash. Most people can work on only one main task at a time; multitasking refers to those related to the main task and those readily observable. An animal attack while building a wooden boat is a related task because a successful attack would interrupt the project, though the attack is not related to the wooden project.

Either too much or not enough does not conform to Tao, Confucius stated. The right amount of outward focus with a small amount of inward attention finishes a job on time without a hitch. With no inward attention, a spirit cannot be online to watch the whole picture afar from a point where the focused mind does not see. Having a spiritual presence all the time does not just benefit the doer to be happy; safety is another concern.

When a male or female shoplifter hides merchandise in her purse or his undergarment, she or he would keep an eye on whether any store employee is watching. After sneaking it out of the store, he or she watches out whether police would spot her or him or whether a shrewd expert would recognize the stolen goods. The constant wary mindset steals a spirit since the critical mental area is swamped with alarms.

The constant weariness disrupts the ability of the critical mental area to communicate with the spirit. This area must be constantly kept in serene condition to wake up spirit, the main reason why meditation works and why a thief's mind fails.

One should always maintain a peaceful attitude to guard against the intrusion of one's own critical mental area. A calm person may be upset about what happened an hour ago, but a peaceful person soon moves on after coming to terms with what transpired. The peacefulness likely is at a minimum influenced by the spiritual connection which tunnels light from the spirit. A peaceful person would appear calm, but a calm person may not be peaceful at heart. A person with lots of SWM may appear calm but never achieve peacefulness at the subconscious level. Disclose and repent now.

Even an avid spiritual practitioner must work hard to guarantee spiritual wake up all the time. A bothersome person, an injustice without provocation, or strong weather can throw a person off balance. All things are possible especially for spiritual people; envy, jealousy, or other nonspiritual emotions can abound to thwart the possibility.

Before living in three dimensions, a spirit exists as a single point like mind. Spirit is flexible like the number zero or one, which can potentially grow to infinity; sky is the limit for spirituality. Similar to air or water filling up a bottle, a spirit can expand and gradually fill up its physical body, especially during physical growth.

Ultimately, wisdom is the key to keeping spirit awake. Knowledge and daily practice ignite the spiritual frame every morning. A keen sense of whether the frame is lit prevents it from being extinguished. When an outside event requires attention, the mind deals with it and returns to the original peacefulness. Only the wisdom of letting go can do it; wisdom is explained further in chapter 9.

Wisdom also resolves nearly unresolvable life problems. Left unresolved, they accumulate into a smelly truckload after months; they become entangled and harder to resolve than before. The hardest problem to resolve is often one from inside a person, not one from the world around. Cleaning the interior of a car is harder than cleaning its exterior; introspection is not easy compared to criticizing.

Here we use *asleep* to describe a spiritual state of not being as awake as the mind. The term *semi-sleep* or *half-awake* is more descriptive than *asleep*. The hearts of dormant animals are still pumping, and they can be woken by disturbance. A dormant spirit does not participate in decision making. Without spiritual involvement is like a zombie; a mind wonders or kills but does not know what it is doing. (Ref 10)

Spirit, Spirituality, and Others Defined

A scientific definition for spirit is formulated after consulting some dictionaries: the abstract life force or principle animating a living organism or existing by itself after the organism dies. After an organism dies, the spirit becomes *a free spirit* with no physical body.

For now, we exclude spirits who never incarnated, such as Jehovah in the Holy Bible, for the accuracy of scientific study; future researchers can add later if they deem it proper. *Organism*, by definition, includes animal and plant, but we focus on animal spirits here as their manifestation is easier to observe than that of plants. Research on plant spirit probably can wait after a foundation is established.

From the definition, spirit is imperceptible to the eye, ear, nose, tongue, or other sensing organs. This immateriality likely posed the most challenge to spiritual teachers like Jesus Christ and Buddha. They taught without proof except words and occasional miracles.

Though a spirit cannot be seen, the manifestation of a spirit on the body can be seen on the infrared image of a Tai Chi master's hands changing temperature mentioned at the beginning of this chapter. With future teaching and research, more imaging methods likely will be invented to validate spiritual existence. Chi is one of many spiritual manifestations; the acts of speaking or listening can also be manifestations if the spirit is awake.

With enough spiritual practice before death, a deceased human becomes a high spirit with unfathomable spiritual power. Without enough spiritual practice, a deceased unable to surrender the body appearance right away becomes a ghost, which is the shadow of a low spirit.

Similar to how a billion people can all have different personalities, varieties of spirits are in the billions. Similar to nice people having similar characteristics, high spirits have similar qualities or an abundance of five merits. With few qualities of the five merits, a spirit is a low spirit.

A broken spirit such as a drug addict or a hardcore criminal is bounded by obsessed thought, materialistic desire, agitated emotion, and unresolved issues. Naming a broken spirit a ghost is unscientific, and the conjured eerie feeling is unjustified. Not ghost, broken spirit can be used to scientifically denote career criminal, druggy, or serious addict of sex, cigarettes, video games, or others.

An academically correct term for low human spirits facilitates research and recovery without shame or guilt, which can deteriorate people with broken spirits further. If regularly demoted as fat or ugly, an obese person may never motivate him- or herself enough to search for a solution. One may intuitively attach to a derogatory term and subconsciously crush any hope.

On the other end, high spirits have lots of the five merits and highly pure thought. To them, hierarchy and authority do not exist; principles and the five merits are the true king for governing. High spirits treat others and themselves the same; low spirits, however, prefer one gender over another.

The equal treatment of genders originates from the deep spirit within. From the definition of spirit, spirit is genderless. For people who know reincarnation well, pure spirit is neither male nor female, so it can incarnate into either without rejection. With a preference, a low spirit can sexually attach to either gender. The attachment binds a spirit to reduce its level.

A strong attachment to either gender can lead to rape, sexual abuse, or sexual addiction. Without the obsession, the mind can focus attention inward toward its own spirit and practice spirituality. Writing from a purely spiritual viewpoint, the authors do not endorse the movement of same-sex marriage.

In chapter 12, we will discuss Tao, which is the essence of spirit, and how Tao can create from nothing to yin and yang. Being born as either gender is inevitable in carnation, but as the wisest among animals, humans can transcend the restriction of yin and yang via knowledge and practice of Tao.

From the definition of spirit, spirituality can be defined. Most dictionaries and encyclopedias do not define it scientifically, so we ponder on all fronts to facilitate future spiritual education and research. The first definition is an ideal spirit with or without a physical body. A couple of prime examples are Jesus Christ and Buddha, who taught with their own experiences.

The second definition of spirituality is the study and practice toward an ideal spirit. Most immediate disciples of the five saints were forerunners of spiritual study. Their work might not be totally scientific, but their devotion and practice built today's foundation. The motto of this definition is that everybody can have an ideal spirit given time to study and effort to practice.

Achieved, an ideal spirit can readily and fully understand anything and anybody, ideal or not. Natural and universal rules readily comprehended, an ideal-spirited person knows the meaning of his or her own carnal life and strives to maximize the meaning via teaching spirituality and Tao.

The third definition is a spirit striving toward ideal. An example is a student of spirituality. Nearly nobody inherits an ideal spirit; thereupon, learning to become ideal is inevitable. Carrying people across a river full of dangers, the ship of spirituality can itself be a danger like the Buddhists who reverse the priority of Buddha and dharma in chapter 10.

As a side note, the word *spiritual* can describe the qualities of an ideal spirit or a spirit striving to achieve ideal. A daily practitioner is spiritual, so is a believer who studies spirituality.

Being spiritual does not necessarily mean being religious, but some people inundate the word *spiritual* with intent to escape religion. If a "spiritual" life has few qualities of the five merits, it is mostly empty, and the person is not truly spiritual. On the other end of spectrum, being religious but not fully knowing or practicing the five merits is no better than those "spiritual but not religious." Submission and freedom have the same root; problems happen when one submits to religion prior to his or her own spirituality. (Ref 11, Ref 12)

A spiritually healthy person likely has the following qualities. First, the person would devote at least some time daily to develop his or her own spirituality, such as when in meditation, repentance, pondering truth, reflecting on self, or discussing spirituality with others.

Second, a healthy spirit would open mind to a potentially spiritual experience. A strange painting understood by few can be inspiring at the right place and time. Meeting a serendipitous stranger can turn out to be a day saver, a headache eliminator, or even a companion. An accident initially a mishap can turn out to be a blessing. A past dis-favorite can illuminate misconception. A once discarded idea may reignite after additional realization.

Third, a spiritually healthy person appreciates an inconvenience or sorrow for inspiring and boosting spirituality. Buddhism teaches that worry means meeting one's own spirituality; avoiding trouble is worse than confronting it as an opportunity to meet one's own spirit is lost.

Fourth, a healthy spirit treats others as he would treat himself. A low spirit forgives him- or herself before forgiving others. It reflects on others' wrongdoing before one's own sin. An ideal spirit reflects and forgives others no different than for self. However, overly forgiving others is as bad as criticizing self excessively. Justice cannot lean on either side of a scale; righteousness sees Ren as a counterweight rather than a saboteur.

Fifth, a healthy spirit trusts its own spirituality and believes in high spirit. When a doctor of philosophy, or PhD, does not even trust his or her own spirituality, the knowledge has little root and will soon dissipate. If a person does not believe in any authority, arrogance overtakes respect to stop spiritual learning. When empty, humbleness can learn more spiritually.

Sixth, joy is found in gradual advance of life meaning and spirituality, despite the sorrow and pain of daily life. Joy is from the increase of spiritual meaning; happiness is from matched wishes from happenings. Tribulation is painful to mind; spirit confers joy like rain after a drought. Without drought, rain seems insignificant. A life is precious, particularly a difficult one which experiences much pain and sorrow. Such life gains meaning not from abundant wealth or experience, but from transforming pain and sorrow into spirituality.

Saving a life is worth more than building a temple, particularly a spiritual life. The other day a friend of ours fell ill both physically and spiritually, so we treated him to Red Lobster despite our limited financial resources. He felt better soon after talking with us.

Seventh, joy is found in boosting spirituality of others. The joy comes whether the recipient is known or unknown to a person and whether the recipient accepts the offer or not. Wishing and praying are powerful as long as from spirit. A generous spirit wishing others well boosts healthy spirituality of community, society, city, state, country, and world behind the scenes. On the other hand, a selfish spirit demotes world spirituality in backdrop. Eighth, the promotion of world spirituality comes from healthy spirits.

Ninth, a healthy spirit half closes eyes and ears toward spiritual deterioration and corruption. Bad news, hideous intention, past personal trauma, physical or emotional loss, Donald Trump, communism, tyranny, arms race, and potential future disaster are but few examples that ought to be paid less attention to. Why worry over things one has no control over? Why take the unnecessary burden when one has no influence over it at all?

To facilitate a scientific study, scrapping the unhealthy terminology is as important as promoting the healthy ones. A name defect can funnel religious connotation into a scientific field; it may violate the scientific spirit of being fair and unbiased.

In Christianity, pneumatology refers to the study of the Holy Spirit and seems to deny or neglect the existence of human spirits. Excluding human spirits, this term ought not to be used in scientific study. Often used to denote the study of Christian theories, the word *theology* ought not to be used in science either unless its meaning is broadened to other religions.

One of the authors took some religious study courses in college but was disappointed to find that the courses taught only Christianity and no other religions. Most Christian churches regard all other religions as heresy, but religiosity is rapidly declining among new generations in the United States. (Ref 13)

To promote the essence of religiosity—i.e., Ren—appropriateness, consistency, righteousness, and wisdom, and to include the teachings from other major religions, religious study courses in college should include other major religions such as Buddhism, Confucianism, Islam, and Taoism.

Spiritual Study in University and Public School

Personal religiosity should not be mixed with school study of spirituality, but religions are the most fertile ground for studying spirituality before spiritual science takes off. In our vision, future PhD candidates should study many religious teachings in depth before starting to write a thesis. A possible topic is parental love found in various religious teachings such as Buddhism, Taoism, Islam, Christianity, Confucianism, and ancient philosophers.

Other potential topics are to compare righteousness, consistency, appropriateness, and wisdom among religions. Yet another potential topic is to compare creation theories among various religions and cultures. Comparing successful practice methods among religions would be useful in helping each spiritual student choose the best practice method for the individual.

Though our last book criticized some PhD holders and PhD programs, we admit that most PhD programs have pushed science forward through research and publication. A PhD program in spirituality would produce many motivated spiritual researchers to write dissertations and books in the scientific field of spirituality. However, the spirituality program ought to have some extra requirements that other PhD programs do not have.

PhD programs today are mostly knowledge based that besides abilities to reason, to present, and to organize in a field, practice of the knowledge is often not required. A PhD candidate in petroleum chemical engineering is usually not required to have any experience in operating a refinery. A PhD in spirituality, on the other hand, ought to have minimum experience in practicing the five merits beyond mere knowledge of the five merits.

The practice of spirituality can only be observed; it is not possible to validate a student's progress via written examination as done in nearly all college education today. Abstract as spirit, the practice of it cannot be done in a factory as the engineering example above either. Beyond reasoning ability shown on a thesis, the ability to repent personal sin, wrong, and mistake ought to be carefully scrutinized by the advising professor. Sin, wrong, and mistake, or SWM for short are defined and discussed in chapter 11.

The level of spirituality should also be observed that a candidate is free from any obsession or addiction. A person unable to refrain from sexual addiction, drug or alcohol abuse, and aggravated assault ought not to even be admitted to a PhD program.

Even people with spousal abuse suspicion, frequent cursing, and repeated rudeness should not be admitted. A president may lie before or after an election, the standard for a PhD candidate is stricter than that for a public official. It would be a laughingstock for a lying PhD graduate to teach courses on the merit of consistency in spirituality. In Chinese, truth, goodness, and spiritual beauty are the three basic qualities of spirituality.

A key part of the written exams would test a PhD candidate on personal dilemmas so that the ability to apply the five merits into real life is certain to exist. Furthermore, without any prior notice, a candidate ought to be tested in real-life situations to see how solid his or her practice is and how he or she would react by instinct.

For example, an actor or actress can use seduction to see if a candidate can hold on to the merit of appropriateness and not transgress sexually. Not for hideous purpose, a candid camera can be set up to collect evidence for such a hidden test. Transcending lust and materialism is one of the requirements before graduation. Though not required to be a saint, a spirituality PhD is required to at least constrain personal materialism and lust from overrunning personal will.

The office and living quarters of a PhD candidate ought to be inspected without any prior notice at least a few times a year. The inspection is not to promote military lifestyle where everything must be in strict order all the time; the purpose is to examine organization and diligence in daily life. A pile of books mixed with leftover food is a strong indicator of disorganization and procrastination. Many such signs can fail a candidate.

Under some circumstances, disorganization or being dirty can be justified. A person with regular depression cannot be expected to be clean and fully organized all the time. Disorganization and filth may wake up a mentally ill person, similar to a pungent smell waking up a sleepy person. Not much can be expected of someone who just lost a family member, pet, or even a favorite pair of sunglasses. All possible explanations should be taken into consideration.

From past encounters of some authors, some PhD holders do not keep offices halfway organized though their dissertations were likely well organized to graduate. What is known and what is being done can drastically differ. However, keeping too clean or overly organized may not indicate good spiritual practice either.

Against some "common sense," being too orderly or clean may indicate obsession, which shows the demerit of appropriateness. This obsession often adversely affects other merits by reducing the available time and effort for them. Keeping all things organized and clean is not necessarily nonspiritual; rather, prioritization skill and motivation for being clean and organized should be further scrutinized.

Prioritization is one key knowledge and practice in spiritual study; chapter 9 expounds on it further. Confucius teaches *when priority is straight, Tao is near.* Nearly no one achieves all wishes in a lifetime, and not knowing Tao and spirituality, most achieve what is not spiritually desired. If the first step is wrong, do not claim success.

Differing from a military inspection, a PhD candidate should be self-motivated to stay organized, instead of being forced. Hell and heaven are both clean and organized; the major difference is that one is forced while another is self-motivated. Military is not implied to be hell; the vital self-motivation in spirituality is the key point.

In the future when spiritual education is populated in school, high school students ought to be required to write their own living wills and be encouraged to update them at least once a year. The will of a PhD candidate in spirituality ought to be inspected at times to determine the level of spiritual realization and practice. The wording and intention of each item on a will can show the level of spiritual practice.

When a person is ready to die at any moment, his or her life perspective and mentality differ from those of the unprepared. The mental readiness for death should not come only at old age; happening at a young age, it greatly explores one's potentials and innate genius. Nowadays, not pressed by their own death, most people bury their potential and wisdom under a huge pile of materialism. The adage that one is drunk at birth and dreaming at death describes this gravely unaware of life direction.

One crucial aspect to be examined is the amount of improvement at the weakest point of a PhD candidate. Everyone has an Achilles' heel; the key is how well one reduces or even eliminates the heel, which is easy to mend if the spirit is active. If the spirit is asleep, this weakness can be very hard to heal, even harder than the real heel due to subpar knowledge or insufficient willpower.

For instance, the Achilles' heel of a molesting priest in the Catholic Church is his obsession with boys' genitalia. To improve, he must first confess to a teacher and think hard on how to overcome it. Not only providing suggestions, the teacher should also monitor the progress. One of the scientific ways to monitor is to scan brain image while showing a picture of a boy's genitalia; less arousal than before means progress. Not aroused at all would be a saint, but few can completely heal one's Achilles' heel.

Consummation is never easy. Moments before physical death, Jesus Christ cried to the Father; extreme pain was difficult to overcome with no extreme righteousness within the spirit. From our conjecture, the karma from his healing of the sick, which was less than totally righteous, had a causal relation to his extreme suffering, even though his volunteered suffering saved billions afterward. Even so, we respect Jesus the same. As discussed in chapter 10, imperfection is expected rather than criticized, even for high spirits. None of the authors is even near perfect.

Not just healing of alcohol or drug addiction must start from awareness and acknowledgment, the healing of all addictions must start there too. For a chain smoker to quit, the detrimental effects on the body or the innate disgust toward cigarettes must first be perceived. Without the internal awareness, advice from others sounds like wind passing the ears and causing only slight irritation.

Not really confessing, a PhD candidate in spirituality *reveals* to the advising professor, who is not a priest or affiliated with any religion. Though revealing personal secrets may reduce guilty feeling according to psychology, what is revealed may or may not rise to the level of real guilt. For example, obsession about cleanness violates spirituality, yet it is not a violation in common law or even spiritual law. The main purpose of revelation is for a candidate to improve.

Even if a revelation likely transgresses common law, the advising professor should be allowed the discretion to decide whether to report based on professional opinion. With consideration, a psychiatrist does not always report cases of murderous thought. As a hypothetical example, a PhD candidate reveals a murder committed years ago. Though in the eyes of common law all murders should be prosecuted, circumstances must be considered in the eyes of spiritual law. We will discuss spiritual law further in chapter 11.

The revelation can help a PhD candidate to improve and help the advising professor to monitor. The progress of an ex-murderer on refusing to kill or eat animals might be more than that of one obsessed with cleanness. The revelation between a pupil and a spiritual teacher can be adapted in public school to facilitate spiritual learning. Many teenage crimes can likely be prevented with the revelation and monitoring.

A PhD in spirituality should be both knowledgeable in spirituality and possess a certain level of spirituality. Candidates who fail to restrain their own obsession, who fail to minimally bolster five merits, and who do not practice ought not to be graduated, no matter how perfect the dissertation and the oral presentation are.

Despite our past criticism of PhD programs, one grander point of PhD programs over religious teaching is the humbleness of most advising professors. Most religions are authoritative and thereupon assume that a newcomer is inferior to seniors in charge. Albeit respecting elders does conform to the merit of appropriateness, a senior is not necessarily superior in knowledge or practice to a junior.

Though some PhD students shot and killed advising professors before probably caused by the arrogance of the advising professors, most PhD advisers are humble and realize that the progress of science needs the new generation to be better than the previous, even more so in spiritual research. An arrogant spirituality PhD adviser should be immediately removed due to the violation of the very principle taught. Hopefully other PhD programs will follow suit.

Similar to the new sustainability major in college pushing to conserve the Earth's resources, the start of college courses on spirituality would whirl the wind of spiritual knowledge and practice to the whole society. Coupled with the establishment of a spirituality PhD program, teaching spirituality in public schools can soon take off. Youth is the best time to learn spirituality.

Spiritual teaching and learning will boost standards of learning and teaching in other disciplines. The reason is simple: studying and learning is mostly about the student, less about the teacher, even though the teacher is a bit more important than the student in the beginning. "A good teacher inspires" is a maxim in education; a spiritual mathematics teacher is more likely to find ways to motivate learning. A spiritual student is easier to inspire than a nonspiritual one.

The purpose of studying spirituality is to wake up one's spirit, which transcends mind and body. People with sound mind, body, and spirit can uplift others to be more spiritual. From close friends of a spiritual few, spirituality can, over some time, expand to a society. In The Average Mentality of a Society graph, the societal mentality can be boosted by only 20 percent of the population due to their spiritual influence upon close others.
(Graph 1, Average Mentality of a Society)

In fact, many people we met strongly advocated our idea of spiritual education in school despite their nonreligious beliefs. One of the authors rented a car to drive for Uber for a week near areas of downtown Los Angeles. During a casual conversation with a female passenger who was also a film producer, she expressed intense interest in our idea of learning spirituality in school and wanted to purchase our last book right away.

Regrettably, that author neglected to keep a copy in the car, though his spirit thought about it. The producer requested to pay via PayPal, but that author realized afterward that he neglectfully gave an email address not registered with PayPal. Though disappointed with a loss of sale, that author has been glad to learn that a nonreligious person can strongly support spiritual courses in school.

Spirituality Is the Root of Psychology and Others

Not only itself a scientific discipline, spirituality roots many other scientific fields, particularly psychology and psychiatry, which started with theories of mind and deducted from animal experiments. Most psychologists and psychiatrists did not learn the root of mind or spirit. At most, they know subconscious mind from the theory by Sigmund Freud, but many of them do not believe it, let alone the deeper abstract spirit.

Their spirits asleep, most psychologists and psychiatrists do not even know the existence of their own spirits, let alone study them. Without learning spirituality, they miss half of the whole picture, particularly the interaction between mind and spirit, which is crucial in concocting remedies for mental illness.

Some non-psychiatrist doctors see psychiatrists as pill pushers. Most mental medicine suppresses the symptom but does not cure the disease. Not knowing spirituality is comparable to recognizing only the existence of a tree while denying that of the root, which can be as far reaching as tree branches. If a farmer applies fertilizer only on the surface of leaves, the tree likely will not grow well. Psychiatric medicine is akin to spreading fertilizer only on leaves; the absorption is very limited, and the effect is minimal on the root cause of spirit and subconscious mind.

Treatment missing the root cause is likely to work very slowly, to mitigate only symptoms, or not to work at all. The constricted viewpoint that psychology is found only in material brain severely limits the potential remedial development for fully curing illness or for improving general mental health among the healthy.

Many root causes of mental illness are cached in the subconscious mind or even spirit. A spirit which has never been woken up would likely present less problem than one that has been awakened once; a person who has never been born may not cause any problem than one who is murdered by the mother. A spirit which has been woken up once but later been forced to sleep may initiate an illness to protest.

With intense practice, one of the authors woke up his spirit during his teenage years. Later, the practice was stopped to search for academic and career success. After the goals had been achieved, he failed to return to spiritual practice. With a chance of bad luck and circumstances, the discontented spirit turned his life upside down with mental illness and loss of job.

Diagnosed with anxiety and depression, nearly no medicine worked. One medicine worked but caused a side effect of initiating yet another mental illness; the medicine did not cure him but suppressed some symptoms. Exhausted all remedial options, he went back to college to learn psychological principles. The study benefited his illnesses greatly but did not help him to realize or alleviate the spiritual root cause.

A few years later, he realized that some fundamental principles in psychology did not match the reality, especially those related to the realm of spirituality and the subconscious. Gradually, he discovered the spiritual root cause of his mental illnesses and started to work on the spiritual connection. He wished that spirituality as a potential root cause of mental illness was taught in college. Such a study would probably have shortened time and bettered his chance for recovery.

For several years in the early stage, he was addicted to video games caused by the illness. The realization of the huge waste of time did not help him to escape. He absconded after being mentally fatigued and exhausted by its repetitive nature. Tasted for the first time the enormous sucking power, he has since realized why addiction to cigarettes or psychedelic drugs is so entrapping and so nearly impossible to eradicate. Once sucked in by an addiction, one is nearly doomed like a hooked fish.

A major field in psychology and psychiatry, addictive medicine remains not very effective in curing addictions. From just-say-no to full-out battles, many police and soldiers have perished while fighting it. But addiction problems continue to snowball. With no spiritual knowledge, even substantially abating addiction is unlikely. Spiritual study not only can potentially cure many mental patients, the national crisis of addiction to drugs, alcohol cigarettes, gambling, and others would also be greatly reduced by the new research focus of scientific spiritual remedy.

As mentioned in our last book, most medical researches do not explore the mental causes of physical illnesses, despite how psychology has long recognized many such causes. Research on spirituality can trickle down to enlighten addictive medicine. This research money is worthwhile, more than the increase of budget on fighting drug smuggling. With little demand, supply stops automatically.

Other medical fields are also likely to be boosted by spiritual research. The origination of many cancers is likely caused by sleeping spirits, which oncologists have not yet learned. An inactive spirit not only can reduce oxygen intake via reduced breathing, but it can also block oxygen supply to some body parts. Lack of oxygen in an area promotes cancer cell growth. Besides cancer, other illnesses are likely to be reduced by increased immune response from an awakened spirit.

Public education is the next major benefactor of spiritual study. A good-spirited pupil is more likely to learn and memorize in a field he is intensely interested in than a somewhat-reluctant non-spirited student with minimal interest in many diverse fields. The latter is the status quo in today's educational system.

As happening today, learning different study techniques at the same time confuses elementary students. The large disparity of characteristics between mathematics and language makes their simultaneous study awkward and inefficient. The training of mathematics should be at a different timeframe than that of a language because their best study techniques differ on many fronts. A student is likely to study better when the same technique is used regularly on similar subjects at the beginning of learning a subject. We will expound our points further in chapter 15.

Spirituality is also the root of most social sciences where people are the major players. Sociology is hungry at half of the pie without taking into account spirituality. Some weird or outrageous social phenomena may be completely normal looking from a spiritual perspective. From a spiritual viewpoint, same-sex marriage or homosexuality are fully explainable. Economic cycles probably can be explained after shedding some light from the cycles of mind explained in chapter 12.

No doubt in the business world well-managed companies are more likely to succeed than those less aligned. Teaching spiritual wisdom of organizing and prioritizing would produce more qualified supervisors and managers than today. The election of higher positions except the top level would hike harmony and efficiency in a company, as covered in chapter 13. As mentioned in our last book, archaeology would draw more interest to resolve many existing archaeological mysteries caused by the less paid and less spiritual people in the study.

A discipline of social science, criminology, and law enforcement would be easier to handle from an initial viewpoint of spirit than today from that of mind. When police and most people stick to spiritual peace rather than mental fighting over disputes, managing social peace becomes smoother. Retracting one step, such peaceful people can be born only if most citizens can be privileged to approve all laws and regulations passed by the government. Elected and highly paid senators and congressmen are no longer average citizens but part of a government. This subject will be expanded in chapter 13.

The wasteful habit of one person may seem insignificant, but collective waste can make a huge difference on the environment. The per capita waste generated in the United States almost doubles that of Japan. Spiritual education focuses on personal performance, not only on the size of acquired knowledge. In general, eastern education focuses more on doing than the western does. It was likely due to the East's moral tradition and family oriented values since the time of Confucius. (Ref 14)

Other fields such as art and sports can also benefit from spiritual study. Spirituality is already part of artistic principle; spiritual study on abstractness can further elevate art appreciation. More civilized and caring less about winning, spiritual ballplayers are less likely to use drugs to boost their competitive edge. Even some pure scientific disciplines can benefit, such as astronomy, which finds that nearly 70 percent of energy in the universe came from nowhere. This dark energy could be easily explained with spirituality and Tao.

Without looking into all scientific fields, we list above only what we see in plain sight. Other fields likely will somewhat be benefited by new spiritual education and research. The influence of Tao and spirituality on knowledge and practice will likely be widespread globally.

Mental Preparation to Study Spirituality

Many new immigrants do not speak English despite their high school English courses. High schools in many countries teach nonnative languages, but few graduates can speak fluently. Is learning a nonnative language really so laborious and hard to achieve? Mormon missionaries can master another language within a few months. On YouTube, we found many lectures on mastering a language within six months.

If one knows that one's own spirit can greatly help learning a language, six months for a language is really no magic. The tongue and vocal cords do not grow inside a brain, so a brain learning to control them would take longer than a local autonomy. Part of unconscious mind, local reflex is frequently used in speaking a language. A brain likely tells the unconscious only the gist of what is to be said, not controlling every muscle movement when speaking.

Spirit directs the unconscious mind to train local muscle reflex for a nonnative language. Once the tongue and vocal cord reflex are established, the language foundation is established, and the brain needs only to conjure up the intended meaning to speak. Speaking a nonnative language fluently within three to six months is not a miracle; rather, high school language courses have failed as they violate the nature of learning. Learning a language from grammar or words instead of custom tones and sentences is against spirituality.

Modern linguists take pride in correct grammar and spelling, but they miss the big picture of human spirituality. Educators blindly follow this gigantic blunder and teach pupils to start from memorizing words and grammar. What a huge tragedy in the open that few see it, or most refuse to see it! Modern education similarly fumbles on teaching chemistry, mathematics, physics, and other scientific disciplines.

Here, nonnative language learning serves as only an example of the failure of modern education. It shows that an education against the nature of spiritual flow is doomed to fail from the start. The motto is that education on the right path must conform to the nature of spiritual flow to achieve the maximum and quickest result. Mathematics is even more abstract than language; with no spiritual education, modern educators no wonder struggle with it.

Being abstract, the study of spirituality is like that of mathematics. Nevertheless, children likely can learn spirituality better than adults because their object permanence has not set in yet; by the same token, their abstract-thinking ability likely is also better than that of adults. Children can think better in symbol, sign, picture, and concept than in word, itemized instruction, and concrete book. In fact, that is what a good education should be: from abstract to concrete, not the reverse.

Though the wisdom needed to understand spirituality is higher than the intelligence for the tangible, grasping the tangible becomes easier once the intangible is understood. The spiritual component of a chair is to be sat on or to place items above ground. The spiritual context of a table is to be used on its top, not its bottom. The spiritual context of a house is to ward off rain and sun directly on people and possessions. Children can understand the abstract context even if they do not know their physical structures.

The spiritual context of a person is the meaningful actions and purpose in a lifetime. Even if one did not fully achieve an action or purpose, at least one tried. The attempts and trials already have meaning. A nonspiritual person sees a goal interrupted as failure, but a spiritual one appreciates the chance to start and to try. Embarking on a journey already carries its meaning; when a goal is reached, the extra meaning is icing on a cake.

Each spiritual purpose can be served by hundreds or thousands of mental purposes. Before symbolically receiving a bachelor's degree, the mind must have waded through many books as well as a bunch of quizzes and exams. Before selling one hundred cars, a car salesperson must endure those in-between customers who did not buy a car. Spiritual meaning is above mental meaning because most spirits wish for abstract success and most minds desire mere material satisfaction; abstractness trumps materialism.

Understanding spirituality is one step further than knowing science. The hurdle in between must be ventured across to know spirituality; the needed abstracted wisdom is even higher than that for religious belief and science. Each inch of brain muscle needs to be excited to a high energy level to observe and master spirituality. For a hundred years, both religious teaching and school study have been preparing generations for this deeper domain where few ventured into.

Modern education and science focus totally on the outside of body and insufficiently on the inside. As a result, most people focus their attention only on physical body and superficial mind. The deeper mind and spirit are mostly left barren, uncultivated, and fruitless. Introducing spiritual education will direct attention inward. People will be more capable of perceiving their own spirituality and deep mind.

The fictional movies such as *Planet of Apes* are not likely to happen. With insufficient wisdom to know their own spirits, other primates have intelligence only to use some tools. The phrase *Homo sapiens* means wise human, which actually derives from realization and understanding of humans' own spirituality. With little material possession and desires, our ancestors were actually more spiritual than modern generations.

Many educated people regard themselves as smart with books read and knowledge acquired. In a way, our ancestors were more adaptive than modern people. Many of them navigated thousands of miles of ocean with no chart or instrument, can we today? Many of them endured extreme weather and hunger for months, can you and us? Their innate spiritual wisdom to conquer the earth was likely of human uniquely. (Ref 15)

One key to our ancestors' spirituality was likely their limited knowledge and intensive focus toward tasks at hand. Nowadays, we learn so many things in diverse areas that much of what is learned is soon forgotten. Increased knowledge can often divide our concentration. One main reason for the popularity of video game is likely its help on focusing scattered minds created by excessive education and media.

Nevertheless, some people lose sleep due to their video game addiction. It helps to focus but can drive people mad. Not easy for mind to focus on, spirituality is abstract. To focus on one's own spirit, the mind first must be independent with no material desire, which buckles down mind like heavy weights around waist, making one unable to walk.

In summary, tools to study spirituality include immense mental focus, ability of understanding abstract, and being good-spirited.

CHAPTER FIVE

Ren (Empathy, Kindness, and Love)

With no proper direct translation, *Ren* or Chinese 仁, means fruit kernel, kindness, empathy, or unselfish love. Ren is a merit innate to human spirit. Animal spirits may have Ren depending on the animal's characteristics. Many docile dogs likely have Ren as some news of dogs rescuing their injured master showed. Some waited years for their master's return; some sacrificed themselves to protect their master.

A small apple seed cannot be seen from outside, but it can germinate into a tall tree. In size or shape, a seed does nowhere near resemble a tree, but they are directly connected, similar to the spiritual link between an injured person and a rescuing doctor. No other animals are unselfish enough to care for a sick fellow being.

Life is precious due to its spirit, which is the kernel invisible to the naked eye. Ren was heavily studied and advocated by Confucius. Buddha's Ren was so powerful that he advocated not killing even ants without a proper cause. The concept of Ren is commonly known in China and Taiwan.

From 1966 to 1976, the Cultural Revolution destroyed a lot of Ren in China, so many who joined the revolution are often described as cold and cruel even today. The new generations have since slowly picked up the Ren concept. People in Taiwan, or the Republic of China, never lost it in the first place.

Unlike in the East, *empathy* is a less often used word in the West, but frequency of use does not necessarily indicate its existence in people. Primarily yang or overt, the western world focuses more outward than the yin East with primarily inward focus. From divination, high spirits or God say both East and West have little Ren, likely due to their high percentage of spirits being asleep. One should develop Ren if perceiving self to lack, but one's own spirit must be woken up first before growing Ren.

With empathy, one is kind to others and animals. This kindness derives from the knowledge that all are the same spiritually. A human may be smarter than an animal, but their spirits have the same essence. High and low spirits do not differ in size or quantity, but in quality. Ren in high spirit is more abundant than that in the commoner; consequently, a high spirit is more likely to help when injustice concurs than a commoner would.

Kindness without spiritual Ren is often false. Giving out a candy bar to a homeless person is certainly a kind act, but whether the giver has Ren can probably only be discerned by high spirits or God. The practice of false kindness is analogous to traversing a river with a paper boat, which will sink before reaching the other bank. Only with Ren is the kindness likely real.

Love can be false just like kindness can be. False or impure love cannot pass the test of time or eyes from high spirits. Love between opposite genders can especially be impure; loneliness or lust often is mistaken as love. A love purity test toward a mate is to ask oneself whether one truly loves one's own parent and sibling. Living together for long, their weakness and strength are often known. Able to love another after knowing the weakness, the love is not selfish.

The practices of empathy, true kindness, and unselfish love consummate Ren, which with the other four merits consummate to Tao. The insufficiency of any of the three likely will not form Ren. Like a stem cell that can create other cells, only Ren can generate true spiritual power and spiritual life. From Ren to the whole spirituality is the right way, or Tao.

Humanity comes from Ren. Ren is without bound; the limited brain size limits the amount of Ren explicitly expressed, but Zen can be expressed beyond what the brain comprehends. Most affections between young couples stem more from physical attraction than from unselfish love, though pure love may later be composed. True love needs no reward. The main reasons of *Homo sapiens's* success on earth is not only due to wisdom but also love.

Love is intangible; it cannot be seen or touched. It can only be played out from the context of life or drama. Manifesting love usually has to be induced from one with the deep capacity; love is often hidden in daily life. When love is revealed in few life events, the events only illustrate a small part of love like an iceberg showing the top one-tenth.

True love gives out heat and light to grow every body and mind. The color green symbolizes this phenomenal expansion from a tiny seed. Time is needed for growth similar to that of a tree. A fully grown tree also takes some time to die out. A physical death is due to growth stop, not due to life stop. Nearly all illnesses are from lack of love.

Physical living and growth by love are two very different things. Living is to sustain life with activities and rests. Growth is to refresh and to improve mind and body. A life can sustain with no growth, but only growth starts a life. One of the purposes of life is to grow, not just to live. Many animals and some people have short lifespans because they stop growing through love.

When in school, we were not asked why we should not kill animals unnecessarily, let alone humans. Take a moment to ponder the reason not to kill. Spiritual love is it, but a spirit must be woken up first. Modern education excludes spiritual education, so love cannot be taught directly or with absolute certainty. The love of most youngsters stays dormant within spirits; it dies out soon.

The cases of serial killers testify to current failed love education. Take a look at Graphs 1A, 1B, and 1C. Each dot represents the spiritual level of a person, and the middle line shows the average spiritual level of a society. Graph 1B shows high average spiritual level, where the lowest dots or the lowest spirit are above the minimum standard. Therefore, they do not need to kill to satisfy innate needs.

High Standard

Average

Low Standard

High Standard

Average

Low Standard

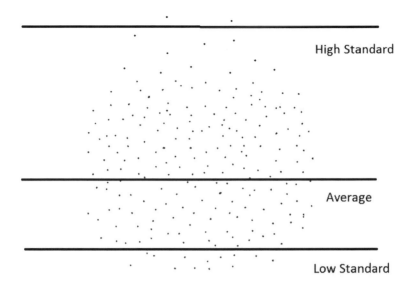

(Graphs 1A: Medium Average Mentality. 1B: High Average. 1C: Low Average.)

Graph 1A shows that the lowest dots are close to the minimum but do not fall below it. They may be mean but not completely heartless. Graph 1C shows low average spirits with the lowest dots below the minimum; they kill others to satisfy their animal instinct without remorse. Repentance and regret are unique to humans; animals do not regret killing, even killing their own species.

Graph 1B shows the spiritual level of many exceeds the maximum, or over sainthood. True saints need not to be validated by a church; their joy and satisfaction are rewarding enough. At times suffering, they stick to a spiritual goal throughout life. Persistent practice makes their lives meaningful and worthwhile. Wealth should not be used as a yardstick for life success, though some succeed on both fronts.

The most common meaning of love refers to the one between a woman and a man during mating. Is physical attraction toward the opposite sex truly love? Even psychologists and psychiatrists are not sure, but they do agree that the desire for a mate can lead to true love later in life. Some try to find true love throughout life, but most never do. What is true love?

Basic Love between a Parent and a Child

Though whether the love between couples is true is uncertain, the love between parents and a child has nearly no doubt. This love grows out of physical creation, duty, blood connection, and investments of material, effort, and emotion. Basic and instinctive with many animals, love is in nearly all people.

Though this love does not distinguish human from animal, it does paint a crude picture of love.

Love between parent and child is not guaranteed to exist forever. Many children do not like one or both parents when grown up; some hate them so much to even kill. Love is in spiritual domain at birth; hatred is in mental domain at maturity. At birth, no child dislikes his or her parents. The dislike and hatred accumulate from the interaction between them.

With no memory, children do not know to dislike someone. An overly restrictive parent can cause dislike or even hatred. A parent should know that no child is exactly like the parent; a child is not from a copy machine. Communication to understand a child is the key for not overstepping any nerve.

Keen parental observation is even more important than communication and should start before a child talks. With love, a parent should respect the privacy of a child, who has autonomy at subconscious and spiritual levels. Discipline with no forewarning or explanation accumulates like snow in a child's mind. Repeated snowfall leads to frozen ground or hatred.

Love and respect go hand in hand within a healthy relationship. Love without respect hurts faith and confidence on both such as an unexplained discipline. Respect without love betrays itself soon; for example, today's people have less trust in governments than people thirty to fifty years ago did. With strong spiritual strength, a child can often sense insincerity or disguise of a parent. Love starts out pure, but accumulated displeasure sabotages the once innocent bond.

Any parent without being taught how to maintain a good relationship with a child is like a time bomb after becoming an actual parent. Today's parental education is too short and covers too few topics, especially child psychology to prevent potential family unhappiness. Frequently, the teaching is also too late after conceiving. Parental education should be a basic requirement of elementary school.

A person without learning youngster psychology ought to be discouraged from being a parent. Nowadays, most parents do not even know psychology, let alone of teenager and child. We do not mean to teach parents to be an expert in youngster psychology like those content-rich college books. However, excluding unpractical and inapplicable materials, parental psychology can be condensed for children.

Some may think that children in elementary school are too young to learn parenting techniques. What are too immature are the minds of top educators like school superintendents or EdD or doctor of education. A girl's menstrual cycle begins between the ages of eight and fifteen, and a boy's puberty begins somewhat later. Forcing them not to have intercourse is probably against nature.

Looking from the viewpoint of a child, children who learn parenting techniques would understand the hardships their parents endured. The parenting lessons not only prepare a child to be a better parent, they also teach a child to behave better. Furthermore, the lessons would prepare them to better deal with hormone surge in their teens. The authors wish we had such lessons before our puberty.

Embarrassment is another major hurdle that needs to be overcome while teaching children parenting techniques. Today's educators had known this big hurdle for decades, but they have had little progress. The problem is adults' embarrassment, not that of children. Adults are really those who need to be educated about not being embarrassed, not children. Focusing on educating the young is another major mistake of modern educators.

This mistake of educating mostly the young is the result of many misconceptions. The first misconception is that children can learn better than adults and that learning difficulty increases with age. Today's phenomenon of older adults having difficulty learning is due to learning being stopped after college, not due to aging or bodily deterioration. With spirit being awake, anything is possible.

Nowadays, most people totally stop learning after college due to the cramming techniques used in school and college. Especially, schools cram knowledge into students without first deciding their interests. As a result, not only do students lose real interests early, but they also grow tired of intensive pressure in school and college. They may learn well for the first twenty-five years, but they are totally exhausted and give up afterward. Some drop out even earlier.

Each period of learning should be followed by at least a period of working to consolidate what has been learned. We will touch on this topic further in chapter 15. Without being burned out in a long stretch of school and college, people would be more likely to accept another period of learning in their forties and fifties, or even sixties. With the sponsorship of industries in college education, landing a job in a different field should be a walk in a park.

Before eliminating adults' embarrassment about teaching children parenting techniques, adults' embarrassment on their own sexual education must first be rooted out. Current adults must be willing to eliminate their own embarrassment by accepting the fact that their sexual education was inadequate and by agreeing to embark on another education that they lacked when growing up. Such an acceptance needs faith and courtesy toward the later generations. With love toward future generations, all things are possible.

Love between Couples Needs Spiritual Link

Among animals, a mated couple often does not stay together. Love enhances the bond between human couples. The high divorce rate in today's societies is the direct result of no spirituality education in school. Even if children attend church worship, which often teaches religious bias more than spiritual lessons, it is at most one day a week, but they go to school five days a week. With spirits asleep, spiritual love is less likely. (Ref 16)

Unknown to many, public school has mostly become the new faith replacing church and temple of the old days. The lack of spiritual education and the atheistic topics in school are likely the major contributing factors to the high divorce rate. It is true that English, mathematics, history, social science, physics, chemistry, and geography, etc. are very scientific, but they are largely inhumane, or lack human touch and elements. Sewing, cooking, and hunting, etc. are humane but they are survival skills becoming less needed.

An old adage states that one reaps what one sows. School education has been highly exalted that nearly nobody sees this major contributor of social problems. Drug addiction, mental problem, lack of reading interest, degenerated family relation, and social isolation, etc. all originated at least to some extent from such an educational system. Knowledge and abilities to read and write cannot be the sole measuring stick of academic success. People are not inanimate.

Not only with wisdom, humans have Ren, respect, faith, and righteousness, particularly we have spirits, awake or not. Spirituality means changeability, flexibility, and out-of-the-box creativity. Two graduates with the same K-12 education will find that they know pretty much the same things. Initially sounding very good that both are well and similarly educated, it will backfire later on, similar to the marriage between two heterosexuals of the same gender.

Not only physically, man and woman differ mentally and spiritually, so much so to the point of being nearly opposite. Two positive or two negative poles in a battery would not have current flow; only one positive and one negative would. In our last book, we mentioned about square-boxed education, which means that people who have gone through it would be molded into the same shape and size disregarding their original shape or size, including the differences between man and woman.

What is done is done, but majority of adults can reverse it if collected wills align to one same direction. Spiritual education is particularly important to mend past wrongs, especially to benefit those married or close-to-divorce couples. Equating to potential materials to be bought later, money is what is argued about most among couples. Without learning abstract spirituality, most people are stuck inside what can be seen or touched, such as money.

We cannot stress enough the abstractness and invisibility of spirituality. If mind values spirit over material, money greatly reduces its arguable role between couples. Money comes and goes, but the key point is the meaning served by money. Money was originally created to serve humans, but many end up serving money instead. Do not let it happen to both you and your spouse. Study spirituality seriously together with your other half.

Invisible spirituality can help a couple to deal with third-party intrusion. Realizing temporariness of material, a couple would look beyond physical or material attraction of a potential third party. Nearly nobody can keep beauty or fitness at old age; most become less pretty and weaker. It is nearly inevitable that one would cross paths with someone more beautiful or stronger, but both can overcome it if they know abstract spirituality.

Inherently, love between couples is harder than love between parent and child. Initially, lovers are strangers who know almost nothing about each other. Even if they know each other since childhood, most people change after growing up. Therefore, work is needed to maintain love between couples. If either side does not perceive or accept the changes of a mate, the marriage soon falters.

Observation and communication transform a couple simultaneously. Careful observation is vital before talk begins; nonverbal communication should precede verbal. A woman wishes to be a policewoman or firefighter after a marriage; the mate does not like the idea and leaves her. Knowing spirituality, one should understand the uncertainty of life. Nobody can guarantee a mate being alive the next day even if he or she is not in a potentially hazardous profession.

A spiritual person knows relations do not last forever. Losing a mate is not the end of the world. Frequently, the more one tries to grab on to something, the more likely that it will disappear soon. A spiritual one does not mentally or spiritually depend on a mate. A practitioner would not lean on a mate so much to the point of being unable to live without.

Only between independent spirits is spiritual connection possible. Without spirituality, at most a couple can connect through mind or body. Nowadays, most are connected through physical and mental levels only; the mental caprice and slowly aging body make high divorce rate nearly inevitable. A couple going to the same church does not guarantee their spiritual connection.

After a couple links spirits, courtesy and respect are the second most important. Unlike a parent with higher status than a child, each of a couple is mostly on equal standing. In a male dominated society, the female usually controls some living aspects which the male is either unwilling or unable to decide such as cooking or sewing. Disrespect and contempt cause dissatisfaction more than material dispute, which often hides actual reason of conflict.

No fixed formula exists for love between couples. An awake spirit naturally springs love while ignoring physical and mental blemishes. True love bolsters one to be respectful and considerate toward a mate. Two halves do not really make a full circle; only two full circles can connect perfectly in spirit, mind, and body. Do not expect a mate to fulfill what is missing internally; otherwise, heartbreak is likely to be inevitable down the road.

Love between Siblings Made of Blood and Friendship

Most siblings in a family have diverse characteristics, but the sibling love naturally flows due to same blood and childhood. Do love siblings as they come from the same root. Only spiritual love can overcome personality difference, so do exalt one's own spiritual level, and do not let one's own dislikes of a different personality block sibling love, especially at one's young age.

Sibling feuds, like most conflicts between couples, are mostly about material things. At a very young age, toys and uneven parental affection are the most likely. At old age, money and property handling are the majority. Sibling friendship starts with the recognition that the bond is for life; regular greetings and communication are absolute necessary to constantly rekindle this friendship. With no maintenance, all relationships decay over time.

Adding friendship to sibling kinship can create a lifetime bond. Nearly nobody is lucky throughout life. At trouble, siblings may be the few who can save one from a total disaster, especially after parents have passed away. Call or visit siblings regularly, but do not get too involved in their lives. Similar to any good friendship, excessively frequent visits may turn into an intrusion, rather than a genuine concern.

Due to different characteristics, siblings can often be good advisers. Not to replace parental counsel, a sibling's perspective can prevent a potential trouble in the near future. Buying a house or a car, marrying someone, or other major decisions may impact the life beyond imagination. A view from another angle may save the day before trouble comes into the door. Do heed the voices nearby, whether desired or not.

Though from the same womb, siblings are different after all. Respect sibling's boundary and privacy regardless of closeness, even identical twins. Similar to any intimacy, a boundary must be drawn between two souls. This boundary is to maintain spiritual and mental autonomy to preserve the two full circles.

With high mate-selection standard and high divorce rate, many old people are lonely. Despite available nursing homes, a sibling is the best choice nearing the end of old age. Some authors used to visit nursing homes and hospices to console the old and the sick. Loneliness, not pain or suffering, was found to be the most dreadful by most. Start a stable loving relation with a sibling at youth, and sustain it to the end.

Similar to love between siblings, love between good friends demands the same spirituality and respect. Having learned to love a sibling, one should have no problem extending the love to good friends. Lifesaving advice is also likely from good friends.

Ultimate True Love Is Toward Strangers

Many animals like primates love family members, but few can love strangers as humans do. The maximum number of monkeys and apes in a family remains small, usually no more than fifty, which is smaller than most human societies. Humans' exceptional ability to love and provide for strangers is the main reason for sustaining large societies. Most primates do not share food or territory with outside strangers who walk into the territory.

Spiritual love toward strangers made large cities possible. Without unselfish love, groups of gangs would brutalize and shrink even a small town, like most animal societies do. Some may argue that law enforcement creates cities, but from results of harsh laws in history, one can probably conclude that rules alone were insufficient in maintaining social harmony.

Rules and laws are built on people's trust and confidence in a society. This trust must be established on mutual respect in order to form a working society. A respectful society can function only with love toward strangers as a starting point. This flow of love, respect, trust, and law is the major skeleton of most human societies that sustains mutual trade of provisions, from food and clothes to constructional material.

It was a long journey from parental love to stranger love. Not new today, philanthropy was not as popular in ancient society. In the old days, skills and properties were handed down to offspring and rarely to strangers. Few of such unselfish acts were done by some spiritual people, but they were exceptions. The level of spiritual love has steadily increased over the span of human history.

The old, the sick, and the crazy were readily abandoned in old societies. Today, many countries provide care with love. Though spiritual love was not explicitly taught in school, the essence of this love had been secretly propagated by high spirits and God behind the scenes, though some egotistic humans like to take credit. No matter who is credited, people have the right idea to love strangers, and it is what truly matters.

The Holy Bible was written in a time of closed societies where the sick and weak were abandoned. Yet in the Bible, the sick were exalted and the meek were protected. Writings in ancient China pictured a future world with the sick and the meek being well taken care of. This teaching started to become popular only in the last few centuries.

Some of the unselfish mentalities were due to abundance of food and material created by the industrial revolution, and some of them were due to higher standard of ethics and morality. Nonetheless, many remain selfish like protecting initially sand pearl with shells. Being unselfish does not mean dispersing all wealth to the poor; it means readily giving to those who need it. It is about choice, not about material gain or loss.

One ought to keep the holiday season's giving spirit alive year round. Serving the poor during Thanksgiving is good, but serving year round is even better. Buying a luxurious house to preserve wealth may be induced by selfish desire for comfort and enjoyment, which may ultimately hurt one's own spirituality. Using that excessive money to buy food for the poor would be worth thousands or millions within the giving spirit. The more one gives, the more one gains.

Many governments have become charity organizations which support the old, the sick, and the challenged. The main reason that no government in the world accepts donations from its citizens is governmental waste and excessive spending. After budgeting decisions are returned to the control of citizens as described in chapter 13, many would be willing to donate to the government.

Governmental charity would be one of the best examples for citizens to learn from and emulate. The unselfish and spiritual citizens likely are more productive than the selfish and nonspiritual. If a rich person wants to hide assets out of country, the net for taxes likely will always have holes. Despite its care for the poor, sick, and disabled, a selfish government exemplifies and compels its citizens to be selfish.

Similar to how smoking parents almost always rear smoking children, a government setting a selfish example can hardly expect its education to succeed in producing unselfish citizens. Most elected government politicians do not know that leading by example is the most efficient way to govern; they resort to law and regulation instead. More regulations and laws probably create more holes for the selfish, who likely exist in many more hearts of populace than in real criminals.

Spiritual Education of Love

After an unselfish government is established, classes of love toward strangers can commence. If unable to even love parent, sibling, friend, or associate, one likely cannot love a stranger. Family love can extend to friend and coworker, and later to stranger. Love for strangers carries elements of respect to acquaintance, of trust to human decency, of righteousness, and of wisdom to invent. Love and its education move everything forward.

A picture is worth a thousand words; a meaningful movie is likely worth more. Education today places excessive focus on reading and writing, and it forsakes love education hidden in many movies and dramas. The 1997 movie *Firelight* draws a picture of a mother's love well over a thousand words. Despite the clear existence of family love, science excludes its study; study of love in psychology is mostly limited to affection between courting couples. Without the study, research, and teaching of spirituality, the light of love even in family is diminished gradually by atheistic education.

In the beginning, the components of love in a movie cannot easily be seen without guidance from a tutor or teacher. Circumstance and environment usually hold the key to finding such components. The above movie tells how a mother treats a wanton child with patience and persistence. These qualities manifest true mother's love due to the large sacrifice without complaint.

Any drama, play, or documentary may hide such a good lesson. For centuries, literature has taken pride in this kind of unscrupulous hidden meaning. Most educators can decode and explain it in plain language, but they seldom do. A hidden message not perceived by a reader has no impact whatsoever. Spiritual education ought to clearly spell out meanings in spiritual senses, despite the abstract nature.

A single story in a movie or play can hardly paint the whole picture for a lesson of love, likely not even close. At least four or five good dramas can probably portray a rough draft of a picture, like a pencil outline of an oil painting. Ten to twenty such movies may detail a pencil outlining, and a hundred such dramas may analogize to the full color of an oil painting. Spiritual education of love is a lifelong learning that may never end at one's physical death.

After learning the first twenty movies, a child is ready to express thoughts of love based on the understanding. One of the best ways to solidify a concept of love is to express it in writing or playing the role in a drama. As discussed in our last book, a child is more than ready to write a book provided a dictionary, an encyclopedia, and a research tool like the Internet are available.

Writing class in today's education is ridiculous that a pupil is asked to write a trite subject with no real meaning required in the content just to see the organization of a paper. Understanding of spiritual love requires deep pondering to match reality. To learn spiritual love, one must organize and express different aspects of love within each movie to really absorb the essence of love.

Today's education reverses the order by putting what needs to be learned first to the last place and what needs to be learned last to the first. The whole picture should be put at the last stage to catch what has been missed. Rather, today's educator presents the whole picture of a discipline at the first year of study. Education should move from partial and abstract to whole and concrete, not the other way around.

This method would teach a basic idea of spiritual love. At least, one is not likely to become a serial killer anymore. Afterward, one can watch more movies and write a book if interested. This intrinsic study and research would answer many questions not easily answered by a rough picture from watching twenty movies.

Due to its abstract nature, spiritual love cannot be described with few paragraphs; it can only be told one story at a time. Spiritual love probably cannot be directly taught or learned; it can only be perceived and realized through stories. Unable to be truly expressed in words, love can only be practiced for people around in daily life. Only after one's love is enough to reach strangers can one be said to really have spiritual love.

Owing to good tradition, love still exists in many families. Many divorces likely happened due to failure of seeing beyond material. Spirituality is a power house for renewing love, not science or education. Knowing little spirituality, today's youngsters tend to act like animals. Classifying human as an animal without any clarification was likely a wrong move by science and education.

Though many animals like the elephant, monkey, and ape show affection toward family, few rise to the level of spiritual love. For example, only humans demonstrate sacrificial behavior for a family member, a friend, or even a stranger as told in many news. When the *Titanic* sank, the captain volunteered to die. Only spiritual love makes a person unselfish and willing to sacrifice self for another fellow human being.

A monkey watching a love movie would not comprehend its portrayed love. The capacity to love and to understand love makes humans distinct from other animals. Without love, some people can easily fall prey to their own instinct to kill others with no remorse. With no love within the spirit and mind, most serial killers derive pleasure from killing others. In the beginning, love sets humans apart from animals; toward the end, humans consummate love via sacrificial spirit.

Hidden tears often tell stories of deep spiritual love such as silent sacrifices, quietly absorbing losses, and compromising reconciliation. Despite the burden, parents feed, clothe, and labor for the children with little complaint. Going to great lengths, a philanthropist suffers for strangers without knowing their names. Such suffering and sacrifices perfect humans. The spirit within each human can and ought to consummate that person.

Spiritual love renders heat and light to make all things possible. It is the power source of nearly all human activities. Our love goes to you through our books, which we spend lots of time and money to realize. Your receipt of this love can ignite your spiritual love within you, and you can hand it down to people you know or do not. Maybe one day one of the authors unknowingly will benefit from such a spread of love throughout the world too.

As a close, the movie *The Miracle Worker* portrays how a stranger, Anne Sullivan, could teach blind and deaf Helen Keller words from scratch against the will of Helen's parents. After Ms. Sullivan lost a brother in an asylum at childhood, her love was transformed as governance for Helen. Without Ms. Sullivan, Helen might have never learned any words, let alone attend a college later. Love inspires others' wisdom like heat and sunlight on all earthly animals and plants.

As a counter example, the French movie *24 Days* can be used to teach what would happen when people lack love toward strangers. Several kidnappers hid a hostage inside a high-rise apartment building with many residents; somebody in the building saw suspicious activities, but nobody reported them to the police. Today, humanity is recognized as an important characteristic existing in all humans. However, the lack of love toward strangers, or apathy, frequently goes a full circle to ironically hit one's own home sooner or later.

CHAPTER SIX

Spiritual Appropriateness
(Respect, Courtesy, and Others)

The second major merit of spirituality is appropriateness. Pure spirits are fundamentally serene, tranquil, peaceful, balanced, and calm. To achieve all these qualities, a spirit must appropriately act on all facets of life to uphold this merit. Respect and courtesy are the specific qualities of appropriateness for relations with various people and the spiritual world.

Other specific qualities spread out to many facets of life such as etiquette, tradition, ceremony, personal hygiene, burial, congregation, agenda of meeting, dress for fitting situations, dance, gathering, party, celebration, travel, table manner, house cleanness, and office organization. If done appropriately, above settings help with relational development between people and spirits, with physical body or not. Appropriateness may be cultural, social, or individual specific; what is appropriate for one culture, society, or individual may not be appropriate for another.

Maintaining friendly relations with others is important for each individual, society, government, or country. But at times hostile relations need to be resolved through lawsuit, riot, terror, war, or threat. The way of handling unpleasant or hostile relations need to be appropriate as well. Using a cruel method to kill an enemy is inappropriate in this increasingly civilized world. Humanity does not exclude the proper treatment of an enemy. This appropriateness toward an enemy is an essence of spirituality; some may call it conscience. Like a mirror seeing whether one dresses appropriately, watching out to being appropriate is the mirror.

The condemnation of the world community upon the use of chemical weapons by Syria is justified through this merit. If no such merit exists among human world, it will soon be turned into animal kingdoms where respect and courtesy no longer matter.

After Zen is seeded in the spirit, respecting and tolerating others' differences become much easier. In Graph 1A, each individual occupies a unique dot without connecting other dots. These spiritually independent positions describe the uniqueness of each spirit compared to other spirits. People are different mainly because of their spiritual differences, which result in the differences of mind or body. Able to respect one's own spirit, one should not have any problem respecting spirits of others.

Most of us are not as great as high spirits or God, and we still have a long way to go. No other people can make one great except self. Each person has a unique spirit and the mind and body following it. Some may wonder why spirits differ from each other so much. Each spirit has many tiny parts, just like a molecule has many atoms. Different parts arrangement produces different spirits.

DNA illustrates how all spirits differ; four letters create billions of distinct individuals. Being unique is intriguing and good. One ought to treasure this diversity from others; it belongs to one and one alone. Be proud of it. When we were taught to respect others, the reason behind was not explained. The supporting reason is diverse spirituality and its merit of respect.

One same word uttered from different people can have very subtle different meanings. Amount of spirituality expressed counts for a large portion. When speaking, one should always express the heart, which is a synonym for personal spirituality. The light emitted by one spirit differs from the light emitted by another. No one can borrow another's spiritual light even if one tries. God and high spirits can bless believing spirits, but they cannot lend light to them.

Do polish one's own spirit to emit the light by highly respecting one's own spirit. This light shines and sees the way, truth, and life the same as Jesus's. Universally the same, the way, the truth, and the life manifest personal spirit. In our last book, we emphasized that all are from God, a spiritual parent. Though the lights emitted differ slightly from one person to another, the ultimate way, truth, and life is the same: the spirituality or the eternal spiritual life.

Few pearls created in one oyster can reflect various lights, not to mention pearls from sundry shells. Siblings in one family are already very dissimilar, let alone people from diverse families. Invisible and untouchable by others, one can only delicately perceive this deeply buried spirit. Excessive materialism, extravagant desire, and obsessive thought can block this spiritual shine like a layer of dirt covering a pearl.

Many search for material wealth or beauty, but most do not realize that the richness and beauty exist within their own spirits; they only need to be uncovered. Wants other than basic food and water are mostly in vain as spirit is abundant enough to create. Some can hold hunger and fast for a few days, but many cannot resist. Excessive desires lead to addiction, which often leads to perdition of soul. Such a fruitless hunting only ends in zero net gain, like graves of many.

Many who do not know spirituality see differences in people as distasteful or undesirable, rather than beautiful and likable. Made from flesh and bone, mind and body are restricted in three-dimensional spaces. With unlimited dimension, spirituality is a true source of beauty and wealth. Like a mountain spring that nobody can tell where the water comes from, a strong spirit exerts power from nowhere.

This endless source of energy is the reason why one ought to respect his or her own and others' spirits. From a mental and physical perspective, energy source from nowhere is a miracle. But to spirit, it is just its nature. To mind and body, levitation in the air is an against-gravity myth, but to spirit nothing is impossible. To obtain that limitless fountain, one needs to return to zero, the humblest of all numbers. Rich in material feeds possessive mind, which moves people away from zeroes.

The zero in spirituality also means infinite possibilities in each spirit. Educated as single-minded in school, most today do not know innate changeability and flexibility hidden inside one's own spirit. This flexibility is not unfaithful or disloyal; rather it is an easily transformable morph to suit all things. Not respecting one's own spirit leads to rigidity and unchangeability, which in turn can lead to alienation and divorce.

Respect Is a Uniquely Human Characteristic

Some animals such as chimpanzees and elephants mourn their deceased by staying and watching silently. Human beings are the only species that buries their dead with ceremony. Scientifically and physically speaking, burying a dead person does not have more significance than leaving it exposed in open air, unless the death is from a contagious disease. Preventing disease was not the reason why our ancestors started to bury corpse underground. So why do humans bury their dead with ceremony?

Burial ceremonies for the deceased are likely uniquely human. Capable of knowing spirituality, a human more readily than other animals knows the difference between life and death. With no spirituality, a person is not much more than an animal. With a residing spirit, a person is respectable. Paying respect to the deceased, a person mourns the loss of an incarnated spirit on earth.

Humans' respect toward each other and the dead is the extension of empathy toward another person. Capable of generating spiritual power, this respect is one level higher than affection among animal families. Though most people may never fully utilize this spiritual potential in a lifetime, the intelligence enables people to tap into this resource readily.

A unique aspect of human respect shows in the clothes. Other animals do not weave or wear clothes even in extreme weather; human clothes are not just used to fend off cold. Wearing clothes in public, a person shows respect to strangers of various ages, genders, and statuses. This respect toward total strangers registers one of the greatest human traits.

This big difference between humans and other animals might be the exact reason why Confucius emphasized very much on teaching respect in worship and ceremony. With no respect, humans are not much different from other animals. With respect, spiritual aspect is prominent, and spiritual dignity is restored despite remnant animal nature inside humans. Spiritual respect renders human humane.

Humanistic respect has existed for so long that many respectful gestures have become heritage or custom, which many view as granted. Dining table manners, etiquette, social gathering traditions like baby showers and bridal showers, and saluting senior officers in the military are good examples of respecting one another. It is sad that many such traditions have become a formality and lost the respect element originally intended.

Before the frequent communication and travel between countries began around early twentieth century, extensive respect already existed within nearly every culture. Despite the language barrier among countries, spirituality was the same. Ingrained in spirituality, respect created abundant respectful traditions in each society. The common spirituality manifested respect within most societies.

From simple salute of nodding head to burying the dead, humanistic respect has been a strong tradition in nearly every culture. It was sustained for thousands of years, long before the scientific and technological big leaps of the last two centuries. Sadly, science receives more attention among educators than respect. It is time that respect is put back to its respectful place since early human history.

Without respect, science and technology alone render humans less humane. Most machines eventually wear down and grind to a halt. With respect, science and technology can be tools of humanity. Global warming is likely an indicator of this overheating enthusiasm toward inanimate tools. Humans have used tools for thousands of years; do not let the tools be the user rather the used, simply because they become sophisticated.

Being Humble is the First Step

Zero and infinity exhibit similar characteristics. What is composed of nothing has no restriction, so the potential for changeability and flexibility is limitless. One who wishes to maintain strong relations with family or relatives ought to first learn to be humble, preferably to the point of zero or nothingness. Any slight ego may hinder or even ruin the development of a relationship right away or somewhere down the road.

Self-esteem differs from ego, though both have the element of self. The self in self-esteem means to respect one's own dignity and decency without spurning others; the self in ego disdains inferiority of others. Any slight ego prevents one from being as humble as zero, and the respect can never be totally sincere. To have no ego, one needs to shrink self to total nonexistence.

Some may wonder how self-esteem can exist without the person existing. Spiritual self-esteem does not require a self to ignite; the spiritual essence would naturally permeate this esteem, kind of like how liquid water cannot be squeezed to less volume than it already occupies. When the mind and body disappear to the point of being directed by the spirit, this ultimate humbleness respects all inanimate and living entities.

This tiptop humbleness needs lots of self-inspection. Most egos are learned habits from parents, teachers, and leaders. Born innocent, a child has no egotistic thinking; in fact, no thinking at all. Ego is the byproduct of a thinking process that is learned in the subconscious while the conscious mind is taught to discriminate.

When a parent compares his or her own child with a child from another family, egocentric cognition is likely formed. When a medal is achieved, personal superiority may creep up in hidden psyche. The separation and struggle between self and others creates ego. It is a tragedy that today's educational, political, and athletic systems encourage this psyche. Thinking retrospectively the meanings of many achievements, one may soon realize the emptiness of many crowns.

Thinking deeply about the meaning of many things in life, one may realize some of the titles and honors are useless. When a student studies history, the stories seem to be quite a distance away. When a person is making history, the lessons of history are often missed completely. Without shedding the burden of entitlement, one may never totally shine one's own spiritual light through.

In the truest sense, zero means unloading all mental freights one carries, whether they are good or bad. Those seemingly good freights only weigh down self and create ego to hinder spiritual growth of respect and courtesy. Zero is for all and all is for zero. Each person must empty the mind to grow spiritually. Some knowledge might have helped, but it is time to dump them to make room for something useful and productive.

The youngest of the young looks up to everyone; the poorest of the poor is the humblest. One is not likely to be humble if a past glory is insisted to be kept like a tiara on head. Mentally speaking, staying at the top is easy; lowering to the bottom is not. Wiping out the plate is the way of nature. No one takes earthly possessions along at death.

Respect High Spirits and Learn from Them

As discussed in chapter 1, high spirits are spirits who have been tested on earth and exalted to a high level through validation by God or other high spirits. Their experiences are worthy of learning. Before beginning to learn, one ought to first respect them and their suffering. Frequently, pain and suffering are not easy to endure, especially when they are taken up voluntarily. Jesus volunteered to be nailed on the cross; the thieves were forced to.

Such voluntary action has been particularly vulnerable; any slight regret can easily tip one to withdraw from the tribulation brought by the willful act. Some high purpose or goal must lead the way. If one can imagine a future success and try to stick to it, one probably has succeeded halfway. Mother Teresa set out to give her love to the poorest of the poor and the sick. She succeeded by sticking to her goal, not by the number she served.

Frequently, it is the heart and the journey that count, not the actual steps or achievement. Hurdles and adversity are mostly inevitable; heartache and stress almost always come along. Endurance is not just a word; it's a reality. Doubt or wobble may shake spirit to the core, but it is for the good. Gold mixed with dirt would not show its luster without high burning temperature.

High spirits and saints do not just exist in religion; each country has many greatly respected heroes who sacrificed for the good of the country. As mentioned in our last book, such sacrifice has never been in vain. The respect from fellow citizens and later generations is no less than that for religious saints. No saints or heroes are perfect, but what counts is not perfection. The heart and the deed count the most.

In mental domain where eyes are attached, seeable perfection is often the goal. In spiritual realm where mind is attached, a good heart is often sought. This heart in the subconscious is linked to the spirit. Not from outside, strength and power are mostly from the deep heart. Most people are stronger than they realize.

Saints and heroes were born no different from us. They started to learn at about the same age. Most of them were not genius having superior memory or intelligence. The key distinction is their spiritual goal and determination. Rome was not built in one day; thirty feet of snow cannot be accumulated from one stormy day. The making of a saint or a hero was not an accident; their persistent mind and determined will were two daily requisites for years prior to any incident exposing the practice.

High spirits and God are not an earthly authority; they do not directly supervise any people or government. Rather, they have been guiding and protecting righteous people. Those who have faith and practice Tao are particularly guided by high spirits. The more high spirits are respected, the more likely they will help to build a better government and society. Lack of respect draws mean spirits who can cause chaos.

The choice is for humans to make. The death of all humans amounts to the extinction of a species like other extinct animals. Though egos of many exaggerate a human's pain and suffering, they are really no different from those of other animals. The real tragedy is the spiritual death of humans. This death of all humans extinguishes potential spiritual lights on earth.

Respect Peers like a Double-Edged Sword

Most kitchen knives have only one edge; a double-edged sword can hurt either way, depending on its moving direction. Treat peers even more carefully than handling a knife. The school system today throws many students into a class for years without much student choice. Befriending seems to be easy in such a system, but many end up in disaster.

People with docile appearance may be fierce inside, or become so after excessive push by others. Not being taught respect, some school students bully the weak to test their control power, kind of like what Hitler did. News of the revenge by the bullied comes from time to time. Some of those being bullied ended their lives. The unjustified school environment is the main culprit.

Even after school environment upgrade as described in chapter 15, one should respect and fear peers as toward an authority. The influential power of peers is often overlooked and can result in tragedy such as a drunk-driving accident of a full carload of young people. Other likely influences include but are not limited to addiction to cigarettes, drugs, and other substances, as well as subtle interjection of personal bias.

Being overly friendly can kill because peers do not wear a hat spelling out the content in their brains. Each person is like a book, and each book can be contaminated when situated too close to one another in school or college. Determine one's interests early on in life and stick with them throughout life. Sidetracking to addictive interests may prove to be deadly at the end though innocent at the beginning.

Showing love and respect by lending a helping hand when necessary, but keep an eye on their spiritual level and mental attitudes first. Before appreciating another's talent, assess a person's nobility first. Excessive talent with no sign of high spiritual level often lands a person in prison later in life. A famous lawyer in New York created a prominent law firm with hundreds of lawyers, but he ended up being incarcerated for fraud and white-collar crimes years later.

Respect Mean Spirits and Keep a Distance

Though mean-spirited ghosts are invisible, mean-spirited people can be spotted. Manner and appearance may say a lot about how respectful one person is toward others. First, the choice of clothing and its color can show how one sees others. Overly flashy and flamboyant clothes may illustrate inner vanity toward high power and control. Mundane clothes may demonstrate inner humbleness.

If capable of keeping oneself clean but not doing so regularly, one may show inner contempt toward others. When respecting others, one would try to keep outer appearance neat and clean for the consideration of others. We may not show inner self explicitly but exhibit outer self like a mirror for inner self. Like an ambassador who represents a country, the outer self readily reveals the inner self.

Manners of a mean-spirited person usually show disrespect through careless speech and vulgar language. Dirty language itself may not be offensive, but the careless use of the language may reflect what is deep down: a disrespectful spirit. This disrespect often stems from ego formed since childhood. Typically, the smarter a person is, the more likely that person may develop disrespect and ego toward others.

The imperfect and mean spirited still deserve respect; they may change someday and become great when their spirits wake up. At the minimum, they deserve to exist and be respected. They often need a lot of space to vent anger or frustration with no forewarning. Their needed space exceeds that of a person with respect. Their meanness likely came from environment in childhood or teenage years.

In physics, an action creates an equal reaction. In human psyche, this analogy works to a degree, though not completely like that in physics. Injury in soul is often created from sometime in one's past. Many forces may mold a soul's meanness, which may either lie dormant or erupt from time to time. Some seeds must be planted somewhere and somehow before adulthood. If one with mean spirit dies before such seed germinates, a mean-spirited ghost may be born.

In fact, mean-spirited people or ghosts deserve sympathy. They may not be a good example for us, but we can be good examples for them. Though keeping a safe distance is necessary, lending a helping hand at times might just encourage them to conquer their internal meanness. A dark corner wishes to receive sunlight; illuminating this dark corner of a mean-spirited person may be an act of love in God's eyes.

Respect the Weak Like an Authority

Since most know that an authority can wreak havoc one's life, respecting authority does not need to be explained. Respecting the weak may be more important than respecting the authority. The strong and powerful physically, mentally, or financially often have plenty of respect already, but the weak often do not. Spiritually, the weak are often closer to spirit than the strong due to the spiritual essence of tranquility.

Spirits may be invisible and contain nothing, but they draw strengths from faith and endurance. What appears weak may be stronger than the strongest. What appears empty may be richer than the richest. A small bug may be weak; one can be stung and discover its strength. Able to respect the weak, one can probably respect anything. So respect even the smallest animal even if it needs to be killed.

One of the most important benefits of respecting the weak is to strengthen self. Frequently, one cannot eliminate one's own weakness due to not respecting the weak. Ego often acts as a blindfold to prevent one from seeing one's own weakness. Unable to respect others' weakness, one is not likely to acknowledge one's own weakness. Without this admission, repentance and correction of self is mostly impossible.

Holding a fogged or blemished mirror, one cannot distinguish whether a spot is on the mirror or on one's face. High spirits and God bless the weak who take in insult and desertion; people with respect should also bless them. A spirit not fixing the inner weakness would be like a lamp not wiping off dirt and not shining. The criterion for deciding whether a spirit is high or low is not its strength, but its weakness.

Introspection to fixing weakness requires a strong inward-facing mirror for dark corners of a very deep subconscious mind. Most people have their mirrors facing outward; such a mirror acts as a barrier preventing one from seeing deep self. Most people repent at weak moments. When one is vulnerable, that mirror caves in and breaks into pieces, like a shy person who has no place to hide but revealing self. The one that most people hide from is one's own deep subconscious, where one's conscience also lies.

No one likes to be weak and vulnerable, but take the opportunity to discover and mend one's own weakness. One main reason why most do not see their own weakness is due to it being covered up by their own strength, especially when one is strong. When respecting weakness in others, one restrains one's own strength from overshadowing weakness, which becomes easily seeable and correctable.

Through respect, one can become stronger not only by mending his or her own weakness but also by strengthening love toward others and self. One who respects others respects the self as a whole that does not separate one's own spirit and deep subconsciousness. This constant respect for self is like a powerful light constantly shining upon one's own deep soul. Via this light of self-illumination, the spiritual power becomes accessible, and the real power follows.

Love and Respect Complement Each Other

Love gives birth to respect, but respect complements love. One can hardly function to its full potential without the other. Love with no respect jeopardizes sincerity of love for touching another's soul. Respect with no love is prone to be invaded by superficial rite and empty ceremony. When love and respect work closely together, the true relation between people is born.

With sufficient love for strangers, one should have no problem respecting them as well as self. Grown out of love, this respect is like heat flowing to warm hearts of others as well as one's own. Upward flowing of heat is like a person always looking up to a respectable person. In cold winter, this warmth keeps people from freezing. Having light or heat is not a sufficient condition to transmit it; willingness to share can touch others in the proximity.

When a person loves another but does not respect another's privacy and dignity, it is like a fireball destroying any just-built bridge. Respectfulness is analogous to a bridge between people; without it, real connection is nearly impossible. Without this connection, material transportation between both sides of the bridge stops. Like a village being cut off from the outside world, the spirit soon runs out of supplies of goodwill and blessing.

With respect but without love is like a beautifully built bridge with nothing to be transported on either side. If both sides of a bridge are equally poor, they cannot provide anything to each other. Love is a real thing to be given to others, whether a warmhearted greeting or material donation. Without love, goodwill for others runs dry and becomes depleted. With love, even a kind and considerate word constitutes love toward others.

Love alone or respect alone produces less power in establishing bridges between people. The most vulnerable people are probably not those who live along, but those who cannot connect with others. A connection is not simply greeting or conversation, but real interaction that shovels goodwill toward each other. After establishing respect from love, do not lose love by withholding good heart and loving spirit.

The ultimate respect is toward an enemy or disliked person. Competition in sports or career fields is not an excuse to lose respect. Quite the opposite, one should respect more toward an enemy or competitor. Many world progresses have been done due to friendly competition, not hateful revenge. When the enemy is respected, goodwill keeps the peace, rather than mutual destruction.

Even an enemy or disliked person has some minimum merits. Mean-spirited people are not bad to the bone; they still possess some good qualities, which are worthy of respect and learning. Though keeping a distance from them is wise, respect toward them would glorify one's spirit into the spiritual world. This revelation feeds back to boost spirituality of self.

One example of how love can complement respect is the behavior of Donald Trump during the election. His locker room talk stirred a lot of controversy regarding perspective toward women. Such dirty talk was not respectful, and he suffered a setback as a presidential candidate. A lot of women and men decided not to vote for him at the onset of the news. His apology along with the testimony of his family likely saved his campaign.

Despite his derogatory view toward women, Donald Trump probably had not done anything rising to the level of against the law. Ethically, he might be wrong, but legally he likely was not. Like Bill Clinton, Trump was likely just being human and exhibiting his male side. Trump's apology along with his wife's testimony likely revived his campaign to the point of upsetting Hillary Clinton's expected win. Love and respect are more in actions than in words, which most citizens probably saw clearly.

Teaching Spiritual Respect through Good Examples

Spiritual respect is an intricate quality that any lack of respect permeates through mind and body readily. Especially sensitive, children can often sense insincerity, disrespect, contempt, and other subtle emotions. Not teaching them this vital lesson of fostering their own spiritual respect is likely to affect their later lives adversely, and they may never learn what exactly goes wrong later. Some experience career or relationship failures repeatedly without knowing this simple internal underlying problem.

Some end up in prison due to this lack of respect in life. Today's schools trying to teach respect without edifying the importance of one's own spirit does not achieve much success. More often than not, people grow up not truly understanding why they should respect others, animals, rules, and the environment. Furthermore, influence of television sports and violence hint to children that being strong is one of the most important things in life.

Teaching students to regularly say *sorry, thank you,* and *please* is only the beginning. More important is the history and significance of human respect sprouting since our early ancestors. *Sorry, thank you,* and *please* become just words if one has no knowledge of their profound and vital importance to being human. If a human is meant to only survive like other animals, such a life is not worthy as a human.

The best way to teach respect is to do it first by self. Teachers of spirituality cannot just utter the words about spirituality. They must demonstrate the innate quality to literally teach it, especially while teaching respect. Respect exists in the spiritual realm, not in the mental realm, so knowledge alone does not help students much to learn by doing. Demonstration of teachers is the key.

Respect is more about actions and performance toward others than love does. The interaction between a teacher and a student teaches more about their actual relation than words. Respect ought to be conveyed through daily interactions to affect the teaching.

If a teacher who teaches a lesson on improving lung health smokes cigarettes in class, this lecture is likely to be ineffective. If a teacher does not sincerely utter *thank you* or *sorry* to students, this lesson on respect will likely produce little result. Respect is more of a heartfelt intention than a simple ceremony or word. The sincerity would permeate through the words and ceremonies if one does really respect another. Spiritual meaning manifesting in mind and body is likely the best lecture for respect.

Internationally, *sorry, thank you,* and *please* are the three most often used words among people of various cultures. Polite parents nearly always produce polite children. Imitation of words is likely less important than imitation of hearts behind the words. Saying *sorry, thank you,* or *please,* one also expresses the heart stemming from the spirit. This revelation of heart overtakes the words to touch the heart of another.

Like a resonance between instruments, a tune can be very contagious, especially when it follows the natural flow of fluctuation. Good music resonates in the heart for weeks after passing the ears. A touched heart via another's sincere respect remains vibrating at the same tune for weeks or months. One who hears this music should relay the vibration to others. When one passes this wonderful tune to others, social harmony is improved.

Every word and move can have spiritual meaning of respect. When a trash can is near, an act of dropping a speck of dirt onto the floor can do a disservice and disrespect to a janitor. An impolite stare of a passerby can subtract integrity of one's own spirit and can set a bad example for a watching child. Do not overlook small moves or words; it matters to one's own spiritual core as well as those of others. Respect others by first respecting every small move and word of self.

Make small respectful word and move a habit in daily life. Respect should be injected into every word uttered and every small move made. Respectful intention ought to be behind the actual words of *please, sorry,* and *thank you.* Make words count by putting up respectful intention and heart toward others, or better yet to the point of vibrating their spiritual cores. This reach of vibration is far and boundless.

Movies and plays are suitable for teaching spiritual love, but spiritual respect in movies may not produce effect on a student. The essence of respect exists in respectful moves and ceremonies. At a distance watching someone paying respect seldom conjures up similar respect in a watcher. In other words, love is an open circuit that encompasses all onlookers or bystanders, but respect is a closed circuit that mostly affects only the acting parties.

A film of religious ceremony, in fact any kind of ceremony, is often boring. The details of a ceremony have little significance to an onlooker, but a performer inside it would perceive the impact of every detail upon the soul. Most ceremonies have little real meaning from each act or behavior alone. The meanings are often hidden in the symbolic gestures or props utilized, not in the ceremony itself.

Because spiritual respect is a practice-oriented lesson, observing how a child shows sincerity and respect during a ceremony is very important. A heart seldom lies even when a mouth does at times, especially during a ceremony. Though respect can hardly be imitated only from learning some behaviors, the serious solemnness such as at a flag raising ceremony or church worship do impact a child's psyche at least to some minimal degree.

Eyes are the windows to the soul; observing how a child looks at an object can reveal the level of spiritual respect. Similar to how behavior reveals one's personality, how the eyes are watching a subject can reveal the depth of spiritual respect. Much such traditional wisdom in military went into training as part of its discipline. This good training practice in military should be transferred to schools when teaching spiritual respect.

Besides asking students to repeat practices of respect in customs and ceremonies, they should also be taught to learn the importance of practicing humbleness. Lessons of respect ought to begin and end at being humble. Without humbling self, one's respect soon is lifted like flood water carrying drifted furniture away. Humbleness is also like a paperweight that ties down one's wandering mind effectively and constantly.

Dangers of Overly Appropriate and Respect

Moments ago one of the authors wanted to use the restroom badly due to excessive water drunk half an hour earlier. One man sat down beside us to use another computer. Soon after, he started to grunt, and none of us knew the reason because we were not doing something disgusting. We thought he was grunting at the content of his computer. Later, we realized that he was grunting at the author who needed to use the restroom and was unconsciously touching his private area in an attempt to control it. After the author used the restroom and came back, that person continued to grunt at him and showed signs of disgust.

From his divination and our discussion, we found nothing wrong with touching one's private area through pants in public. He did not expose his private parts, and particularly the grunter had the same gender as him. In fact, that author said that he always covered up his private parts in the men's shower room in the gym to prevent arousal of a homosexual if one were present. Consequently, we decided to expand this chapter to discuss the topic of excessive appropriateness.

Confucius said that a Tao-practicing gentleman should not look or watch during an inappropriate situation. That grunter watched that author intensively to announce that dissatisfying grunt. A spiritual practitioner would not have even looked at what that author was doing; even if one did, he or she would have looked away. What that author was doing had no concern to that grunter whatsoever, and the unwarranted watch likely was caused by his existing disrespect to others.

A Chinese proverb states that one ought to clean up the snow in front of one's own front door before criticizing the snow above a neighbor's roof. Noticing a small noticeable error of others before cleaning up one's sin, wrong, and mistake is grossly inappropriate, a lot more so than the grunt itself. One should first attend to one's own faults before trying to correct those of others.

Furthermore, we discussed the inappropriate disgust for another only due to a flatus. The western world is particularly true for this disdain than the east since all authors saw it only happening in the west.

The overemphasis on table manners, etiquette, and cumbersome ceremonies in many European countries and America, especially in the old days, had many dislikes and are slowly changing. A laugh or disgust at a flatus still needs to be eliminated by the next few generations. No similar kind of overemphasis occurred in the East beginning from the teaching of appropriateness during the era of Confucius. A habit is harder to eliminate than to have no habit at all from the beginning.

Though one probably can hold a flatus and go somewhere else to release gas, doing so is not healthy for the body. In fact, smelling a flatus can prevent cancer, according to modern research. Anything against physical nature is likely inappropriate. Not only practicing Tao spiritually and mentally, one should also practice in physical realm. Another example is that holding urine too frequently or too long can cause serious internal diseases.

Over respect for an authority can be very bad. As we will discuss in the next chapter, the most faith one should have is the one toward one's own reasoning, followed by faith in high spirits, followed by faith in a close family member, and so on. The German people in World War II excessively respected their government to the point of blinding their own conscience. It set the wildfire of killing millions of Jews and other innocents. Same excessive respect happened to the Japanese then too.

One should properly respect another based on the quality of the mind and spirit, not the title. Though most authors dislike President Trump, we respect him as a straightforward person who dares to say what is unpopular. His efforts in teaching children and running companies is worthy of respect.

One ought to establish a hierarchical system to assign amount of respect according to merits. Respecting one's own spirituality ought to be the highest, followed by high spirits or God, parents, siblings, and true friends. They ought to be followed by favorite movie or music stars, by government authority, by acquaintances, by strangers, and so on. With no good cause to reverse the order, a reversal may be against Tao or one's own spiritual reasoning.

Respecting a living high spirit in a person more than parents might be justified if one is sure that the merits of that person is proven and worth it. Accordingly, faith can follow the respect order. Otherwise, a proper order from proximity to distance and from known to not-well-known should be followed when assigning the right amount of respect.

CHAPTER SEVEN

Spiritual Consistency
(Faith, Trust, Credit, and Others)

Spiritual consistency is the close match and synchronization between the subconscious mind and spirit, between the conscious mind and the subconscious, between deed and the mind, between earlier and later, between left and right, between the conservative and the liberal, between plan and execution, between in and out, between two family members, between two enemies or two friends, between human and high spirits or God, between teacher and student, and between the husband and the wife.

This synchronization does not mean that both must be on the same step as in a military march; rather, it means they are on the same page with a similar goal or purpose. Two enemies are not likely to have a similar goal but maybe a similar purpose of achieving world peace, though their definitions of world peace may be quite different. Exactly whose definition will pan out is likely decided by who is closer to Tao.

During the first Gulf War in the early 1990s, the coalition forces won over Iraq, which did wrong in its unprovoked invasion of Kuwait. In other words, Iraq violated the international agreement not to unjustly use military force against another nation. This agreement complies with the spiritual merit of righteousness, so the coalition forces were apparently closer to Tao than Iraq.

Agreeing with some popular criticism, some authors initially disagreed with the decision of President George H.W. Bush for not fighting all the way into Baghdad due to the concerns of additional casualties and of long-term management difficulty. Contrarily, high spirits indicated that the decision of Bush walked on Tao. We surmised that the spiritual world was forgiving and gave the Iraqi government and its President Saddam Hussein a second chance to correct themselves.

Also to the surprise of some authors, high spirits indicated that the decision of President George W. Bush to start the second Gulf War in 2003 walked on Tao. This time, the popular criticism was even more heavily against President

Bush for the later found unwarranted reason of withholding weapons of mass destruction. As stated in our last book, we sided with the criticism and blamed President Bush for starting the second war unjustly.

Apparently, many authors were wrong in blaming President Bush for starting the second Gulf War. We surmise that President Bush was correct in invading Iraq after the 2001 terrorist attack on US soil in order to foil terrorist bases, albeit that he cited an erroneous reason about weapons of mass destruction.

More precisely, synchronization is more about complying with Tao than being in sync with each other. The two opposite decisions between both presidents, one to stop invasion and another to start one, were both righteous despite their difference on the surface. As another food for thought, high spirits or God indicated that the decision of President Lincoln to start Civil War was righteous and walked on Tao.

Faith is the consistency of belief. Trust is the consistency of people. Credit is the consistency of behavior over a time period. Other consistencies are the matching of what we listed in the first paragraph. Yet other consistencies are the orbit of Earth around the sun, the courses of galaxies, the seasons, and the social development of humans. The first three stable phenomena pertain to the movement of heaven and Earth, and the last is for human species. The former belongs more to Tao than spirituality; the latter relates to human spirits.

Tao will be further discussed in chapter 12. Based on the Holy Bible in the West and the various writings in the East, many authors conjecture that two Gods, a male and a female, have been governing all spirits since the beginning of time. This observation is also based on drastic difference between the western world and the eastern world. The West is extrovert or yang, and the East is introvert or yin.

Likely, the male God governs the West, and the female God governs the East. The father of Jesus Christ is probably the male God appearing throughout the Old Testament. He is a God of many words as illustrated in the Bible. Not with many words, the female God probably prefers concise orders to high spirits and has not been on many literatures, probably due to her reclusive nature. Both Gods likely are concerned about the wellbeing of human spirits, and they probably have been adjusting human courses behind the scenes from the very beginning.

Strict hierarchy likely does not exist between high spirits, but the seniority likely counts. The respect between high spirits is likely strong and consistent. The two Gods are the creators of all high spirits. When alive and with eyes that can see spirits, Buddha likely knew the existence of both Gods, but he chose not to mention them probably based on the reasoning that such a teaching might not help his disciples.

The two Gods probably adjusted human courses at times to force humanity to walk on Tao. Whether a person would succeed in taking over a regime was likely not left to chance. More or less, the two Gods probably decided who would win in a war. A high spirit has just indicated to one author that the loss of Vietnam War by US to North Vietnam was intentional to preserve the cultural innocence similar to what happened in China in 1949. The female God likely distasted pending corruption coming to the East being tagged along with technological advance.

The human histories were likely consistent in the sense that the male God modified the history of the West and the female God the East. This modification was likely not based on preference of the Gods, rather based on Tao. If any preference ever took place, it was likely due to their liking of a particular person's spiritual quality. In our last book, the marine medic who dodged bullets in WWII was likely the working of Gods or high spirits based on God's directive. Either way they operated with very few knowing.

The consistency between spirit and the subconscious likely will become particularly important when spiritual education becomes popular. The mental illness of an author was caused by his spirit and mind being inconsistent. His spirit became awake in his teenage years, but he failed to sync his mind with the spirit later in life.

The internal clashes between his spirit and his mind resulted in mental illnesses, which were induced by burdens of purposeful injustice secretly arranged by high spirits or God. Suspected for over a decade, he verified this inducement a moment ago. It was for his long-term spiritual benefit, instead of short-term monetary gains of roughly three more decades. Without his mental illnesses, our two books were likely not possible.

Waking up a spirit constitutes a promise to the spiritual world that Tao will be enforced in this person. No matter how slight, the inconsistency between an awakened spirit and a crooked mind is a violation of Tao and may deserve retribution or tribulation; the latter was upon that author. A PhD student in spiritual study holds similar promise and can be severely punished by mysterious forces if not being cautious in personal life and one's own SWM. High spirits decide on whether to retribute or to tribulate, not the student. Not so much the known, one should always fear the unknown. An immunity is even less likely for a graduated PhD.

Before the twentieth century, not only transportation was limited to animals, two-way long distance communication was expensive and not widely available. A benefit of local message transmission was that choosing a faith was simple. With the explosion of transportation as well as telephone, computer, and satellite, choosing a faith became increasingly difficult, in addition to the atheistic influence of school and college.

More than half of the graduates today have some doubt about the church or temple they attended in childhood. Choosing a faith is like choosing a lifetime mate; it can impact one's whole life. In the old days, people locally had limited choices of mates. With abundant Internet choices today, many are at a loss in choosing a suitable mate online or in person. After all, the subconscious mind of a person is often not readily visible like the inside of a house.

Unable to decide which faith is the truest, many opt to choose nothing or to fall back to the safe choice of science. After all, science can be seen and touched. However, being safe does not mean it is the truest. Dark energy and many other unexplained phenomena on earth indicate that the ability of science is not limitless.

Certainly, science should be trusted as most of its disciplines took a long time to develop and its methods of development were carefully examined by generations of scholars. Nonetheless, it is time to recognize and to admit the limitation of visible science, particularly by scientists. People should trust science but should not put complete faith into it. Recognizing its limitation in some fields is the first step in finding a suitable solution.

Addiction medicine is a prime example of the limitation of science. At the best, science can avert addiction through developing psychological techniques and some help from medicine. Addiction is often deadly and completely ruins a life. Cigarettes, alcohol, and drug addictions are already a handful for addiction medicine. We refer mostly to addictions like computer games, overeating, sex, pornography, shopping, sports, and routine work, which are dangerous hidden killers.

Another major limitation of science is its lack of subjectivity. Science prides itself for being objective, but lack of subjectivity becomes a pitfall. Though being objective is good scientific practice, human subjective nature cannot be totally shunned away. Each individual is different and unique, but science emphasizes objectivity so much that most people have lost their subjectivity after twelve years of school.

Yet another major pitfall of science is its atheistic nature. Though some scientists may be religious or believe in spirituality, the inherent atheistic nature of science educates many students to believe in atheism, or at least to doubt the existence of spirits. May or may not rise to the level of denying the truth of the Holy Bible, Darwinism is a good example of scientific atheism. Both atheistic, science is no better than Communism in this regard.

Without teaching spiritual faith in school, people believe in many kinds of symbols: money, law, power, system, or strange theory. Though some real power exists in some of the symbols, we are saddened by the fact that many people put one of them as the highest priority. Spirituality, love, respect, faith, righteousness, or real wisdom becomes less important than one of those symbols.

For example, putting money as the highest priority, one becomes nearsighted with focus only on material gain. Possessing large property, struggling to be big, and earning huge income are all done in the name of money. Though people cannot live with no money, putting money above one's own spirit is like putting a carriage in front of a horse that is not likely to go anywhere.

Not actually going anywhere is probably the most common sickness of graduates today. Working full-time or starting a family does not have real meaning by itself. Being a billionaire alone is even less meaningful. Security can protect the material shell without injecting meaning into life. Though life meaning must be attached to movement of material, material alone does not carry a meaning.

As children, we liked to ask why about almost everything we did not understand. After growing up with a lot of education, most of us stopped asking why. Why did we stop asking why? Focusing so much on acquiring material into brain, we ceased to ponder the meaning of all obtained.

Next to money, people without spirituality believe in power and control. Money and power often are connected. Money is needed to fight a war and to control acquired territory. In World War II, the strong military of Germany invaded other countries to control wealth. Also, the strong Japanese military invaded neighboring countries to control needed mining resources. Frequently, only the affluent can afford to run for public office to gain political power.

Money corrupts; putting power as the highest priority also makes people arrogant, aloof, egotistic, and lose touch with reality. The belief of Hitler that bigger weapons were always better partially contributed to German loss in battles. Many emperors were doomed soon after conquering other nations and becoming arrogant. Placing power as the foremost authority often clouds judgment and clear thought. Believe what the power can do, but do not believe in the power.

Many without spirituality believe in the law. To them, order is the highest priority. Social stability becomes paramount over personal freedom and choice. The number of laws and regulations grows out of control, but the crime, lawsuits, and corruption keep growing. High-level public officials and representatives can even start to corrupt legally under the law they make.

Those who believe in the law are more likely to also believe in the system. Is the system a political system, an economic system, or a government? Seeing many Ford Model Ts, which is the first car introduced around 1910, running on the streets of New York today, one likely would have wondered whether they time-traveled back to 1910. Sadly, people use a political system for hundreds of years and do not feel the need to improve like they do with cars.

Actually, talks about changing the system have been around for a long time, but none of them materialized. This procrastination was partly due to the potential impact to many people and partly due to the difficulty of garnering enough votes. In chapter 13, we will elaborate on how to change a system steadily and surely.

People without spirituality also tend to fall prey to strange theories such as Scientology, religious cults, and terrorism. With the faltering of religious values and the rise of atheistic scientific values, many spiritual needs are not being met. An attempt to crown science to the level of religion had led to the creation of Scientology, which, however, lacks real spiritual content. Many religious cults were reported on news as mass suicides or sexual exploitation. Some others rendered their believers fruitless.

Some cult leaders might originally have had some spiritual awakening, yet most of them likely did not achieve a full blown spiritual connection regularly. Even the authors do not dare to claim a constant spiritual connection despite daily effort. Spiritual connection needs the consummation of all five merits; even if only one merit is missing, it may not connect.

One main reason why terrorist groups such as ISIS could recruit people to sacrifice themselves was the lack of spiritual education in school. Joining a terrorist group boosted many to spiritual existence and belonging. Many people are literally dying of thirst for spirituality. Physical death in exchange for a spiritual life can be more attractive than a spiritual death.

Faith is the soil where spiritual seed germinates and grows to become love, respect, wisdom, and righteousness. Without this fertile soil, the spiritual seed would attempt desperately to land on another place. The result of a mass absence of spiritual education is a society full of lost souls who are ready to latch on to money, power, law, system, and heresy. Spiritual education of faith, trust, and confidence is likely the true and only salvation.

Subjectivity and Non-logic of Spiritual Faith

One believing in everything is basically as pointless as one believing in nothing. A choice of which and what to believe is more important than a literal step of executing the choice. A proper belief is the zeroth step before the first physical step, as we discussed in our last book. If the zeroth step is wrong, all the steps after the first will be wrong. Choosing what and which to believe is a very subjective and personal decision.

Emulating scientific objectivity, psychology study today is too impersonal to adequately fit into personal agenda and thinking process. Subjectivity should be a major study area of psychology. The perspective of looking from inside of a mind can drastically differ from that of looking from outside.

Many scientists have difficulty understanding the mentality of a suicide bomber willfully dying for a belief. The problem is that scientists have formed the habit of looking at things and people from outside. Looking from inside would incorporate the strength of belief and the spiritual power. In other words, a whole person, including what is hidden in the subconscious and the spirit, is counted.

Psychology studies motivation, which is at the door of stepping into one's inside; it fails to step further into the soul where the personal power lies. Without stepping into the subjective realm, psychology cannot recognize this deep hidden power within. Spiritual power is proportional also to subjectivity. The more subjective a person is, the more powerful the spiritual faith is.

In a beneficial way, subjectivity boosts confidence into spiritual faith and power. An umpire needs to be objective to judge both players impartially. If this fairness is donned onto a player, it would reduce the force and motivation of the player. The same process can be transferred to personal decision making, which is also subjective in nature. Study of subjectivity within psychology may focus on understanding this power and determination and finding ways to increase them.

Reasoning or logic has little to do with spiritual faith; it is a pure personal choice. Similar to choosing clothing to wear, a belief does not need a reason. It is what it is; explanation is not needed or even possible. Reasoning and logic may be utterly useless in deciding a particular belief. One's fate is mostly unknown and cannot be determined before it happens, just like faith.

The lack of logic in choosing a faith illustrates the danger of believing in everything one sees and hears. Science believes only tangible and proven theory; Albert Einstein tried to avoid them, which led him to discover relativity and quantum physics. Our eyes and ears often blind and baffle us more than we realize or wish to admit. Likewise, intelligence and reasoning can thwart belief.

Protestors and demonstrators are blessed for strong beliefs. A belief is a motor propelling one into doing something purposeful and meaningful. Following daily routine to merely survive is like a wandering animal. If one believes one's own spirit, then it does exist to help. If one does not believe, then the person does not feel its existence.

Unlike a tangible table or chair, our spirits and the faith inside it cannot be seen or touched. With no logic or explanation, faith spits out logic and reasoning, like a fountain spurting out water year round. The loss of faith conduces to reduced reasoning ability. Though churning out logic, computer chips are assembled from non-logic diode arrays.

Like easily dissipating air, a weak faith soon disperses spiritual strength into surroundings by a slight wind. A strong faith can resist strong wind like a deep-rooted tree holding on to the ground in a hurricane. Concentration and intense focus is the key to strong faith. The worst sin of a person is probably not to believe even his or her own spiritual existence.

Faith also increases efficiency to achieve life goals. Instead of focusing toward outside tasks, focusing inward toward strengthening faith is like growing the root of a tree. Though the root is not seen, the foundational strength is greatly enhanced. Continuous faith is like a powerful motor of an electrical car which pushes it forward.

Signs and Symptoms of Lacking Faith

Some signs and symptoms of lacking faith includes being unkempt, depression, anxiety, complacency, hunched over, easily frustrated, easily addicted, empty headed, with no personal opinion, relying on others, and prone to digestive illness. When many of these symptoms occur, one is likely to have little spiritual faith. Increased depression and anxiety in a society often indicates a social problem of generally lacking spiritual faith.

Faith is like a pillar of a house that other beams depend on. One with a deep and strong faith tends to stick his or her chest out and hold his or her head high. A person frequently lowering his or her head or bending his or her back indicates the lack of deep faith. Faith is the foundation of life; lack of this foundation often renders a person either goalless or with too many goals, both of which have no supporting pillar.

With too many life goals, one overextends self to try to achieve dreams to near exhaustion. As a means to an end, time and effort for chores are cut back to feed a nearly impossible ambition. A person falls prey to being unkempt and neglecting hygiene and disorganization. Like a mad scientist trying to achieve a research goal, one does it at the expense of losing one's own spiritual faith.

One important sign of lacking faith is being easily frustrated by failure or interruption. People rushing to accomplish multiple goals often find standing in a shopping checkout line or a traffic jam irritating. Time is never enough for them, and small loss of time is sufficient to induce frustration or feeling of being set back. Having little time to stop and think deeply or to plan at a grand scale, they are lost within themselves.

With no life goal, one is easily distracted by beautiful sight, smooth music, delicious taste, soft touch or feeling, opposite sex, entertainment star, and other worldly dazzle. The world becomes a playground full of toys for those adults who never spiritually grow up. Like a rocket not having its own propelling power, it can be sucked down from the sky by any small amount of gravity.

An addiction can easily attract and glue a faithless person; others' opinions tend to have undue effect on that person too. Faith is the central belief that forms the base of other beliefs. With a shaky foundation, a building would not be sturdy enough to withstand an earthquake. The higher the building is, the more dangerous it becomes, especially after one overextends to multiple goals.

Without the basic core belief, all other beliefs become shaky and easily detachable. The thinking process of a person relies greatly on this core belief. Without it, one likely has difficulty in even thinking straight, let alone creating anything. Over a prolonged time with no core belief, what is learned is soon forgotten, just like a porous sieve unable to retain water. Like a zombie's brain, the head of a person with no core belief is empty like a soccer ball.

Without a core belief, one can hardly stand up, like a spineless vine that must cling onto a tree. After a marriage, interdependency can set in to depend on spousal support for all emotional and spiritual needs. This heavy burden can result in a surrender or divorce. Likely, nobody can carry another on shoulder forever; the huge exhaustion can easily be imagined.

With no core faith or life goal, one often neglects to check other goals and grows complacent at routine or living comfort. A car without a destination would wander around and waste gas. A best life goal is one that is unlikely to be fulfilled in a lifetime no matter how hard one tries. A saint often did not totally accomplish his or her life goal indeed; faith makes up the rest, like Jesus did.

People may think saints are fools; in fact, they are the smartest as they initially set out to perform the impossible.

With no strong core faith, one wobbles from side to side. This constant switch of positions often leads to digestive tract problems such as diarrhea, constipation, bloating, high acid reflux, or other digestion discomfort. Similar to a liquefied soil easily flowing away, most nutrients do not stay long to be absorbed. After years of depletion, a ground becomes stubbornly hard, and most plants cannot grow on it.

After long deprivation, depression and anxiety can set in unexpectedly. Like ten feet of snow not likely resulting from one storm, a development of depression and anxiety often results from the combination of multiple incidents and factors over decades of spiritual depletion. A spirit is fragile and needs to be cultivated daily to preserve its freshness and tenderness, like a newborn baby or newly sprouted vegetable.

Food and Exercise for Healthy Faith

Like a person who needs food and exercise to function properly, a spirit needs a daily dose of faith intake to be alive and well. A faith-lacking spirit is like a ball without much inside; it is soft and empty. Better yet, fill the ball with a solid material or even heavy metals such as silver or gold, whose quality stays stable for centuries. A solid inside may require decades of faithful practice.

Frequently, after one is attached to someone one likes or dislikes or is tormented by material gain or loss, faith is lost. One easy way to pump up faith is to read something spiritual. Sutras, the Holy Bible, or other religious books written by saints are good choices. People who have reached the shore know better on guiding toward the worry free kingdom.

As discussed before, human senses deceive people more than most are willing to admit. Seeing things needs lights, and hearing things needs air. This world of materials is made of wallpaper and holographic projection, which will eventually fade away. Spiritual words from successful saints testify and remind people of this fragile and temporary existence, which is not much different from virtual reality.

Righteous words can be particularly helpful. While other merits often cannot be personally felt, being righteous can often be perceived deeply. A person with faith often can more readily sense responsibility and duty, which correspond to righteousness, than other merits. Words of saints infuse lights deep into a soul like a magical pill to revive faith.

Another food for boosting faith is to pause before consulting high spirits or God. This brief pause gives one a chance to consult one's own spirit. Frequently, a baffling doubt becomes clear suddenly and eliminates the need for divination. As a person transforming from less spirited to more spirited, this self-consultation can increasingly be easier and more important.

Most are confused by diverse choices or opinions. This confusion often is due to messed priority or excessive desire. The light of one's own spirit can shine into a clouded mind by reminding one of true life priorities and ultimate life goals. Once a priority is set straight again or an excessive desire is recognized, the choice can suddenly become clear.

Mental exercise should be used frequently to strengthen faith. While reading spiritual words all the time may not be healthy, memorizing and reciting some favorite spiritual words can propel one to move toward spirituality while doing something else, such as a chore, a walk, or a wait. Similar to physical exercise, mental exercise keeps one spiritually fit and burns off excessive fat of a mind. Do care for spiritual body more than physical body.

The excessive fat includes but is not limited to comfort luxury leaning, tasty food craving, soothing music adherence, and other attractions. The mental exercise aims to place one's own spirit at the highest priority than the mind, body, and other trivial things. Some trivial things may be important, but placing any of them as the highest priority would reduce life meaning and motivation. Also, do not be satisfied with only the knowledge of putting spirituality at the highest priority. The mentality of putting spirituality at the highest priority is even more crucial.

Each of us has a customary way of thinking which we seldom pay attention to. This autopilot in our thought process becomes second nature to us, similar to driving a car for years. Right after sitting in the driver's seat, one knows what to do next. If the highest priority is not spirituality for decades, the mere knowledge of putting spirit at the highest priority is definitely not sufficient. A mentality such as the second nature of driving a car is needed; it may take years to place one's own spirituality to the highest priority just as the time needed to form a driving habit.

The longer a customary way of thinking has formed, the longer it will take to adjust self to a new way of thinking to put spirituality as the first priority. Kind of like a person who wanders deeply into the wood, the further one is lost inside the wood, the longer it will take to walk out. The subconscious mind is a deep wood. Do not give up or be frustrated if mental hard work does not seem to be effective. Given enough time, it will.

By reflecting a customary way of thinking or an addiction into the spirit, the mind can gradually change after some time. Even then, do not expect changes to take place within weeks or months. It often takes six months to several years to rid a wrong way of thinking or an addiction. The mind is flexible but is often sticky; to unstick it will likely take a lot of time and serious mental work. This is why we repeatedly stressed mental persistence in our previous book.

Closing eyes frequently may help people addicted to beauty. Sitting quietly alone for a long time may help people addicted to soothing music. Staying away from video games for a few weeks may help to shed the addiction like a lizard shedding a used skin. Whatever the addiction is, stop it for a few weeks or months to perceive the difference. One may find one's own peace and tranquility from being free of the constant disturbance.

Another way to escape an addiction is to swamp oneself with the addiction to the point of sickening. Like a flood killing all living things on its way, a flood of addiction can wake up a mind by swamping it to the point of exhaustion and of asking for mercy. Exhausting a desire to the point of nausea can be risky, though, sometimes, but it might be the only way out of a stubborn addiction. The mind in the brain is made of flesh, which is bound to decay at some terminal moment. Although risky, a fire can at times be used to extinguish another fire.

All born with this tranquility, we often neglect to compare this complete silence with noises. Our spirits were originally peaceful with no sight or sound; we gain sight and sound through senses to facilitate survival, not to be blinded or deafened. Reaching one's own spiritual peace, one soon realizes nothing in this material world is comparable. Spirituality is total silence. Only total silence can reach spirituality. When a mind becomes totally tranquil, one reaches Tao and spirituality. Gold is silence.

Physical exercise is yet another way to motivate the mind and spirit. When walking, swimming, biking, or running, the mind and spirit are shaken by physical movement and less likely to fall asleep. Night sleep is for mind and body, not for spirit. Too much sleep bores the mind, which affects the spirit. Sleep-wake cycle pushes the mind and body to move forward. Closely following this cycle increases spiritual power; disobeying it drains the power, like a steady rhythm of breathing during a marathon increasing endurance.

Most physical bodies are destructible. Most bodies are also limited in strength, flexibility, and stamina; exceeding the limit risks injury or death. Not only realizing one's own eventual physical death is important, the belief in one's own physical limit is equally important if not more so. The disbelief of this limit is rampant among teenagers who are experiencing rapid bodily growth. They should be instilled this belief before puberty starts, just like sex education and emptiness of sex by itself. Many injuries during youth are caused by this disbelief of one's own physical limit.

Even though most physical bodies have limits, this ceiling can be slowly pushed higher through training. Most people cannot eat a jalapeño raw within a meal. Knowing that the most difficulty of eating jalapeño being in the tongue receptors, one can train oneself to gradually increase tongue tolerance to the point of eating two to three jalapeños a meal. With enough time and endurance, most physical limits can be raised to greatly exceed average. Patience and perseverance are the key.

Defend Faith with Reasons like Country Boundary

As we repeatedly stressed in our last book, all faith must build on the belief of self, especially one's own spirit and spirituality. Without this foundation, faith or trust is not stable and does not last. Most religions emphasize on believing in their religions, but they failed to point out the basis of faith in one's own spirit and spirituality. This fundamental error has resulted in many unstable faiths and blinding beliefs.

The outward tendency of mind can often shake this basic foundation of spiritual belief if not well established at the first stage of life. The basic of most hand combat is a sturdy foundation of lower body. Without this sturdiness, one can often fall and be defeated. The foundation of believing in one's own spirit should be fostered from childhood as the first step. After children's minds are busy learning knowledge, they have missed the prime time of establishing this most basic foundation.

With belief in one's own spirituality, doubting other people or things would be all right. The faith for God must also be based on the faith in one's own spirit and spirituality. The faith of Jesus in his own spirituality probably enabled him to cure others. Without a root, no plant may grow. Many social problems likely originate from this lack of faith in people's own spirits and spirituality.

After this innermost fortress of soul is established, one should defend it like guarding a border. Do not just draw a line or put down a landmark to defend this belief of one's own spirituality. Fight tooth and nail if needed to prevent it from being occupied by others or authority. No authority is higher than this foundation. Not just defend it, expand the territory from there on.

A person with faith in his or her own spirituality is ready to believe in higher spiritual power, be it God, saint, or another person. As we will discuss later in chapter 10, the shaky faith of those who believe in Confucius and his teaching likely stemmed from their shaky faith in their own spirituality. With no strong home country, attacking other countries may be doomed to fail. Probably lacking faith in his own spirituality, Confucius suffered hunger while attempting to preach Tao to other countries.

After building a home country, expand the territory daily to fill the heart and conscious mind with this faith. The subconscious and conscious are personal soil and should be sacred without intrusion from others or authority. Elementary teachers ought not to misguide that believing in one's own country is more important than faith in one's own spirit and spirituality.

Like the softness of brain, mind is inherently soft and easily persuaded. It is a tug of war between two choices while growing up; choosing to believe what others say or what one's own spirit reasons is a vital switch which can determine one's fate in life. Use one's own reasoning to occupy all conscious and subconscious mind inch by inch with daily work of faith in one's own spirituality.

The important strategies of this vitally important war are keeping the pressure constantly, no rush or shortcut, and attending to the subconscious mind. Being soft, mind cannot resist constant pressure and persuasion. One who has built a basic fortress of faith in his or her own spirituality must remind him- or herself of this vital territory regularly. This is the compass of finding a spiritual home at physical death. If this compass is lost, returning to God's kingdom is nearly impossible even if they allow it.

The constant self-reminder keeps pressure on one's own mind, like a sentry keeping an eye out for any potential external or internal danger. The watchful eye must be careful and not rashly be done. A small neglect can lose the home territory of faith in spirituality. Not just outside influence needs to be watched carefully, subconscious mind is equally important to watch.

When an enemy attacks, reason and principle are the best weapons to counter the encroachment upon personal sacred space. Sharpen one's own reasons and principles to ensure that they are absolute and not opposing with one another. A ship machine gun able to turn 360 degrees is likely to damage the ship inadvertently. Only absolute reason and principle do not risk hurting self in foot. Absolute reason and principle do not contradict with each other.

Only absolute reason and principle are sharp enough to kill enemies. Ambivalence and hesitation dull weapons and aiming precision. Ponder extensively to avert any uncertainty. Faith cannot be built in a day, just like the city of Rome. Knowledge is the most glorious when it inspires to resolve an internal confusion. Before one knows how to defend, learning to offend is futile; reason of self ought to be sound before starting to learn reasons of others.

Only absolute reason and principle grow absolute faith in spirituality. Do not borrow other's absolute reason. Based on individuality, various people have their own absolute sets of reasons and principles. Referencing and learning from others' reasons is all right as long as one filters them with one's own careful thoughts. This borrowing of reasons and principles is the spirit of education.

Daily caution and hard thinking make sharp and absolute weapons both for defending self and for choosing others' beliefs. Given diligent effort, one's faith in spirituality and eventually Tao will grow daily. Faith is the source of strength and power, particularly the faith in one's own spirit and spirituality. With more abundant faith, one is more likely to withdraw from it when needed; at crises, faith in self is scarce.

Belief as Foundation of Faith and Trust

Belief is the foundation of faith and trust. Many beliefs toward one target build a faith or a trust. Strong faith results from internal cooperation between wisdom and righteousness. Trust results from external consistency linking appropriateness and Ren.

Like glue, faith and trust bond people together based on spiritual consistency. Only consistency at spiritual level can truly align mind and body at all fronts; otherwise, an internal consistency may fall apart soon. A married couple may or may not have a true bond; if not, they may soon separate or divorce. In the old days, couples stayed married due to social distaste for divorce, not necessarily because a true bond existed between them.

Trust other people or spirits with at least a slight reservation. Overweight on trusting can tip the balance and reduce one's own faith toward one's own internal strength. A book cannot be fully judged by its cover; a person cannot be totally evaluated by few superficial contacts. Few truly know the deep lake of another, even between spouses. A subconscious mind for the most part is not totally known by one's own conscious mind, let alone by another person.

Never completely trust a book, another person, or a rule. An adage says: "If an individual totally and wholeheartedly trusts a book, it is worse than without that book." All must pick up the weapon of reasoning while reading a book before consuming the stated belief. Our books are no exception, nor the Holy Bible or the Ten Commandments of Mother God. Most words once uttered or written carry potential bias or flaw. They can lose the spiritual transparency or all-encompassing trait. Lao-Tzu said that words of Tao that can be said no longer bear the whole truth of Tao.

Instead of words, the foremost to believe and trust is one's own reasoning and spirituality. Just be sure to double check that the reasoning conforms to spirituality.

Most politicians are strangers to most voters. By nature, a politician cannot possibly know all voters in person. Also a citizen cannot possibly know all people in a government, which is made up of thousands of people, so a citizen cannot possibly trust a government. This false trust is the result of governmental propaganda and citizens' mental blindness. This is the main reason why we suggest that representative democracy is replaced by true or direct democracy as outlined in chapter 13.

Though not to be totally trusted either, the Bible, Quran, sutras, and spiritual books such as ours are at least in the open and not hiding anything. Even so, they should not be digested without a deep thinking. A wrong food can seriously affect one's spirit or mind. They might not be poisonous, but they can induce trance to hibernate a spirit. The constant spiritual wakefulness is vital to one's whole health, not just food and exercise.

Faith should come before trust. As discussed above, no one perfectly knows others. Many couples do not even communicate with each other fully on personal secrets. Even if they do, they may not fully understand the reason or principle behind the secret due to the barrier of propensity between male and female.

Hence, one must place faith in one's own spirituality above trusting another individual. If one were to draw a picture of faith and trust, it would be shaped like a mountain. The mountain peak is one's own spiritual faith, and the middle section is the trust for others. This hierarchy should be crystal clear for a mountain to be sturdy. A mountain with the center part missing has a high risk of being toppled by earthquake or other natural force.

Teaching Spiritual Consistency, Faith, and Trust

A change of mind or personality does not mean a change of confidence or faith. A sugar dough can be made into various shapes before being baked in an oven. Once baked, the shape no longer changes, and any attempt to change the shape can destroy it. Unfortunately, today's school rushes to fixate the shape of young minds by teaching them fixed things way too soon and too early.

Like solid clay sticking to a particular principle's mold, spiritual consistency is one main reason that God and high spirits do not easily change promises. Consistency and loyalty are like Earth's rotation around sun or the moon's around Earth, churning out routine day after day and night after night. Slight variations from one day to the next consummates to four seasons. Too many changes too quickly can destroy crops and kill people.

Changes revolving around a steady principle can be as long lasting as gold. This kind of change is good for mind and body, which is perishable flesh craving for change. Spirituality is the pillar of a person that remains steady. As one keeps spirit pure like a year-round mountain spring, the change can be endless, but the resulting spring water is always pure and drinkable. If the source of a spring is contaminated, all things downstream a spring are contaminated.

This unchanged source is the faith or confidence, the foundation or basics, and the eternal life or truth of the true self. Faith in one's own spirituality and its origin, or God, makes life and all things on earth possible. Without this faith, nothing is likely to succeed and all success is likely to fail eventually. Be sure to keep the faith in proper proportion. Faith in one's own spirituality should be the biggest, followed by that in high spirits and God, followed by that in parents, followed by that in members of family, followed by that in social leaders, and so on.

Modern education reverses this natural order by asking students to trust political systems and community leaders before believing in their own spirituality. This produces many lost souls, not to mention the breeding of a corrupt political system and many corrupt leaders. Only after majority of citizens have placed faith in the right priority does a nation have a meaning collectively.

Only spirituality breeds consistency, and only a person with faith in his or her own spirituality treats others as fairly as treating self. Unable to treat others as equal as self, one is likely to be bounded by greed and misplaced intelligence. Righteousness cannot exist with no solid faith or consistency within one's own spirit.

CHAPTER EIGHT

Righteousness

Spiritual righteousness is the knowledge and doing of right principles. Right principles are those originated from spirit. Doing a good deed due to a learned principle that doing good deeds is good, one probably does not truly believe or understand the principle. This good deed likely counts almost nothing. Doing a good deed from the heart without thinking, one is likely blessed heavily even if it is a small deed.

Except the person who performs the good deed, most others cannot discern whether the deed is originated from the spirit or not. Judging a person purely based on the deed can be misleading. Also, practice of righteousness at the spiritual level may not always show up as external deeds.

Learning Right and Wrong Principles

Do not be so quick to dismiss that most people already know right from wrong. Telling right deed from wrong deed is easy as they can obviously be seen. The important question is whether a deed has a right or wrong principle. People play football for various reasons, yet not all are good. In fact, many are wrong, such as playing for parents or money. As reasons from external factors, they are probably not originated from the internal spirit. One of the right reasons may be to play for fun.

Wrong principles often lead to wrong deeds like murder, rape, abuse, theft, or assault. But good deeds do not necessarily originate from right principles. Above reasons for playing football are good examples. If a deed conforms to spirituality, it is a right principle; otherwise, it is a wrong principle. Whether a deed conforms to spirituality is not easy to determine. Before one can tell a right principle from a wrong one, one must be in touch with one's own spirit at all times.

A question one should regularly ask oneself is whether one is constantly in touch with one's own spirit. Without touching one's own spirit, it is nearly impossible to know whether a principle held for a deed is right or wrong. The principle of a spirit is not always right when doing a deed, but the spirit knows the spirituality deep down. Like a person ponders deeply at a dilemma, regularly a spirit delves into spirituality to expound knowledge.

Meditation works on this same principle that a spirit must be extremely tranquil to reach deep down to spirituality. Quietness is the precursor of an action, which not first approved by the spirit and spirituality is prone to deviate from the course, or the way of Tao.

Many dictionaries define righteousness as morally right, which is too shallow and not in touch with spirit. Moral or morality is defined as the standard of good conduct, so conduct restricts the definition of morality. Right or wrong in spiritual sense cannot be judged from conduct, as earlier analyzed; rather, the principle decides a conduct.

More than morality, the scope and depth of righteousness is beyond the concept of most people, whether they are religious or not. Think righteousness as a vast ocean as most people only have a small swimming pool in their backyard. Refraining from doing bad things to others can hardly qualify as being righteous. Only after becoming righteous can one do righteous deeds; deeds do not define a person. Only the pure righteousness within a person defines the person as righteous.

In other words, righteousness is a spiritual state, rather than a mental state. Being spiritually righteous, one is ready to do righteous things all the time, twenty-four hours a day and seven days a week. This readiness comes from deep in the spiritual nature, not the shallow mental nature. Like a water balloon ready to burst and to release water, a spiritually righteous person is ready to do righteous deeds, but not necessarily doing it literally all the time.

In addition, a righteous person must transcend materialism to enact the internal righteousness. A person who cares too much about material possessions cannot enact spiritual righteousness and is not qualified to graduate with a degree in spirituality. Material possessions include the shape and sound of this world like the beautiful figure or sweet voice of an opposite gender. An example is pornography.

As explained above, whether one's principle is right or wrong cannot be judged by others unless the principle is revealed. The right or wrong of this principle is also elusive as it is not as straight forward as morality. Not only utmost tranquil mind and spirit is demanded out of a righteous person, eliminating materialism likely counts for more than half of this demand. Though this learning is demanding and laborious, high spirits can help.

With the help of divination discussed in our last book, high spirits can quench many desires from wrong principles. For example, a person addicted to pornography may desire to spend a Saturday evening at a strip bar. If he asks each time, high spirits likely will advise him not to go most of the time. With enough faith in high spirits, he would greatly curtail his unrighteous trip. Though not a cure for the root cause, it is betterment.

Furthermore, divination can help an addict of pornography to discover and eliminate the root causes if the person wishes. We do not think that porn addiction is genetic. A parent might have instilled some ideas to the addict at a young age or even before birth, but such ideas influence one no different from an advice of a close friend. The key to break the ill advice is to replace it with a better advice from high spirits or good books.

Spiritually Righteous Harder Than Mentally Righteous

Differing from spiritual righteousness, mental righteousness somewhat equates to morality. A person with moral values from school or family can be mentally righteous and be praised for good deeds. To be spiritually righteous, on the other hand, a spirit must be constantly awake. Based on our assessment in chapter 4, about 80 to 90 percent of people have their spirits asleep all the time, but high spirits or God put it at 95 to 98 percent.

Even if trying their best, avid spiritual practitioners may not have their spirits awake at all times. Mentally awake does not mean spiritually awake, as we discussed. When a spirit is awake, one feels the body like an empty bottle ready to be filled with righteousness. Do fill it with righteous thoughts and behaviors.

Intense concentration and little outside distraction are needed to wake up a spirit as we discussed earlier. Keeping self calm and peaceful is a crucial piece of a puzzle in keeping spirit awake. At the moment of spiritual awakening, a principle is much easily scrutinized to determine its right or wrong. This self-examination should be done while mentally awake.

Imagine each breath as inhaling a righteous word and exhaling a crooked thought. When a body is filled with righteousness, it can pop and connect to universal righteousness. A crooked thought may not be wicked. When one is focusing on a task, a desire to hook up with a passerby is likely not wicked but crooked.

Do inject spirit with righteousness at all times. Fill mind with righteous thoughts at times. Focus on doing righteous deeds, particularly when at work. If working as a clerk, focus on thinking a righteous thought for the next customer. Sincerely greeting a customer at walk in and sincerely bidding farewell at walk out is righteous. Greeting purely based on company policy would be not.

While writing a newspaper article, think about how to report a story in a righteous light. While driving, focus on looking out for danger of a pedestrian walking into path, even if that pedestrian runs a red light. Righteousness is not just refusing to covet what does not belong to self; it is also about unselfishly watching for others their precious possessions.

Literally doing what one prays and wishes for is ultimately important. Difficulties and obstacles are bound to arise while doing it. Patience and perseverance are needed to tackle all seemingly endless and insurmountable troubles before reaching the final goal. A wish may be good, but the trial and tribulation will vehemently test the strength of a wish and effort over time. No goal on earth can be achieved simply by wish or prayer.

Slow movement and fast progression likely will alternate. Do not be deterred by nearly stale progression. A locomotive moving forward all the time is not as good as one that stops from time to time to pick up passengers. Watch out for people one may meet or contact by chance. Pay attention to an environment one may be accidentally in. At times, change of people or milieu may be needed to promote righteousness of self and others.

Many letters make a word, many of which make a sentence, a paragraph, a chapter, and a book. Seconds accumulate to minutes, hours, to days, to weeks, to months, to years. A life goal often takes decades to complete, much more than a four-year university study. It is worth the time and effort for a large project.

Literally in one day, one can have thousands of thoughts. Some are generated from outside and some from within one's own mind. A flooding of a gym locker room may spur hundreds of different thoughts from many who wish to use the gym. The origin of an external event often cannot be controlled by one encountering it, but one's thoughts can be. Different people generate different thoughts for an event, but the best thoughts are from those who are determined to finish a life goal or no thought at all.

There is likely little use in complaining, being disgusted, offering blessing, criticizing, investigating, or even offering to help. The gym likely would not want anybody besides employees to work on the flooding. Focusing on one's task probably means the most help for the gym. Most thoughts generated from an outside event are useless, inefficient, and thwarting to self, unless one is directly involved in the responsibility, such as a policeman or a janitor.

Thoughts generated from within one's mind often escape detection as not related to an external event. However, these thoughts can be more substantially trivial than those generated from an outside event. A psychology study counted the number of sexual thoughts in a day to be in the thousands, especially for males. What is the use of having such thoughts if one knows for certain that he would not get it?

Look, watch, envy, desire, jealousy, distraction, attraction, searching, turning head, following fashion, and a host of other words describe these internally generated thoughts. They slow down an individual by sucking away available time and effort. They thwart personal goals immensely over a long period of time. Each thought probably lasts only for a few seconds; nevertheless, the accumulation of thousands adds up to hours per day. Though thoughts can coexist with actions, the enormous amount of sidetracking can greatly reduce the potential achievement of a mind.

Being focused means eliminating all weeds of thoughts, which can account for approximately 20 percent of mental capacity for a somewhat focused person. They can account for as much as 70 to 80 percent of mental capacity for an unfocused person. Confucius said: "Do not even look if something is inappropriate." Though only a brief few seconds, such a glance wastes time and mental energy.

Methods of Practicing Righteousness

One should pay more attention to one's own small deeds than big deeds, which, though, are often evaluated by others. Taking a casual walk, writing a text message, or turning the head to look at a passerby often carry little significance to others. However, they can exhibit more of one's own spirituality than a school or work project. The qualities of these simple behaviors draw a clear picture of one's spirit to tell one's own spirituality.

Without enough seconds, minutes cannot be formed. Without all sixty minutes, an hour cannot be. Without all twenty-four hours, a day is impossible. Without enough days for the month, one is incomplete. A big quantity accumulates from small ones of its components. Every second of one's life counts, not only those happy or exciting moments registered as major memories or life events.

A safety patrol is doing a good job only after watching each second throughout a guarding shift. If a thief comes in during a window of few neglectful seconds by the safety patrol, the vigilance of the whole shift is questionable. Ninety-nine percent of righteous practice may end as an unrighteous life due to 1 percent of letting the righteous guard down.

For a rape to happen, thousands of such thoughts likely have appeared on the rapist's mind. The thoughts are either repeated so many times and finally being carried out or slowly diminished to disappear from mental radar. It is all up to the person. Internally generated thoughts such as rape do not disappear by themselves in a few days or weeks; only constant checking and mental effort can pull all thoughts back to righteousness. A horse that strays too far from the main road may need some time to steer it back to the right track or Tao.

Patience and perseverance may be needed to steer a horse with very wild propensity. Do not give up simply because of repeat frustrations. A spirit is not guaranteed to win the tug of war with the mind. Only constant vigilance can possibly tip the scale. Letting a wild horse go whichever way it wishes, the horse is unlikely to return to the righteous road. A spirit must steer the mind gradually, even if it means letting it loose from time to time.

The daily practice of righteousness is like growing a crop of rice. The process is steady but slow. Do not give up simply because one does not actually observe its growth. Persistence and a long time are needed to see the result. Do not use the distance one travels in a day to measure the speed of rice or righteousness growth. A ruler of one mile is inadequate in measuring one-eighth of an inch a day. Though a practitioner may not see the growth, the inch-up spiritual strength can often be felt.

The End Goal

The goal of righteous practice is to sense one's own righteousness. This sense differs from an emotion or a physical sensation. This abstractive feeling of righteous spirit can be perceived by a tranquil and peaceful mind. This acute sense of a righteous spirit may take months or years of practice to occur, but eventually it will.

An intention of doing every small task righteously and the literal practice of the intention help the subconscious mind to sense the growth of this abstractive righteous feeling. This increased righteous sense increasingly fuels and improves the kinds of righteous tasks performed. After a period of time, this righteous feeling increases to the point of being very obvious to the doer. Then and only then does one fully know what we are talking about here. Looking back at that time, one will appreciate the words we write here.

Between the interval of righteous intention and the actual righteous deed, the thought process needs to be righteously refined as well. Intruding thought that is unrighteous should be stopped when it first comes up. Like weeds, all thoughts not completely righteous must be removed at the root immediately to prevent future growth.

Having a strong righteousness from the thinking process of righteous deeds and intention, one is ready to teach others righteousness. Not only in religion, righteousness exists deep inside spirits like a gold nugget that nobody can steal. This gold is the real richness in a person. Without it, a person is still poor even if materially rich.

On the material level, righteousness is about self-sufficiency without taking anything that does not belong. Here, anything includes lusty need, material want, and personal desire. In a family, basic righteousness exists. When siblings depend on one another for material or emotional help only when absolutely necessary, they have righteousness. Wife and husband who do not depend on one another to fulfill lust or luxury desire also have righteousness.

A major consideration of becoming righteous is to recognize personal desires and not to rely on others to satisfy these desires. This can be difficult due to the emotional tsunami an instinctive desire can weather. Being righteous differs from being nice and considerate, which are covered in appropriateness and Ren. When a person sees another with desirable body and creates a desire with no consent from that person, this desire may already render that person unrighteous.

This may sound strict to most who have similar desires hundreds of times a day. However, in the spiritual world, desire and any mental movement are enough to constitute right and wrong. This is why pornographic addiction can be detrimental to one's spirit.

A desire created when watching a pornographic material may already violate righteous principle, especially when no hormone propels one to do so.

Though mind is at the downstream of spirit, spirit can be badly influenced by mental activities. An unrighteous desire can hurt the core of a spirit like a knife cutting into a living tree. A few cuts may not hurt the trunk of a tree much, but many cuts may wreak havoc on the spiritual life of the tree.

An unrighteous desire hurts spirit more than being inconsiderate because righteousness is closer to the core of a spirit than courtesy is. If you draw a line to cut faith in half, half of them would lie outside and half inside. Righteousness and wisdom lie inside, and consistency and Ren lie outside. Consistency is the outside counterpart of righteousness, and Ren is the outside part of wisdom.

This unrighteous desire is like daydreaming of being materially rich while living in poverty. It's not only unrealistic but also unethical to conjure up a dream thought. Thoughts like this can be compared to imagination of literally killing another whom one hates. The spiritual life of the person who dreams it has been hurt. In some religions, the lesson of forgive and forget aims at spiritual root. When a person thinks of hurting another, that person is hurt already before another actually is.

In other words, righteousness is about living within one's own means and not to covet others' possession. The more one covets, the less likely one will get it righteously. A wicked mind is playing a zero-sum game. The so-called evil spirit or Satan is in impure mind. Righteousness and unrighteousness are like a sword cutting different parts of a tree. The one that cuts small branches will promote growth of a spiritual tree, but the one that cuts the trunk may eventually kill the life.

As discussed in chapter 4, mind, body, and spirit are closely interconnected. They affect each other like a skin layer being attached to other skin layers. The deepest skin layer may not be seen readily, but the infection of that layer can cause severe damage even if the surface looks fine. The reason why sunburn is so painful is that the heat of the sun penetrates deeply into the deepest layer of skin to cause damage.

A wicked or unrighteous thought is like an infection at the middle skin layer. The skin surface may look fine and beautiful, but the damage caused by the middle layer toward the deep layer skin is not observable or perceivable until the pain is felt at the deep layer nerve. Pure thoughts keep the mind and spirit healthy; impure and contaminated thoughts may sabotage the spirit to the bone unknown to the mind.

Modern medical research has proved that thoughts can turn a clean glass of water to spoil faster than a glass of water without any thought injection. Some Japanese and United States scientists used scientific experimental methods to study the effect of thoughts on water. When many people inject good thoughts into a glass of water, the water later was found to remain fresh and pure longer than a control sample. When a glass of water got many hateful thoughts such as cursing and blaming, that cup of water became spoiled sooner than a control sample. Thoughts can feed or kill. (Ref 17)

After being purely righteous in behavior and thoughts, a person is ready to influence others for increasing others' righteousness. A personal talk, a casual meeting, an upright posture, or even a walk-by can all impact righteousness of another. If one has righteousness to confer to another, the conversation, behavior, and posture can permeate one's righteousness to positively affect others.

Most people likely have noticed that the same smile from different persons have diverse meanings that they can be readily told apart. The feeling of righteousness is similar. Most probably do not know why, but they can just tell. The kind of high integrity and righteousness is contagious that people admire from bottom of their hearts. The way is universal and the same.

One adage in Taiwan and China is that most people have a similar mindset, and this mindset uses similar reasoning, or spiritual way. These similarities between people of different races and creeds are the result of similar spiritual properties. When one does a right thing but does not conform to tradition, most others would recognize it as right and want to follow suit. Most people have the root of five spiritual merits in them, and the root just needs to be inspired to sprout and grow.

Suggested Research Topics

This section does not appear in other four chapters on spiritual merits, but the readers can think about a topic they are interested in that has not been fully discussed in each chapter to write a thesis paper. The following two questions are only a small portion of at least twenty questions we can come up with. Here we list only two as examples.

The first potential research topic is "The relationship between posture and righteousness." Many have seen in a movie how a person can change postures based on mood or circumstances. A depressed person likely slouches shoulders while walking or faces down with arms and legs extended on a bed. A well-spirited person likely sticks out chest or smiles regularly. A reciprocal relationship may exist between posture and righteousness. They may also influence one another If so, working on right posture may increase righteousness.

A second potential research topic is "Why are Ren and righteousness most emphasized in many religions?" The answers to this question may be straightforward or complicated. Love and justice are probably the mostly mentioned words in documentary films. Even fictional novels focus on these two topics frequently. The other three merits, though still getting occasional notice, seem not to appear as often.

CHAPTER NINE

Spiritual Wisdom

As the title suggests, spiritual wisdom is the wisdom originating from the spirit, not from the brain or mind. This wisdom has unique qualities of better dealing with abstract, whole-picture above detail, and calm and steady progress. Other qualities include diligence, thinking out of the box, overall efficiency, and good prioritization and organizational abilities. Also all the qualities are well balanced and not tipping toward few qualities while neglecting others.

To achieve these qualities, the spirit must be awake when the mind is awake. As discussed in chapter 4, only less than 5 percent of people achieve it regularly at a society with no spiritual education. In addition, a spiritually awake person is more likely to be spontaneous, serendipitous, focused, mentally clairvoyant, accurately intuitive, and fast responsive than those spiritually asleep. These characteristics seldom can be duplicated all the time by the mind alone.

Furthermore, some deep qualities include ability to see through the truth, strong capacity to start over by giving up what has been learned or processed, and well balanced in making decisions. Only after at least a few months of being spiritually awake, these qualities of more profound nature can happen. One example of demonstrating spiritual wisdom was the nuclear program of the United Stated during World War II. Another example was the cultures and people of the United States.

During WWII, Germany probably had better grasp of nuclear knowledge and technology for making the first nuclear bomb than the US did. The spirituality of the US attracted people with spiritual wisdom to work in the Manhattan Project. As portrayed in several movies about the project, spiritual people working around the scientists inspired some scientists to design the nuclear bomb better. More than mere luck, the US beat Germany to produce the first bomb.

The military superpower of the US since WWII is also based on this mighty spirituality within the US and its military culture. Building an aircraft carrier takes only money and technology; a strong military force relies much more than those of materialistic nature. The Soviet Union's stubbornly brave military culture beat Germany in WWII with inferior military equipment. The ironic mismatch between poor spirituality, economy, and military technology in the Soviet Union likely caused the collapse of the Soviet Union.

Hollywood spirits is yet another example of the US's spirituality which inspired the world's spiritual awakening, especially from the 1970s to 1990s. Not only the natural and spontaneous quality of the movies, the storyline provoked righteous and empathetic reverberation around the world, like a spiritual tornado. Spirituality sells; likely no God's blessing was necessary. The selling of spirituality carried the price of corruption, addictive drugs, smoking, alcoholism, violence, and other habits of very good nature. All these must from now on be corrected by spiritual education, maybe starting again from Hollywood and the US public education.

Differences between Spiritual Wisdom and Mental Smartness

Probably most have heard that *street smart* and *book smart* differ. It says that people who master academic learning are often not as shrewd as learning from the street. More accurately speaking, book smart should be termed academic smart as people who can master academically are not necessarily well versed in or even remotely drawn to books, and vice versa. Though not totally the same, spiritual wisdom resembles academy smart more; mental smart resembles street smart more.

For simplicity, let us term spiritual wisdom as *wisdom*, and mental smartness as *smartness*. One characteristic of smartness is the sharp ability of being quickly reactive, which means reacting to sound and sight with acute eyes and ears. The Chinese word *smartness* squibs as precisely this incidentally. Contrary from most learning source today from the outside world, wisdom mainly generates learning from the inside of a person. This internal learning can be personal experience, past memory or knowledge, conjugation of memories, and particularly the spirit.

Unlike smart people turning on senses all the time, a spiritually wise person titillates acute external senses only at right situations. A wise one in a study room does not need to turn on knobs; they unplug music to facilitate concentration for the task at hand. The unwarranted use of senses by the smart not only wastes energy but also provides holes for intruding on attention span. A few seconds of security breaching can lead to minutes or hours of sidetracking.

The ability to stop all senses is particularly important at sleep time or meditation, not to mention facilitating peaceful personality. Many smart people we know are overwhelmed by thoughts and senses that they equate sleep as lying down in a coffin due to headache and insomnia. Do not underestimate the importance of this ability of turning off all senses.

Another difference between a wise and a smart person is shrewdness. A joke popular in the engineering field tells a story that an engineer was about to be decapitated at a guillotine, but the chopping block malfunctioned. Naively, he taught the executioner how to fix the malfunction. Shrewdness used at a wrong time can be deadly at one's own peril.

Yet another example, one working decades for a company recently applied for a management position and was selected due to his shrewdness and industry competition. He inappropriately treated his group and caused many mental disturbances. A perturbed employee implicated to harm him, who soon quit his new position and moved to another state due to fear. Timing and circumstance must be adequate to apply one's shrewdness; otherwise, calamity may result for self and others.

Some smart socialites may sometimes lack ability to forget. Christianity stresses *forgive and forget*, but without forgiving, forgetting is nearly impossible. Whether one should forgive an utter injustice is a totally different matter compared to minor injustice. Though religious, a nonspiritual person can have difficulty forgetting, especially a past unrighteous act such as purposely missing an interview to confirm good job performance at the end of a year. This memory can be haunting for the rest of life due to the blame of conscience.

Strongly linked to one's spirit, memory of spiritual nature clinches the brain tighter than the accidental encounter of another person. In fact, a spirit does not forget anything. Within many eastern tales, a dead person soon reviews all that one did in a lifetime in front of a mirror as if playing a movie for things just happened yesterday.

To our spirits, our eyes likely act as security cameras recording twenty-four hours a day and seven days a week, or at least during those waking hours. Our small RAM, or random access memory, which stores short-term data for quick retrieval like in a computer, holds only limited amount of data. The data in RAM are later moved to the spiritual hard drive, which often is not accessible immediately to the person, especially if the spirit is asleep.

Today's education focuses only on strengthening memory and neglects the vital ability to forget. Not only in education, psychology and psychiatry urgently need to learn how to forget; yet, they cannot achieve without knowing spirituality. Only those able to forget can possibly have joy. The happiest people on earth are those who have learned to forget. Most memories are bitter.

To learn this spiritual lesson on ability to forget, one must forego the wish of wanting a good time to last forever or of wanting a bad time to end as soon as possible. The social culture of the United States is to blame for this wrong principle around the globe. Pursuit of happiness results in aversion to unhappiness. This discrimination between happiness and unhappiness creates uneven mentality like a whirlpool in the ocean caused by uneven air pressure. It sucks spirituality into the abyss.

Good or bad time in life eventually ends. This cold and cruel truth of life can never be changed. Enjoying the moment whether good or bad and whether pleasant or suffering can substitute this defective and improper belief fallaciously from the US ancient culture and tradition as mentioned in our last book about breaking the tradition and culture chain.

Smartness and wisdom also differ in linearity and whole picture. In fact, the picture of a spirit is three-dimensional or more, or a concrete picture. Like a straight line, the mind thinks mostly linearly and is often difficult to steer direction like a fast train on a track. On the other hand, the spiritual thinking works closely and directly with bodily senses to explore three-dimensional possibilities. This thinking involves all senses of physical body and is often more accurate and versatile than that of the brain, which can only perceive indirectly through nerves.

This imperceptions of senses and three dimensions empower the brain to deduct logic and to reason one by one, instead of block by block like spirit does. Less capable of deducting and reasoning, spirit focuses on enlightening root cause and principle behind the obvious. A complete match of personal behaviors with these principles is called walking on the way, or Tao.

Innate deducting and reasoning abilities render humans smart, yet they also thwart the utilization of spirituality. To this aspect, some animals demonstrate more spirituality than many humans. Some examples are elephant, dog, dolphin, whale, and cat. Their docile animal natures incarnate them to be more spiritual than other animals, such as ferocious wolf or tiger. Some individual animals in the docile category can be ferocious, however, depending on the spirit of that animal.

A result of disparity between linear smartness and concrete wisdom is impotence of many to discover the truth. The ultimate truth is the spirit, not the words or teaching of any religion from the past to the future. Not just any spirit, one's own spirit is the ultimate truth to the self.

Buddha plucked a flower and showed it to hundreds of his disciples; only few perceived the three-dimensional truth of one's own spirit after decades of Buddha's teaching. It is no wonder that only a handful of spiritual learners out of all religions get it. This grave impotence of perceiving one's own spiritual truth in the vast majority provide the opportunity of fraudulent gangs to swindle money easily. Probably only a popular practice of spirituality can eliminate this large-scale bewildering about the truth.

See through One's Own Death

A model of a human fertilized egg should be shown to the first grader to help them realize how small each of them was. Compared to a grown adult, a first grader may be small in size but is humongous to a fertilized egg. This comparison guides pupils to realize how little one originates from and how drastic a life changes in size. After knowing where they came from, teaching them on their eventual burial to return body to earth can be much more convincing and acceptable.

Another way to learn physical body impermanence is through dissection and anatomy. From the observation of a living frog with eating and sleeping habits, the death and immobilization of a frog can stun pupils to the importance of life. It also reminds them of the preciousness of their own lives, even though only eighty to one hundred years at the maximum. The age limit does not negate the truth of life and its spirit inside, but merely sets an automatic clock which will ultimately expire.

Even dissection of human corpse should be allowed at whatever young age if one wishes. The dissection would not only help to learn human anatomy in future medical fields but also help to see through death. Without it, most elusively think self as invincible and indestructible, especially during teenage years and young adulthood. Of course, this learning is not for everyone. The characteristics of each child should dictate the selection and timing.

The fact learning of body composition of over 70 percent water and bones alone can help a pupil to realize exactly who a person really is. Water, bones, and minerals alone do not make a life; only a spirit does. Genes are codes that need to be decoded to grow a person; the decoding process spells the origin of a human life as much more than material alone. The word magic alone does not cover it.

Yet another way to see through death comprises the learning of body decay process. The stinky smell and ugly sight irritate many, nonetheless waking souls to the folksiness of an alive person contrasting to a smelly dead. The value of life rests not only on activities but the meaning behind the activities. The emptiness of physical body at the end does not negate the meaning of a life.

Observing a burial process and the inside of a tomb unveils the mystery of one life's termination. Something without a beginning has no end. A physical life with a beginning must pass the end, like a two-hour movie reaching the credit screen. Whether the consistency of one life is credible plays out in the end along with all other merits.

The various ways of learning above may backfire without teaching spirituality alongside with it. A common attitude produced is to regard all lives as meaningless after realizing the emptiness at the end of life. Though true that no meaning exists before and after a physical life, a life carries a well-intended meaning within the spirit while it resides in the physical body. This residence acts out meaning into a life, especially the five spiritual merits.

After realizing essentially emptiness of physical body, a child is ready to write a will. Besides conveying the love for close family members, the purpose of a will pinpoints to the readiness of one's own death. This mentality of being prepared to die is similar to the pre-battle readiness that one intends to do the best to glorify one's own life meaning for a greater good. That good is inside one's own spirit.

When a person expects self to be alive the next day, seeing or hearing a family member may be dull. When a person expects to die the next day, such sight and sound may transform into a joyful encounter dramatically, as played out in many endings of Hollywood movies. A trick of making this readiness into one's mind is to constantly remind self of certain death in some future time. Most fear a meeting with an angel of death, but no one can escape.

Probably, only people having a near-death experience have had the sincere feeling of letting go of everything. This feeling helps one to see spiritual self through the lens of death. Most are often too accustomed to living and totally forget that they will die in the future. Through death, people see their own spirits more clearly.

Some believe that nothing is left after death; for them, death means the very end, but they may be in for a big surprise if they find out otherwise after death. Some others have known death is the start of judgment to decide where to go next, and they likely have done their best to prepare for it before death. If one is unsure where to go next, the judgment can be very stressful. A trial and sentence can give little or no clue to a new criminal as to what will happen next.

Therefore, it is easier if one has some practice before the actual death. Of course, one can never experiment with his or her own death to see how it feels or what it looks like, but one can learn to mourn one's own death to know what it feels like. Before the actual mourning, assuming that one has done a lot of sins, wrongs, and mistakes in the past to deserve a lot of punishment is safer than assuming that one will go to heaven. Lowering expectation reduces the fear of overestimating the good deeds one has done; furthermore, the heavenly standard often is higher than human standards.

Killing a bug, one does not know where the spirit of that bug goes; however, mourning the death of self, one soon realizes that he or she may go to the same place as the killed bug. That can be a very scary thought of meeting the spirit of a dead being whom one killed unjustly. How will one face an enemy not being prepared? What will be the scene when one faces another whom one has done serious wrong to? No stage screen can cover up the ugly fight and no place to hide from a conflict.

The next step is to build one's own tomb with a headstone. Seeing the tomb and headstone, one likely has a surge of feelings never been experienced. Mixed feelings of regret, relief, fear, sorry, or others are possible. Life experiences differ, so reactions will differ. Mourning one's own death can be a lifetime experience that few can brush it off. After experiencing how it feels like to be mourned, one is less likely to have excessive grief when a loved one dies.

After being ready to die, one can realize that touring all desired places on earth is impossible, kind of like marrying every potential mate on earth. The number can be in the thousands, and for sure no one can handle that many mates in a lifetime. Life is not just an experience; it ought to have some meaning behind to warrant it and to make it worthwhile.

Going on a trip for the sake of going is similar to eating food for the sake of cleaning up waste; it has no meaning and is counterproductive. Just like going to all liked places is impossible during a lifetime, doing all things one desires in one lifetime is equally impossible. One ought to ponder carefully to pick and choose one's own priorities based on life goals and meanings desired.

A scientific study of the human living process, not just human development in psychology, which is afraid of touching this subject, would discover the above truth right away. Most scientists fear this taboo of studying the subject of limited human lifespan. This fear probably originates from their fears of their own death, which they likely wish to live forever. In their subconscious, they blind themselves like commoners or wish that some new technology will enable them to live forever. It is a pity for the hypocrisy of science to pretend that human death does not occur to all humans.

To overcome this fear, one must constantly remind oneself that physical death cannot be equated to spiritual death. A scientific experiment can be used to verify this truth that physical death is not equal to spiritual death. A computer scale is put under a near-death person to monitor and to record weight. After death, the weight record is then compared to the heart-rate record to determine the exact weight loss at death. We hypothesize that a weight difference at death will not be found.

If our hypothesis is right, one can deduct that something weightless is supporting heartbeat and brain function before death. The weight of a computer connected to a power source is equal to the weight of the computer not so connected. The only difference between the two is the flow of electricity, which is weightless and exists undoubtedly using measuring instrument. That thing of no weight before death is most likely a spirit, as human ancestors have known all along.

One may argue that electricity is lifeless and differs from the living spirit described in our books. Not so fast to term electricity as lifeless, scientists have done experiments to prove water as alive through injection of thoughts daily for a period of weeks or months. Good thoughts and blessing kept a cup of water fresh longer than bad thoughts and curses did. Buddha stated that all things had spirit inside; maybe he was right after all. (Ref 18)

Not just scientists, all should know and regularly remind themselves that physical death is not equal to spiritual death. Repeat reminders inject this knowledge into the subconscious, which will no longer fear death but courageously face it like taking an immunization shot, a small pain that an average adult can handle easily. This subconscious realization is the enlightenment, which if followed by actions to increase its spiritual merits will keep the spirit awake at all times, including after death.

With any more doubt, one can design and perform experiment by following a few videos on YouTube. Those simple tests use water or rice in labeled glass jars to remind oneself whether to curse or bless into a jar. Doing with one's own hands will inspire more than watching alone. One's spirit is in the body more than in the mind, though mind can easily block spirit from shining. (Ref 17)

One may can expect one's own death deep in heart if one can mourn one's own death. As discussed in chapter 4, a subconscious derived from brain infrastructure likely is formed over a long time. The longer one lives, the harder it will be to change the subconscious. One strongly believing in one's own physical life may need more time to change the subconscious mind than one who does not cling to physical life as strongly.

Another reason for being unable to convince oneself may be the body postural habit since childhood. After verification from our divination, a body posture is part of a subconscious mind just like a brain infrastructure is. Brain structure is one mindset, and a body posture is another. A subconscious is the combination of these mindsets and possibly others. All the characteristics of these mindsets form the property of a subconscious mind.

A Confucian teaching is about righting one's own mind and repairing one's own body before aligning family members to Tao. Each family member can affect the whole family; without all family members on Tao to put their own spiritual lives at the very top, the whole family suffers due to few clinging on to physical life. Likewise, with most families in a nation not transcending physical life, the whole country suffers. Repairing a body may need months if not years because body postures may have been fixated for decades.

Some people who do not have enough determination in practicing Tao or who have deviated too far from Tao may never be able to return to Tao within a lifetime, especially if they have never been exposed to spiritual or Tao education since childhood.

A third possibility for being unable to return to Tao within a lifetime is the weakness of spirituality in the spirit. Some spirits are inherently stronger than others due to their origins. A personal spirit formed from a few thousand ants may not be as powerful as another formed from the splitting of Jesus Christ. Recycling of spirits, whether to heaven or to hell, is for their own good to increase their spiritual strength from outside pressure. This principle can be applied to the reincarnation of animals. For example, a tiger which is fed up with the same spiritual quality of a tiger may boost its own spirituality to the level of a human later.

The heaven just mentioned above is inferior to the heaven where God resides, which is Truth Heaven or Tao Heaven. The inferior heaven, or Chi Heaven, accommodates those who have done good deeds on earth but have not understood or practiced Tao enough. Most angels, gods, and goddesses are in this category and will eventually need to learn and practice Tao to return to Tao Heaven. Unlike Tao Heaven able to last forever, Chi Heaven will eventually be destroyed along with the solar system.

The best place to learn and practice Tao is on earth, not Chi Heaven or Hell, which do not have perishable physical body. The growth and decay of physical body is like a tweezers that pinch the mind and spirit hard into reality. This often painful pinch can force one to realize the folly of being overly materialistic or overly abstract because Tao is exactly and precisely halfway in between.

Prioritization

One main characteristic of spiritual wisdom is to prioritize based on spiritual principle. Having good priorities in life is the prerequisite of spiritual success. A bad priority based on all kinds of materials, including but not limited to, money, power, achievement, opposite gender, or physical health likely does not last after the material is obtained. The meaning for a self-made billionaire to get richer than himself is pointless. Setting spirituality as the highest priority conforms with one's own spiritual nature and takes a lifetime to succeed.

The highest priority in one's life should always be to practice oneself spiritually, mentally, and bodily. When setting as the first priority, this practice can consummate achievements of material nature, such as wealth or family. Like a carriage must have the horse before the cart to function properly, a person with wrong priority likely would not accomplish anything major in life. Even if they do, they often end up losing it all. A billionaire cannot take any property away at death.

Improving self is easier than trying to change others through compelling laws, words, or actions. The motivator is the natural flow of spirituality from inside outward, which is more powerful than laws or words. Without a good priority, a life often dissipates into trivial surrounding. This practice of oneself influences others to imitate and to practice on their own. An entire family and society can be so uplifted.

This practice on oneself differs from being selfish. A person focusing on improving self can still have a kind heart and readily give or help others. Only after one substantially improves oneself can one help to improve others. This self is the center of attention to work on, not others.

This focus on improving self cannot be achieved without some daily practice first. Most have learned to prioritize spending of money on a purchase that matters the most. Food purchase should be before an alcoholic drink. Extra clothes should be placed at low priority if food is scarce. The number of clothes and shoes that can be worn in a lifetime is limited, so is consumption of food. Limited lifetime needs limited supply.

Any waste is not likely if limited resources are available. Buying only what one can consume saves not only the wallet but also limited food source. A choice between a dozen eggs and a gallon of milk may be difficult, but between soda and a meal should not be.

A personal life goal should have higher priority than other life trivial matters. The time of a person's life is limited. Sickness, growing up, and senility further reduce the amount of available time for a life goal, not to mention time spent on accidents, chores, and other trivial things such as music or news.

Time conservation helps to achieve a goal. Doing two or three chores at the same time can increase time available for a goal. Without watching out where time goes, one may spend hours shopping for a few trivial items. This waste of time often occurs when one does not actively pursue a life goal.

Despite the importance of setting and achieving life goals, recreation balances mind to prevent overheating. After all, the human brain is made of flesh that needs rest from time to time. The amount of recreational activity should be appropriate to the degree of tiredness, just enough to regulate the mental fatigue. Excessive rest and recreation can result in wasting time and failed goal. Healthy diet consists of mostly carbohydrates, protein, vegetable, and fruit, yet the body does need some fat and sugar to repair body and to nourish brain.

When a short-term goal is completed, set another one to keep the mind busy and the spirit alive. The biggest time stealer is probably wandering around without any life goal. Prioritize what is important before starting a day. Without this prioritization, most only try to survive like animals, and the opportunity of expounding spiritual meaning is wasted, like a drunkard who passes time by immersing him- or herself in liquor.

Organization

Organization is another spiritual wisdom that is often underemphasized. Though most school and college graduates have some organizational skill, this skill often is learned from other fields instead of by itself alone. Learning to organize can probably start from sorting toys and personal clothes. Toys of similar characteristics such as ships, cars, and trucks can be placed into the same bin; while, all the mental games such as jigsaw puzzles and crosswords should be placed together.

Writing can be used to learn organization. Well sorted words help the memory because the human brain is wired to remember similar things. When writing a book, similar words and sentences are used over and over again to illustrate a central theme. The natural flow from word to sentence to article to book helps one to learn organizing skill which can be further applied to other fields.

Before writing, one should start with an outline of ideas. From this outline, an article can be fully developed. Good writing is all about good organization. Thinking on the level of a whole picture or outline differs from thinking on each paragraph. If an outline is not well organized, the so-developed paragraphs would not be organized either. Another advantage of outlining is to think in terms of logical flow of ideas instead of detailed wording.

The thought process of mind is linear like one sentence following another, but the process of spirit is by the block like one block after another. The connection between blocks may not be obvious at the beginning, so comparing between ideas should be done beforehand to line up ducks. The thought process of outline is to connect blocks of ideas.

Organizing toys or clothes in a closet is dealing with something visible, which clearly exhibits its property based on functionality. On the other hand, abstract ideas or qualities cannot be seen with naked eyes; therefore, they need some imagination. An ability to imagine facilitates organization of abstract things in nature. The advance of computer technology and virtual reality makes the imaging much easier by transforming the abstract into something concrete within a short time.

One important aspect of organizational skill is to recognize and eliminate what is redundant and unnecessary. An onion is inappropriate among banana, apple, and orange. Removing an extra not belonging to a particular group makes the group pure. The ability to reduce a group may need willpower or determination to speak out or object. An unrighteous tolerance is no different from letting go a cancer cell, which soon spreads to other healthy body cells.

This organizational ability can help greatly to achieve life goals. Learning to organize can make one work in a more organized manner. Organization during learning may determine the success of this learning. A well-organized army is more powerful than an army in disarray. An organized writing is often easier to read and more convincing than an unorganized one.

Already abstract and difficult to grasp, a disorganized spirituality may be bound for a disaster rather than a powerful helper. The organizational wisdom rests in the clarity of organization which separates good from bad and superior from inferior. Like picking out bad ones from a just harvested pile of apples, spirits prefer all things abstractly in order than in disarray.

In organization, less is literally more. Ten apples are easier to arrange than one hundred of them; one hundred apples are easier to handle than one thousand. A large quantity tends to create more organizational problems than a small quantity. A wise one with organizational skill often prefers less over more. Though more accommodating, a large house with eighteen rooms is substantially harder to clean and maintain than a small house with only three rooms.

Big Picture and Decision Making

Education of spiritual wisdom of seeing the big picture and making good decisions should start from a young age. In fact, this education for children should be easier for adults, who often have a habit of paying too much attention to detail. Focusing attention on an individual tree in a forest, one may not see the forest as a whole. Not that they do not actually see the forest, but their attention and focus are somewhere else.

Youngsters who speed excessively and cause accidents have not learned the wisdom of seeing the big picture. Being quick to reach a destination is by itself not a wrong wish, but this wish is the tree instead of the forest. Without a healthy physical body, the spirit cannot perform. Risking bodily safety to obtain an extra few seconds or minutes of advantage overlooks the importance of a healthy life compared to time saving. Time saving must be done within the parameters of safety.

Without a life, a life goal is impossible, so it is better to be safe than sorry. The physical body is destructible, not to mention the unnecessary pain and suffering caused by a car or any accident. Rock climbing with no rope support may be a gamble with death; this is equivalent to the risk of excessive speed on a road. A wise person seeing the big picture of the preciousness of one's own life seldom takes on the risk or gamble.

It is a good idea to show a mangled car to children. To state it mildly, this mix between steel and flesh is brutal. Attention of the driver is the key to see the big picture of other lives carried in the car. Not just car accidents, the consequence of any risky behavior should be illustrated to help children see the big picture of a spirit behind each life.

Through the realization of possible consequence of careless or wanton behavior, a child can soon learn the big picture of every action. Otherwise, they often do it without thinking. Although physical body is not real and is bound to eventually reach the end of its service life, the spirit it carries is very real and meaningful. Letting a life go to waste due to one second of risky behavior simply is not worth it. One can only see a big picture when stepping way back.

After seeing a big picture, one is ready to learn to make good decisions. A big picture also facilitates prioritization, which can help with decision making. Life direction and achievement are all about big and small choices along the way. Do not underestimate the potential impact of small decisions. Relatively speaking, the decision of President Nixon to allow some of his people to illegally wiretap was a tiny decision during his presidency, but it brought him down.

Without seeing the potential impact of a small decision, one can be adversely affected or can be led to demise. Buying clothing may seem a small decision, but the color can affect the wearer positively or negatively. Feng Sui may seem trivial, yet it can lead to misfortune or missed opportunity. Certain small thing can hugely impact some people.

The divination tool introduced in our last book can assist a person enormously in making the right decision. Not only capable of correcting life course, high spirits can inspire one to see the big picture when making a decision. For example, one learning to see through death asked the high spirits to indicate whether his mother would be all right at ninety-five years old. This question is likely to be answered sarcastically to teach a lesson. All spiritual practitioners should learn that all die eventually, including a family member.

Perceiving the inappropriateness of similar divination, one can learn from high spirits about seeing the big picture. Not that high spirits like to answer divination sarcastically, the learning of seeing the big spiritual picture outweighs a straightforward response. Learning from high spirits is more of an art than a science, which we will discuss further in chapter 12 on Tao.

All decisions made by an individual should relate to the individuality, not being influenced by other people or decisions. The originality of a decision would guarantee it to be pure, unbiased, and spiritually correct. Near white is not truly white; it carries a hue of some impurity. A line not completely straight can topple a skyscraper; an impure decision can cause damage later.

A decision wrongly based on a previous similar decision can easily be committed by someone not experienced in the decision-making process. The fact that a previous decision had a good result does not mean all future similar decisions will end in the same good way. Consideration of the point of origin, or the ground-zero point, should weigh heavily in a decision-making process. When the root cause for a decision is not clear, the steps following it can all be wrong.

The most important part of a tree is the root; without it the tree will die. Following someone else or a previous decision to make a decision is like feeding a tree at its leaves; the benefit is limited and may result in its death. The big picture of a person is the spiritual root, which should be the motivator of decisions; otherwise, a decision may deprive the spirit like feeding at tree leaves. Much such deprivation can lead to spiritual sleep or death.

Many dislike science or mathematics simply due to dislike of their teachers. After trying out many religions, some are not satisfied with the teaching of every religion. Most teachers or religions are biased, but the knowledge of spirituality is unbiased like science or mathematics. The key lies in a deep-thinking study to familiarize and to practice its essence. All roads lead to Rome as long as one is determined and persistent on reaching the goal of perfecting one's own spirituality.

Some fashion was accepted for good reason by majority of population such as the 1946 bikini trend, which could expose more skin to increase vitamin D absorption. Some are not as good, such as high-heeled shoes, which can deform the feet to cause body damage. Before accepting fashion, ask the reason or principle behind it. Reasoning with the root cause ensures a decision is based on the ground zero and not blindly following a fashion.

Blindly following others can lead to big sin. The Nazis could conquer Europe within a short time likely due to the blind faith of the people in Hitler and Germany. At the same time, the same thing happened in Japan, where the military and emperor were blindly believed. A collective blind faith in one's own culture, country, or leader often leads to disaster or atrocity. A built-in check and balance in government may not work if majority of citizens have blind faith in either its leader or the country.

Similar tragedies happen even today. Many violent gangs thrive on the exact same blind faith. Many governments are trying to eliminate terrorism, but they fail to recognize that they are also part of the problem. A not completely righteous government is bound to breed unrighteous and even extremely violent gangs. Later in chapter 13, we will further expand on this subject.

Whether to use traffic lights or to build a jump road for a railroad crossing is not a science but an art of seeing the big picture. A traffic light for a rail crossing is less expensive but less convenient, especially when a long train passes. For a city, a good balance between rail signal and rail jump road would facilitate traffic and reduce impatience of drivers at the same time.

Above consideration sees the big picture of overall city traffic and inconvenience of drivers. Most considerations have two sides: advantage and disadvantage. A planner needs to carefully decide on each decision along the way by checking every disadvantage and advantage. The disadvantage especially deserves attention as being safe at all times is better than being sorry later.

Be Versatile, Not Just One Interest

Being naturally linear, mental smartness often sticks to only one interest and nothing else. The prevalent college education of studying only one major and of working on only one job through a lifetime demonstrates this linear nature. Many religions ask their followers to believe in only one religion, which appeals to this nature.

Human ancestors who traversed many continents with limited knowledge and tools mostly relied on their spirituality. Food tastes the best when one is hungry. This hunger comes from survival instinct of spirit. Being totally abstract, our spirits do not care which interests we are taking at the moment. The interests of a spirit are extremely diverse; only a mind would pick and choose one most favorite.

In our last book, we stressed the importance of exploring multiple interests in series stages of a life. Even a genius like Einstein later in his career ran into theoretical staleness; it might be due to a long period of adherence to physics. Returning to learn deficient German or other languages could have triggered Einstein to pick up his edge again in theoretical physics. In today's school and workplace, expecting a student or a worker to stick to only one area is against their spiritual nature.

Today's college education demands a balanced program to include English and mathematics in all majors. Yet this educational theory still misses the mark of spirituality; the versatility of a spirit extends beyond mere English and math. An all-encompassing college program should require that a student verses in diverse disciplines, preferably a mix of totally unrelated fields such as engineering and economics, or social science and physics.

The spiritual merit of consistency about internal coherence is different from spiritual versatility, which deals with outside interests. A spirit is like a water fountain deeply hidden in a mountain. This mountain spring constantly jets out crystal-clear water, which may run out of water if its source is limited to only one nearby pool. As long as clean in nature, all pools are good sources for a spring.

Limiting one's own interests is mostly the doing of one's own mind. Obsessing with cleanness is often due to a mind's unchangeable direction. Limiting one's mind to only an interest is likely caused by its fear of mystery and unknown. Staying with only one comfort zone or accustomed interest spells the confining and linear nature of smartness. This mental jail is often set up by the self, not others, though others probably have helped through educational push and relay of popular belief.

As explained in the chapter on spiritual consistency, eliminating internal conflicts and realigning all principles eliminates internal inadequacy, which can greatly reduce interests in outside world. Generating good personal credit with banks and other people is a worthy consistency, but it does not affect one's versatile interests. Combined with spirit, mind can be like water that changes direction at any time. Spirit is like a pillar in water; it stays undisturbed with the water flowing around.

As mentioned in our last book, the problem of polygamy likely rests on conflict of personality between many spouses of the same gender. Likewise, the competition of classroom attention by five pupils can be difficult to manage, not to mention five wives or husbands. A spiritual interest in versatile husbands or wives is not really wrong. As we stated, we do not advocate or criticize polygamy, just discussing it from a purely scientific point of view.

Many complain that few are well trained in supervisory or management skill to be qualified for those positions right away. Not only middle management positions, a candidate with balanced qualification is even harder to find to fill top jobs such as CEO, president, or entrepreneur. Modern education should take this blame as it is very inflexible and not versatile at all. Nearly all students are mandated to sit in a classroom for a fixed number of years, no matter how spirited or smart they are; otherwise, a diploma is impossible.

The educational system is the culprit of it all. A major in university takes a minimum of four years to complete, not to mention master's and doctorate degrees. They raise tuition and fees but do not improve educational qualities. Educators are especially wrong for purposely not changing their principle to match needs for supervisory and management skill.

A supervisor or manager needs diverse interests in various fields to handle various kinds of problems. The obsession with a fixed amount of time spent in the classroom is a symptom of Obsessive Compulsive Disorder, or OCD. Many people have diverse interests before starting college, but their interests go away after realizing the number of years needed for each interest. As problem solver, management should be versatile in diverse fields to look at the whole picture to make a better decision.

Worse yet, most school and college graduates cannot even properly manage their own affairs, let alone manage other people or a company. This is sad for future generations as they continue to go downhill and become less organized. To graduate quality supervisors and managers, all students should have been taught those skills in school and college. At least, graduates with the skill can handle their own affairs better. A study on management should be started in early elementary school like the popular courses of mathematics and science.

Being versatile in many fields is a human nature in the subconscious and the spiritual level. A child knows to ask for various types of candy to try each. A spirited practitioner is interested in doing everything by him- or herself just like the advocate of Datong world growing food in the backyard described in chapter 16. As naturally abstract, spirit does not glue to one particular interest, like sticking to a major in university.

The nature of a person to eat and have intercourse does not need to be taught once food or the opposite sex is nearby. In the old days when tribes taught their children, all children must learn all available knowledge to qualify for adulthood. Granted that the vast amount of knowledge today cannot possibly be all absorbed by an individual in a short time, but versatility in several fields such as the combination of engineering, stock market, and art should not be too much of a burden. Again, time required for fixed course requirements blocks an easy way out of the boxed education.

Traversing human nature by unnecessarily demanding minimum classroom time often murders humanity and human nature in a big way. Other means exist to examine and ensure quality of graduates such as administering multiple examinations or oral exams to ascertain the acquisition of knowledge. After all, college professors assign grades based on fair examinations and tests. We do not see any need to ask them to add minimum classroom time requirement upon students.

Nothing Is Sure Until Finished

Many American football fans saw Super Bowl LI where the Atlanta Falcons won big at halftime 21-3 but lost it 28-34 to New England Patriots at overtime. The dynamics of this game show exactly how human minds are linear. With an eighteen-point lead, the Falcons likely thought that their victory was certain and popped champagne at halftime. Though checking far ahead is a good trait of smart people, many overdo it by adding their own complacency when things are going well.

The second half of a plan cannot be expected until the first half fully completes. A train with too much momentum may miss its scheduled stop and abandon a very important passenger waiting there. That train may need to come back again to pick up that customer; it would be a waste of time and money for the railroad company. Do not start a celebration till all things have been done perfectly.

Do not rely on expected time available to finish a life goal, especially at young age. Most cannot foresee what will happen tomorrow except maybe high spirits and God. We stressed this critical point at many places in our last book. Finish a life goal at the earliest time possible within one's limit of ability, situation, and condition. Some unfinished business can pop up at the last minute to delay the intended completion time. One of the authors learned this lesson firsthand while writing this book. He repents his mistake.

During the weekdays, keep on the toes and do the best all the time except the end of a day or weekend when all things are complete. Leisure as a luxury is not to be spent casually, especially when facing a challenge while pursuing a goal in life. A life goal is the most formidable enemy of a person in a lifetime. A goal of saving the whole human race can be overwhelming, as depicted in many Hollywood movies, which imitate life.

A physical life has limits. Not just body strength and endurance, timing is limited too. A perfect timing to finish a task can be gone forever if one is not on tiptoe at all times. A missed deadline can be like missing the last scheduled bus for the day; walking home can take hours. Finish what is needed to be done fast and early; more tasks may pop up later. Use the best focus, attention, and concentration one can afford.

No infants, children, or young adults are guaranteed to reach old age, as stressed in our last book. Cherish every hour of a day as if the next hour may not exist. The preciousness of time cannot be overemphasized. Sickness, illness, accident, intrusion, and attack of verbal or physical nature can occur unexpectedly. Such attack may or may not be one's own fault.

A loss of one's own life due to someone else's fault means the same for the self. Do not be fooled by the futile pursuit of justice in many lawsuit cases as no dead person can be revived. Tolerating the verbal attack from an outrageous passerby or rude driver may just save the day from going down the drain, and maybe saving one's own life as well. The uppermost purpose of seeing through one's own death is to cherish one's own limited time on earth, and the time is literally limited. Time is a whole lot more precious than money as it cannot be bought, so spend it even more wisely and thriftily.

CHAPTER TEN

Coordinate, Balance, Submerge, and Unify

The five merits are like the walls and floors of a house, which provide basic integrity. Any of them missing can result in incomplete protection even with a roof, which provides cover from rain, sunshine, or hail, but not protection from animals. The covering grace of high spirits and God can bless one up to a limit; the rest is up to the doing of the believer. Those with a lot of SWM have little defense against vengeance by others or animals. Most people and governments may look innocent, but they can turn vengeful to someone at wrong circumstances.

As mentioned in our last book, wanton deeds of religious people can conjure calamity despite their moral values and practice. Heavenly deposit from a philanthropic deed is like a roof; merit practices are like floors and walls. One inside and one outside, both healthy heart and robust body are essential to the wellbeing of an individual. The lack of five merits or philanthropic deeds can result in the death of the individual.

Being submerged, a healthy heart coordinates and balances functions with other bodily parts. Good relations with family and friends stitch a network of resources, which supply information and material. This supply sometimes can be vital. Ren without righteousness causes corruption or retribution. Kind but unfairly treating the group, a supervisor can cause some to be disgruntled, resentful, or even retaliatory.

Excessively focusing on one or two of the five merits can unbalance the scale of merits, like an uneven table surface dropping dishes and cups on its top. Refer to the discussions regarding this coordination and balance in our last book. After coordinating and balancing the five merits, the table surface is even, but it still needs strong legs to support.

A network of family and friends provide the legs for a sturdy table. As mentioned in our last book, most cannot survive in this world alone, especially during infancy. More vital than the information and material support from family and friends are their counsel, direction, and criticism. Though unpleasant, criticism can be awakening and salubrious to spiritual health. One should follow the principles of one's own belief, but criticism helps to substantially and extensively correct the course back to Tao, kind of like Donald Trump now.

Including the authors, most of us are in the infancy of spiritual development. Being blinded by a false image of being an adult, we often become arrogant and give up on advice and criticism too early and too soon. This arrogance often ends up severing relations with good people who may later help spiritually. After a bridge is burned, the money and effort needed to rebuild it is often substantially more than that of the original construction; just ask any divorced couple.

A surfaced submarine is more vulnerable than a submerged one; concealing a deer tail may save the deer from being hunted down mercilessly. Arrogance and showiness often summon attacks of past wrongdoings to others, especially for those wealthy and famous such as Bill Cosby and Bill O'Reilly. Jealousy is a mental nature toward unfair distribution of material or attention; a brain does not share like the spirit does. A wise one hides whenever possible.

Like the five extremities of a body, the five merits must coordinate properly to operate complex machinery such as a crane, forklift, bulldozer, or excavator. If the head or one of the limbs has a mind of its own, achieving personal goal may be doomed. Being obsessed with serving needs of others can tip the balance toward Ren, which is the main reason of concentrated homeless. Overly emphasizing righteousness can lead to one's own decapitation such as the story of Guan Yu in the Eastern Han Dynasty in China.

This unification of the five merits requires constant communication among them. Before trying to righteously hand down an execution sentence, a judge or juror should introspect on whether the nature of the crime warrants the penalty. Taking the life of an abuse sufferer might add insult to injury. A serial killer who fundamentally does not believe in the wrong of killing may not deserve to die either.

The Absolute Nature of the Five Merits

Like the absolute nature of spirit, the five merits have no opposing qualities. Ren can only be sufficient or not; the opposite of Ren is not hatred. With insufficient Ren, one author wronged in hating the City of Brea, California, for the unjust appeal process, despite the correct identification of injustice. He repents. Impure love is the opposite of hatred, not the pure love inside Ren. The only way to describe the lack of pure love or Ren is the lack of it. Before falling in love with a mate, examine whether this love is pure, or it may later turn into hatred as some divorced couples have testified.

Likewise, insufficient appropriateness, consistency, wisdom, and righteousness are not rudeness, lying, stupidity, or coveting greed. Rather, they are inappropriateness, inconsistency, unwise, and unrighteousness. The article "Is Truth Dead?" in *Time Magazine* is an example to illustrate the difference between lies and righteousness. *Time Magazine* interviewed President Trump and pointed out many of the incongruence between the reality and what he said. (Ref 19)

What exactly is the eternal truth? It is Tao and spirituality, all others are temporary. Believing in the truth, in the spiritual merit of consistency is not concerned with lies or deceit. Trump might have prevaricated in his speech and writing, but his behavior had nothing to do with the truth, even the truth within him. Two situations exist when a person lies or deceives: one is that the person intends to benefit from the deception, another is that one believes in what is said.

In the first situation, the person violates the truth by willfully conveying something against one's own knowledge and conscience. In the second situation, the belief of the person may differ from those of scientific understanding or common knowledge, but this faith in one's own words should not be placed in the same category as the first situation. A person is entitled to believe anything one wishes, even if it is against common sense or scientific discovery. In other words, President Trump was truthful toward his own spirituality.

Despite the authors' dislike of President Trump, we have to speak the truth from heart and to give President Trump the credit he deserves. The criticism of *Time Magazine* did not violate the truth either. From their perspective, not speaking based on reality violates the truth, as what happened with President Trump. Though the definition of truth by *Time Magazine* is not the same as the eternal definition we delineated, they spoke the truth out of heart, so they are truthful too, despite their misunderstanding of the word truth.

Notwithstanding the conflict of opinions, President Trump and *Time Magazine* were both truthful. This view of both sides being correct can only be taken from the absolute point of spirituality. After the absolute Tao creates yin and yang, they are no longer absolute. An added observation is that the prevaricating habit of President Trump is consistent with his previous behavior as a television personality.

Though hatred, rudeness, lies, coveting greed, and stupidity are not the opposites of the five merits, they are not good due to their nearly opposite qualities. Their inferiority is caused by the lack of good qualities within the five merits. A person with constant hatred is likely devoid of Ren. The spirit of a fraudulent gangster likely has no respect toward any others. One coveting other's possession to the point of jealousy likely is not righteous. A person constantly making foolish decisions of committing the same mistake over and over likely has departed from one's own wisdom.

These inferior qualities render people like space ships traveling far away from the effect of the earth's gravity that their chances of spontaneously landing back to earth are nearly none. The earth's gravity is an absolute existence that no other is the opposite of its existence. The fact that the earth rotates around sun with no outside help proves this absoluteness. Also the fact that the earth has both yin and yang sides exposed to the sun evenly demonstrates its absoluteness. This absoluteness in humans is individuality or personal spirituality. Losing one's individuality to group mentality, the person presumably has forgone the absoluteness of his or her own spirit.

When a spirit does not conform to Tao, one no longer has both yin and yang, kind of like a train which loses one side of its track and soon is stopped by friction. Practicing the five merits from the heart is better than practicing from the mind, and practicing from the spirit is better than from the heart. This disparity is often so huge that it cannot be made up by the length of practice time. This is why many people cannot achieve spirituality in a lifetime.

For instance, one thousand years of practicing Tao from the heart by an attractive fox-turned-human spirit may not surpass one decade of practice by an avid spirituality student. The point used to push a heavy stone block matters; pushing on the right way like using the law of the lever induces rolling of the stone downhill quickly. Without the law of the lever, one may spend hours unable to move the stone an inch. Science is mostly about reasons behind things; a placement of spiritual education at all levels of school and college soon uplifts the spirituality of a whole population. We will address educational reform in chapter 15.

This absolute nature in humans has been gradually lost over the course of history due to lives in a physical world which must have opposing qualities of yin and yang to exist. Nearly all people eventually marry another, often not based on true love but based on loneliness. Once a mate is found, most stop searching for eternal truth and become stuck in this very adversarial world of yin and yang.

The practice of the five merits merely returns a subconscious mind back to its spirit. This return is like going back home after years of working away from home. Using mind only is laborious and achieves less than using mind and spirit. Working at home saves time and money. The combined power of mind and spirit can be much more than that of mind alone.

No place is like home, especially the home of one's own spirituality. Before this return to home, one must fix the illusion that a workplace can last forever. The impermanence of earth makes it a no-brainer choice to resort to one's own spirituality. Only the absolute five merits can achieve permanence and carries each person home. The pull or push of mind only provides an illusion of returning home but does not actually do so with no support from one's own spirit.

Everything in nature grows upward toward the sun; the natural aim of human growth is toward spirituality. This willful spiritual growth results from the practice of the five merits. Tao or the mental practicing of the five merits is the only path home.

This return to one's own spiritual home has nothing to do with changing the self. Many wrongly think that a main incompatible reason between couples is that one changes but another does not. One's mental wandering at a same place or downward spiral does not advance a step toward one's own spirituality, only the daily practice of the five merits does.

The Meaning of Life

Life in its physical form only has no meaning. The potential meaning of a life is in its hidden spirituality, which if not unearthed is equal to no meaning for that life. The formation of family and giving birth to offspring is biological albeit our feeling of family connection. This emptiness of a life can only be instilled a meaning by growing the seed of spirituality.

Whether this seed will grow is up to each individual, and no others. Not even close family can help even if they are willing. Advice can reach only so far into a mind; stubbornness can lead to eventual destruction of the spirit like a piece of paper being burned in a bonfire. Propagation of spiritual education can teach this knowledge to all souls, but spiritual growth from daily practice still depends on each student.

The meaning of a life often derives from the choices by that life. Whether choosing wisely to stay on Tao determines spiritual life or death at the end of a lifetime. Growing a seed can be particularly difficult in its infancy due to the heavy enclosure by surrounding soil. Environment can strongly prevent change like a magnet holding on to a junk car. Frequently, spending lots of effort and time is unavoidable.

The existence of Tao in the universe gives birth to the random encounter in the course of each life. Each decision during this encounter determines whether the spiritual seed will continue to grow or not. Today's public education provides fertile ground to increase reasoning ability of students. Good choice of action can consummate the practices of the five merits to render a life meaningful.

The main purpose of education should not be monetary gain but meaning of life. Not teaching spirituality is the fault of today's educational system, but not firmly and solidly stepping forward on Tao is the fault of each individual. A meaningful life would draw money income, but not the other way around. Large amount of wealth can be a huge barrier on the way toward spirituality, especially when one intends to only hold it. Likewise, overly thrifty hurts one's own spiritual growth.

The divination tool we discussed extensively in our last book is an important tool to realize life meaning. Though not emphasized a lot in this book, it is an indispensable device in learning Tao from high spirits or God. This is especially true at the beginning stage when one's correct Tao orientation is shaky. From experience, high spirits and God know Tao and can guide the spirituality student accordingly.

The possible thirty-two answers from the toss of five objects can be easily calculated by two to the fifth power. Originally with six objects and sixty-four possible answers, the Book of Change, or I Ching, was written several hundred years before Confucius was born. He studied and used it to converse with heaven regularly. Due to its difficulty of being understood, a scholar during the Ming Dynasty converted and simplified the sixty-four answers into thirty-two. (Ref 20)

Divination helps to instill life meaning before one's spirit is strong enough to make meritorious decisions. When a person is dominated by mentality rather than spirituality, decisions tend to be materialistic in nature. The downward cycle of materialism and mental dominance can fuel each other like a fire and a pile of papers. It keeps a person trapped in materialism.

A road leading to the top of a mountain wanders around to reduce the ascending slope; the path to spirituality and life meaning often is not a straight line. This zigzag path is necessary to match the frequent rise and fall of most minds. A saw goes back and forth repeatedly to gradually cut into wood. Interlacing between nice guidance and critical whip pushes and pulls a mind toward spirituality like the cycle of day and night creating Tao.

Two out of the five divination objects can be used to denote yes or no. A positive and a negative indicate yes; both positive and both negative indicate no. As long as a believer is sincere, high spirits and God are likely to direct. The possession of Tao by them indicates their empathy for helping any inquirer with good intention.

The writing process of our books demonstrates how divination can push and pull people to Tao. None of the authors were wealthy at the time of writing our first book. After our idea of writing was approved, we wrote with an initial enthusiasm of sharing divination experiences. But the thought of great wealth from book sales crept into our minds, especially near the publishing time.

High spirits or God approved our request to increase the original price suggested by the publisher, likely due to their understanding of Tao and our unspoken wish of boosting our bank accounts. After a few years, we realized that the book sale did not generate much income, and we also realized our wrong intention. We repent.

Though our initial motivation was right, our later intention to be wealthy from the increased expense of readers was wrong. However, the publishing process brought our materialism to the surface, so we became aware of and could correct this mental flaw of ours. The meanings of our lives were increased after publishing the first book despite our broken dream of becoming wealthy.

With the awareness of our wrong, the writing of this book boosts our spirituality much more than that of the last book. Many of the writings in this book seem to be literally inspired by high spirits to the point that even the authors were all surprised by what we have written. In fact, most of us have gained a lot more understanding of spirituality and Tao than we did at the moment we started to write.

All authors are appreciative of the opportunity and honor of writing these two books. Without the initial approval of our first book by high spirits or God, we might have never been confident or motivated enough to write due to our deficiency in book writing skills. Basically, we had no faith for writing a book at all, let alone two. But now, we sincerely hope that our inspired inspiration can propagate to all readers who are interested in spiritual education.

The Five Saints and the Two Almighty Gods

Before we start to write this section, we need to make it clear that we do not mean to criticize or totally disagree with any saint or God. In fact, we have high respect toward all of them despite their small imperfections. The main reason why we discuss those imperfections here is purely for academic and scientific purposes. Fairly, any spiritual student should learn to criticize even those one has high respect for in order to advance his or her own spirituality.

An unfair criticism constitutes blasphemy or defamation if it is made public. A lawsuit charge of defaming another person is easy to fight in a court of law, but blasphemy can be devastating if the person or spirit has the power to punish without a trial. Before we started to write, we have asked for permission to write these. After we finish writing, we certainly will have all these paragraphs approved.

The five saints we refer to in the section title are Mohammad, Jesus Christ, Lao-Tzu, Buddha, and Confucius, who created the five major religions popular today. The Islam founder Mohammad was very spiritually appropriate in his teaching. Covering a female's face at public places with males who are not family members was appropriate to avert unwarranted arousal if she is appealing to the male. This practice might have prevented many civil conflicts.

Confucius had a similar teaching: "Do not watch, listen, speak, or move if it is not appropriate." The practice of Islam took it one step further than other religions by stipulating that all females should cover up their faces in public to help the spiritual practice of the male. This teaching of covering the female face was very well intended based on the principle of spirituality. Though some females may not like it, it conforms to Tao.

Since the time of Mohammad, the constant worship and serious fasting are very good spiritual practices for Muslims. Rite and ceremony are particularly important for the beginners of a belief. Those processes help worshippers to strengthen their faith via actual behavior and performance. Rite and ceremony still exist in many governments today such as the inauguration of a national president. They are necessary to announce, to formalize, and to boost faith, as discussed extensively in our last book and this.

Watching out for appropriateness is a good practice during a ceremony, but other merits should be worked on while not worshipping. Placing too much emphasis on worship topples the balance of the five merits and hurts righteousness. Paying too much attention on being appropriate on the surface, one often neglects the righteous backbone of a task. For example, a clerk caring too much about being appropriate to customers often does not correct a customer's wrongdoing like cursing or impolite behavior, though an excessive response is not warranted either.

This potential oversight of righteousness is especially obvious among terrorists. Their lack of righteousness breeds jealousy toward other people or countries; the jealousy breeds thoughts of terror to get even. The global terrorist attacks signal the insufficient appropriateness around the world. Excessive payment of top management in public and private sectors, the wildfire of pornographic addiction, and the empty celebration for nearly nothing are only the tip of an iceberg for lots of inappropriateness around the world.

This imbalance of spiritual appropriateness around the globe breeds terrorist thoughts in many. Do not completely blame terrorists. Perform introspection and make fundamental changes in every country to subdue this bad karma. Chapter 13 to chapter 15 detail some suggestions on reform of company, government, and school. Many citizens of many countries can and should think of more ideas.

The deficiency in righteousness among many Muslims leads to jealousy of other people's wealth. After becoming rich from oil sale, many in the Middle East spend on extravagant things such as luxury cars or boats just to show off their wealth. This unnecessary spending spins from jealousy toward the wealth of the western world, similar to the jealousy of terrorists toward technologically advanced countries.

Jealousy of the number of wives possessed by others causes many Muslims to compete for the number of wives owned. Sometimes, it leads to spousal abuse. A moderate competition is healthy for both fun and exercise; excessive competition hurts righteousness the same way as terrorists do. A little bit too crazy are the American football and the world soccer championships. Not being appropriate causes the same ripple effect as the excessively appropriate Muslim. The world has only itself to blame for terrorist attacks.

Jesus Christ was well respected by many people. Few on earth have had this faith and gumption to voluntarily die on a cross, certainly none of the authors. His volitional death has inspired millions, if not billions. The extreme popularity of Christianity in Europe, Africa, and the Americas today largely owes to his sacrifice over two millennia ago.

At the time when Jesus requested to be crucified, the female God did not agree, though the male God did. We just asked high spirits or God and were asked to correct our initial notion that the female God partially agreed. Our initial notion about the disagreement of the female God came from watching a movie on Jesus's crucifixion. In the movie, a female figure walked around the cross with a worried look of deep love, like that of a loving mother. The approval of the male God prevailed as the West was his main spiritual governing area. The reason of the disapproval by the female God was based on Ren that cruel and unusual punishment should not exist.

At the moment of the final death when the pain became unbearable, Jesus called out to the help from the Father. Death by suffering is always inhumane, but most of the ancient Romans and eastern dynasties did not acknowledge this. The concept of humanity became popular only a few hundred years ago. A strong faith drove Jesus to volunteer to die, but he was after all a human. Despite his use of spiritual power to heal others, his promise to God had stopped his spiritual power from warding off physical suffering.

Notwithstanding his sacrifice, a flaw of Jesus was his inability to elaborate teachings in detail. One reason that the New Testament was not very complete in his teaching was likely that he did not educate followers in great detail like Buddha did. This flaw was the result of his strong faith hindering his thinking process. When his mind clenches faith tightly, he lost sight on how to explain what he really meant in detail.

This oversight from the extreme faith of Jesus has influenced many Christians to do things instinctively instead of wisely. Sometimes this instinct is correct, but sometimes it is not. As we discussed in chapter 4, the subconscious mind can fool a person into thinking that an instinct comes from spirit, though it is not.

The hidden subconscious mind can be more dangerous than the conscious, which is in the open. The molestation of altar boys in the Catholic Church stemmed from excessive faith in intuition over wisdom. The dispute about creation of human race is another example. How exactly did humans come to be has little or nothing to do with the abstract spirit inside, so the dispute on Darwinism is mostly pointless.

Based on Tao, we deduct that the choice of Jesus to volunteer for a crucifixion was not totally wise, despite his pious volition to demonstrate faith in God the Father. The strength of one's faith does not need to be publicly displayed to be validated. The redundant wish of exhibiting one's own faith reveals to the placing of immoderate faith above pain and suffering.

When he so wished, he focused too much on his faith and neglected the amount of physical pain he would have to endure; it was also due to his inexperience of any physical pain prior. This oversight from excessive faith caused his final cry for help from God the Father, who probably did. The strong bond between Jesus and God the Father was commendable in boosting the faith of Jesus to such an extreme height. Nonetheless, immoderate faith kills many, as history has proven over and over again.

Criticizing God the Father unfairly can have an even bigger consequence than criticizing the five saints or other saints. We do this humbly as God the Father is still the alpha and the omega, and his spirituality is more perfect than any of the authors. Growing up to become an adult, one may have some better ideas than those of one's parents. These ideas are thoughts and do not always paint the whole picture as authors are humans with potential blockage of mind.

The approval of the crucifixion of Jesus has had bad influence on western culture in general. First, it encouraged the excess of Jesus's faith and further blocked his wisdom. Second, the example of Jesus being crucified was not a very good one for his followers that many have thought the only way to faith is through pain and suffering. Some of the abuses in abbeys or convents and monasteries, were due to this misconception.

Third, this excessive faith has sprung the ideas of country governed by church, unjustified force upon other nations, killing of abortion doctors, an earth with Christianity only, and excessively defensive countries. A country can only be strong either via faith in the system as in the United States or faith in the top leader as in North Korea. Without fostering blind faith throughout a country, a strong worldwide navy is unlikely. When only one country is strong militarily, all others want to develop advanced weaponry.

One prominent description in the Old Testament is the righteousness of God the Father, whom we have great respect for. It is true that on average westerners are more righteous than easterners due largely to the teaching of Christianity, but a person can do righteousness overmuch. Excessive righteousness hurts Ren, as the approval of the crucifixion showed.

For example, a judge who is overly enthusiastic in enforcing justice may purposefully overlook an underlying reason for a crime to suit the righteous mindset. This on-point blindness hurts Ren of the judge. The strong faith and righteousness can weaken wisdom and Ren and tip the balance of merits. Most things moderate is better than extreme, even spiritual merits.

Dominative Christianity and Judaism or even with Islam does not necessarily lead to high spiritual practices by believers. Blended spiritual education from Buddhism, Confucianism, and Taoism has propagated family values and traditions in Taiwan, China, and many Asian nations for thousands of years. It has not stopped working without one dominating religion. The worry of heresy not only stifles spiritual growth but also makes fools out of believers. Human smartness is sufficient to sort it out without being coerced or steered behind the scenes.

Not that God the Mother is perfect. She tends to be emotional and sometimes may be a little bit too loving, like an eager mother who risks the danger of stifling natural growth pace. Words in her writing described bloody tears for her lost children in the world today. Those emotional words greatly inspired some authors to practice spirituality as teenagers. Excessive grief can hurt both self and others, like excessive conservatism can thwart spiritual growth.

A famous Taiwanese folk song has simple but interesting meanings: "The grandpa likes salty food, but the grandma prefers sweet. The fight between them breaks the wok." The words of God the Father in the Old Testament are a lot more than the words of God the Mother in her Ten Commandments as we described in chapter 7, so we criticize proportionally. The wok alludes to the world humans live in.

The Tao of Lao-Tzu was higher than Confucius, but he is less famous than Confucius. When he died, Confucius was twenty years old and had benefited from his mentoring. Shortly before his death, the strong spirit of Lao-Tzu knew it and was walking out of a western gate of the Great Wall. A spiritual gate guard sensed the strong spirituality and asked him to leave a book, or Tao Te Ching, for others to study.

Being extremely humble is the premise of being righteous. The humbleness of Lao-Tzu enabled him to see through all universal truth and the falsehood of human existence. This righteousness so generated, however, hindered his development of Ren, maybe to the point of being callous or cold. Most of his disciples were high spiritual achievers, better than those from other religions, but they were more free spirits than saints. As much as they can, the saints do their best to help people to improve spirituality, but free spirits are less willing.

In the future if incarnated, Lao-Tzu may be the best choice to answer for students the unsolvable questions of Tao. His Tao is praised as so high that even dragon and tiger kneel down and submit to him. As a hermit, he distastes city living where one often loses one's own spiritual life to attraction. When living on earth, he let loose his spirit to roam around the universe and kept in touch with the spiritual world.

Though good, the theory of Lao-Tzu is not flawless. Contrary to Confucius, Lao-Tzu advocated that the general populace should not learn to improve their merits, and the merits in an individual will be manifested by itself. This is probably true before the minds and spirits of most people are contaminated, but it is not true anymore for a long time. Many conflicts and wars since ancient times demonstrated the deterioration of general mentality that they do need to be educated to return to Tao and spirituality.

The original intention of Lao-Tzu was probably not to propagate Tao and spirituality as a fashion where everybody follows it in flock. He likely would dislike today's education where graduates are sent to society by a bunch. Mass production of graduates with the same standard kills all the individuality that comes with each spirit. Murder of individual spirituality is worse than all of the knowledge acquired in school.

Another minor flaw of the theory of Lao-Tzu is his total ignorance of what the general populace need to survive. Most people have to work to make a living. When working, they are inevitably involved in the secular details, which cannot be easily escaped. To totally ignore their mentality and to focus on practicing Tao in the deepest sense has not been accepted by the general populace with great ease.

The theory of Lao-Tzu would be great for those who do not have to make a living. With total focus on the practice, most can achieve high spirituality and Tao fairly quickly by following his teaching. His theory is especially perfect for people living in a convent or monastery. Though much of his theory is hard to comprehend, one can quietly ponder their meanings to tranquilly match them to the nature, which has a lot of similarity with Tao and spirituality.

The deep understanding of Tao by Lao-Tzu enabled him to realize that many writings in his book might not be easily accepted by most commoners. He likely perceived that enthusiasm like that of Confucius might encounter a lot of resistance because the time was not ripe yet. When the right time comes, Lao-Tzu will be more than willing to help all people who are interested in understanding and practicing Tao.

Buddhism is a popular religion in the world, especially in the East. Buddha's teaching was extensive, including many lessons on interactions between mind and body. Practicing his detailed analyses of mind and spirit, a lot of his disciples reached enlightenment. Highly wise, Buddha taught both adults and children and both poor and wealthy.

Some criticized Buddhism for denying the existence of God, which is likely not true. Many of his direct disciples could spiritually travel to heaven and hell. As the teacher of those disciples, Buddha probably had known God the Mother and the Father. Some reason likely prevented Buddha from teaching it in his lecture.

A possible reason was that he might not have revered the Gods as the highest spirits while living in the secular world. In India during his time, the caste system at birth decided whether one would be rich or poor. As the prince of a country, Buddha lived in luxury provided by his people. He disliked the inequality. Likely, he did not want to create a hierarchy in his lecture through introducing the senior spirits.

Whether purposely or forced by the environment, his failure to mention the senior spirits, or Gods, was an imperfection in his lecture. Focusing too much on wisdom, one is likely to neglect appropriateness and respect. Many of his later disciples became egotistic due to this mentality and the dharma learned from Buddha.

They think that the dharma of Buddha they have learned is very powerful, even more powerful than Buddha himself. Dharma becomes a material possession to them like a house or car many collect in life, despite their knowledge of forgoing secular possession learned from the dharma. They have not realized that their knowledge of dharma is also a kind of material possession that can bind their spirits.

Nevertheless, we reiterate our high respect toward Buddha's teaching as many authors have had benefited from his dharma. Some authors learned this hidden flaw only after years away from dharma and a talk with some Buddhists affected by this flaw. Those Buddhists place dharma even higher than their own spirituality, like putting the cart before the horse.

Later in his teaching career, Buddha likely also perceived this wrong path many disciples had walked into. He corrected it by teaching that nothing had been taught, but it was probably too late. Plus, without realizing the root cause of overly emphasizing wisdom then, he would have impacted little with the correction. His course of correction probably tipped the balance only slightly.

Toward the end of his teaching, only a handful out of thousands of disciples realized what he meant when he plucked a flower to point out the higher importance of each spirit than dharma. Some authors benefited from dharma but at the same time fell to the same trap of not realizing the importance of spirituality over dharma. Lately, after years of not being in touch with Buddhism, one author in a conversation happened to discover this reversed priority within a Buddhist leader who teaches many followers. This inappropriateness is probably readily remediable by an introduction of the highest senior spirits to be revered by all.

Confucius was crowned the Ultimate Saint of Forerunning Teacher in Taiwan and China. His teaching has influenced China and many surrounding countries for over two thousand years. Most dynasties after him used his teaching as the primary testing material for qualifying officials in government. People passing the tests were celebrated and announced with trumpets and parades marching toward hometowns and home doors.

The highly regarded Confucius's teaching conjured some jealousy; many of his writings were burned or purposely destroyed. A famous destruction occurred in Chin Dynasty by the First Emperor of Chin. That movement not only publicly burned Confucius's books but also many Confucians were persecuted or killed. The latest disaster was done by Chairman Mao of China and his Red Guard during the Cultural Revolution from 1966 to 1976.

People in Taiwan and China frequently recite the words by Confucius as ultimately true, but the series of destructions has betrayed the teaching's imperfection. His emphasis on Ren was one of the forerunners of advocating humanity long before slave emancipation in the United States. Females in Taiwan and China have been treated more equally than those of the West without a feminine right movement. The first empress in China governed in the seventh century.

The imperfection of Confucius's teaching lies in his insufficient faith in spirituality or Tao, despite his brief consultation in teenage years with Lao-Tzu. In his lifetime, Confucius was materialistic to some degree. Materialism has been a major deficiency among many Confucians. One popular saying of his is "a person rarely possesses Ren if often speaking fluently or expressing too much facial expressions."

Though some authors thought the above quote was probably at least partially right, the divination showed it as totally wrong. As a repeat teaching in the Holy Bible, people cannot be judged purely based on surface demeanor or appearance. A homeless person may have Tao; a rich person may not. Most of us cannot tell from the mere appearance. A performance of philanthropic acts cannot be used to judge Ren or not. The spiritual Ren is invisible and can only be perceived from one with a spiritual eye.

The excessive lectures on Ren by Confucius likely caused his insufficient faith in his own spirit and Tao. If too kind, a person can become inconsistent with his or her own spirituality. For example, a church which serves meals to the poor every day provides the hungry an illusion that those meals are granted and will last forever. The constant meals can eclipse the faith of the poor when the meals stop someday. When Confucius was struck by hunger while traveling to many countries, heaven was trying to send a message to him about his overemphasis on Ren.

The deficiency of faith in Confucius also caused him to say that eating and lust are part of spirit, another popular quote in Taiwan and China. The instinct of eating and lust is in the subconscious mind, not in the spirit, as we discussed in chapter 4. A faith deficiency in spirituality often confounds a mind into mistaking the subconscious as part of the spirit. The nature of a spirit does not include food or sexual desire.

In fact, Confucius probably should not be blamed for this oversight of focusing more on Ren than other merits. Having the wish to teach spirituality to others as Confucius did, one needs to emphasize on one or two aspects to make a lasting impression. It is similar to the technique used for an advertiser for a television program or a commercial promotion. An advertiser has limited time and space to focus on one or two best features.

Neither should any of the five saints and two Gods be blamed for their slight blemish in acting out their internal Tao. The very nature of an act or performance is to do it one scene at a time. In a lifetime, one has barely enough time to reach one most important goal, let alone many life goals. A saint or God does not need to be 100 percent perfect, only the realization of Tao and roughly balanced five merits suffice to return one to the spiritual homeland.

Though Tao itself is perfect, it becomes imperfect after incarnating in physical body. Earth moves around the sun in elliptical shape, and it tilts to create four seasons. Tao uses steady cycles to regenerate. Earth's tilt is 23.43704 degrees and decreasing; it oscillates between 22.1 degrees and 24.5 degrees on a 41,000-year cycle. Only a biologist can answer questions of life impact if this tilt disappears. (Ref 21, Ref 22)

An example of this imperfection in humans is lust. On one hand, indulging lust on prostitution or pornography chips away spiritual appropriateness and respect, which further abates righteousness. A spirit can be so ruined eventually. On the other hand, attempting to rid all lust via suffocation creates an equal reactional force to prevent its elimination, a basic law in physics. A mind with brain matter follows the laws of physics. This conflict between spirituality and materialism exists as long as one is alive.

Some of the authors enjoy nudism at times, but we do not agree that everybody should be naked walking around a library or restaurant. Though some may prefer more skin exposure to absorb vitamin D, allowing bikinis or shorts in public places may not even be appropriate. Overexposure of skin for both genders can induce inappropriate sexual reaction in others. As liberal and free as the United States is, it is illegal to do so in public; this is appropriate as it should be, based on the reasoning of Tao.

Practicing nudism may be objectionable to many religious enthusiasts, yet it can be a tool for a spiritual practice. Some reasons of pornography and sex addiction are unrealistic fantasy and inaccessibility of the opposite gender. Some religions and countries segregate schools to different genders to prevent inappropriateness. Though with good intention, this system fuels more than what they try to prevent years later. Nudism can help people to transcend unreal fantasies and to reduce their chance of becoming addicted to pornography or sex.

We were pondering whether to change the phrase *the opposite gender* to accommodate people who are homosexual. A divination says that loving a person of the same gender is in the spiritual level. It also indicates that homosexuality should be treated as a disability. As material world, nature is not perfect, generating many deformed infants and physical disabilities.

At spiritual level, one can inherently be either gender and can love the opposite gender. This love is unconditional enough to be called Ren; otherwise, family would soon fall apart between male side and female side. The increased prominence of homosexuality points to the insignificance of sexual organs in sexual orientation. The differences between God the Mother and God the Father described in chapter 7 spells potential conflicts between yin and yang properties.

These conflicts are unavoidable because of the differences between their spiritual propensities, but the conflicts are not all negative. Choices between salty and sweet food need to be balanced to avoid heart disease, diabetes, and malnutrition. Plus, there is no fun if no spark ever comes out of a relationship. Arguments back and forth wake each other up as long as they do not become physical. This fighting is more of an art than a science as many psychologists can attest.

A story of practicing Tao can illustrate the benefit of nudism. A male practiced Tao successfully, but a major hurdle was his love of female bodies. When he was sent to heaven for interview, he took one extra look at a beautiful goddess. He was immediately ordered back to continue his practice.

Afterward, he chose to live in a brothel, where he ate and slept with prostitutes while working on immobilizing his subconscious mind about female attraction. After a few years, he eliminated his mental arousal from female attraction, kind of like one being tired of video games after a few years of repeated playing. Here, we want to specially stress that this method is not for everyone as all are different and may need different methods.

Educating children about teenage hormone surge and increased sexual desire prepares them for upcoming puberty. A spiritual education should also be done at the same time to prevent any inappropriate behavior. Touching someone without permission is inappropriate, such as touching when working together or pretending to bump into someone by accident. Rape and sexual abuse particularly can damage one's Ren severely.

Propelled by the fear of being incarcerated, most adults do not even know why they should not rape or abuse another. The root cause of their ignorance is from the top educators who also do not know why either, let alone be able to teach it to children. Even if they know, they are reluctant to schedule this kind of lesson due to fear of attack by media for inappropriateness. The cycle of ignorance is endless, and few with gumption to break it are needed.

CHAPTER ELEVEN

Sin, Wrong, and Mistake (SWM)

Within the last seven chapters, we introduced the scientific aspects of spirituality and how those aspects can work together in unison with each other. All those chapters were like colorful fruits or vegetables we draw on a piece of canvas. They look delicious and nutritious but cannot be eaten or digested. In fact, one may be bored by our words. This is the most important chapter to turn our words into true nutrients that one can digest and absorb.

In our last book, we devoted many chapters to boost one's resilience in following our precise instruction. This resilience is especially applicable in this chapter. To reach enlightenment, listening and understanding is only one-hundredth of the progress. The other 99 percent is practicing and fortifying the practice. Without this 99 percent, the knowledge of spirituality amounts to not much more than a piece of paper with some words on it.

This is the sharpest contrast between spirituality and science that one is practice oriented and another is knowledge based. Without walking the miles, one probably can never fully realize the principles of spirituality. Without doing an experiment hands-on, a student cannot truly grasp the essence of being a chemist. One may understand physics well through pictures and imagination, but not chemistry, especially not spirituality.

We need to emphasize that the sin referred to here is different from the sin mentioned in many religions. The sin in religious literature refers to the sin defined in that religion, but the sin we mention here refers to the blemish defined by one's own spirit. The mind may or may not be aware of this definition in its spirit. When one transgresses one's own definition written in one's own spirit, that person has sinned, regardless whether religious doctrine is followed, based on our definition.

Therefore, one may naively believe to have been following all religious doctrines faithfully but may actually transgress his or her own principle set up by his or her own spirit, so a sin is committed. What matters the most may not be a behavior or a superficial thought; the subconscious and unconscious truly count the most. This is the reason behind our instruction in our last book about detaching from religion.

If a person follows his or her own definition in spirit but this definition violates commonly recognized definition by high spirits, a wrong is committed instead of a sin. As a dramatic example, if a serial killer does not subconsciously think that killing another human is wrong, the serial killer never sinned after killing each human but merely wronged. Satan often operates on this fine line between sin and wrong.

Nazis and white supremacists are wrong, but they may not have necessarily sinned in the confines of the above scientific definition. Even when those believers kill others, they may not have sinned if they truly believe in it in their own spirits, not just mentally. Making only Hitler or Japanese military power of World War II culpable misses the large picture. One who follows another's wrong to commit a sin is even more unforgivable than that wrong. Satan knows the weakness of people's mind.

A mistake is defined as negligence or carelessness while trying to follow one's own righteous principles. If a captain drives a ship into an iceberg with not enough care to cause the death of 1,519 people, he is negligent. Is he more innocent than a Nazi concentration camp officer who executes 1,519 Jews? The carnal law may think so, but in the realm of their own spirituality, they are equal. Though we abbreviate sin, wrong, and mistake as SWM, we want to emphasize that all three are equally unforgivable with respect to one's own spirituality despite the order of being mentioned.

In other words, God and high spirits may more readily forgive the captain than the Nazi officer, but to the spirits of the captain and the Nazi officer, they are equally unforgivable. To explain it with a scientific analogy, the property of light switches from particlelike in grand domain to wavelike in quantum realm. Similarly, the quantity and quality of a spirit can be vastly different when comparing the viewpoint of looking inward with that of looking outward.

Comparing SWM and Carnal Law

The word *carnal* in carnal law is chosen to reflect the characteristics of common regulations and laws, which govern mainly the flesh of people rather than the mind or spirit. It does not contain any sexual or defiling tone or connotation. Religious people may call it *secular law*, but to be scientifically correct and not to sound out of this world, *carnal law* is probably a better name than *secular law* to be taught in school.

To explain their difference in a nutshell, carnal law evolved from human evolution and SWM derives from every person's spirit. Largely, both of them jive with each other well because they both derive from spirit. The major difference is that SWM is personal and private but carnal law is traditional and public.

Here, their purpose, domain, substance, goal, conflict, and justice served are analyzed.

The purpose of carnal law is to maintain social order, and the purpose of SWM is to achieve personal unity of mind and spirit. Without carnal law, most would still feel uneasy and anxious after taking another human's life. Did he or she deserve it? Was I right in taking another human life? A murder causes ripples not only to the relatives of the victim but also to the souls of most murderers. SWM is innate to most people.

Often, SWM and carnal law complement each other. Some thieves and murderers were caught specifically due to personal guilty feelings from SWM. For example, a thief stole from a bank security truck and the case went cold after few months. While walking toward a street police one day, his SWM and guilty feelings roused police suspicion. With a little bit of scaring tactics by the police, the thief thought his act was discovered and revealed the theft.

A guilty mind is often pecked by the guilty spirit to reveal the crime. Many murderers told about their mental relief after being caught and starting to detail the killing. A reflection of SWM is like a second nature to most people similar to females giving birth or males looking for food when hungry. To reach one's own spirit, one just has to fine-tune this innate SWM power to catch and correct even the smallest mistake.

Keeping unity with spirituality is greatly important in a person's welfare. Nearly all accidents are not purely so; the spirit likely has something to do with that "accident." The spirit, body, and mind must work in harmony for a person to be truly prosperous. Otherwise, gained luck or fortune is likely to change hands soon or eventually. Constantly infighting, a sports team of three people likely will lose often.

The main governing domain of carnal law is the outside world, though a query into the mind may sometimes take part. The domain of SWM is mainly to guard the interior world of a person from outside intrusion. After a murder happens, the motive often can only be used to adjust the extent of penalty, but usually not to decide guilt. Some argue on exonerating a murderer purely based on motive. It may hold some SWM ground, but seldom in grand carnal law perspective.

The ability to reflect SWM naturally exists in each individual's mind, body, and spirit. A spirit can purposely cause an accident to warn the mind about infringing on a spiritual principle. A mind may protest the excessive spiritual control by deviating from its usual behavior. A body may purposely become ill, such as a cancer, to protest against the mind or the spirit for corruption or infighting.

Like a three-headed person, mind, body, and spirit can sometimes disagree or argue. SWM is the key to balance and check all three of them to keep them happy, not just one or two of them. The domains of mind, body, and spirit may be independent, but they are interconnected at the root to constitute a whole person. A famous Buddhist tale is about a monk with three disciples going to the west to get dharma. It describes this frequent dilemma along the way to spirituality.

What matters in carnal law is behavior. The major judging criterion of SWM is mind. A spirit is mostly silent and takes part only to resolve conflict between the mind and the body. As discussed earlier, a body has capacity to think independently from the mind. A mind cannot control blushing, sexual instinct, or muscle reflex.

Mind, body, and spirit can all commit SWM despite the fact that the body is the only one able to manifest it into behavior. The root of an SWM can germinate from any of the three. Once grown, an SWM can spill into other two domains and contaminate the whole soul, so watch out for the seed of SWM in all three of them. A natural-born serial killer may be spiritually educated to eliminate the killing motive; it is one of the main purposes of public spiritual education.

A purely scientific mind is dangerous as it cannot tell good from non-good. It can be easily influenced to do bad things by foul seed in the spirit or the body. We use the word *non-good* instead of *evil* to be more scientifically correct and to avoid religious undertone. A famous ancient Chinese proverb states: "An uneducated mind is dangerous, and the mind of the spirit is tiny to begin with." Here the word *uneducated* means not being spiritually educated.

The education referred to in this proverb is also the spiritual education by Confucius and disciples. It is not quite the same as moral education or religious sermon, though they bear some similarity. The former indicates a direct imposition of value that should be faithfully followed, and the latter is even more so with a religious overtone. A spiritual education refers to a scientific study and practice of spirituality; however, without any imposition of value involved.

This education especially does not refer to modern-day public education with only literature and science as main study subjects. The lack of spiritual education not only renders today's education incomplete because spirituality is the root of science, it also wipes out all belief in one's own spirit and spirituality. This belief is the essential survival tool of one's spirit. The resulting suffocation in most spirits in today's society contributes to the increase of illness in mental and physical realms.

A purpose is the reason for achieving a goal. The goal of carnal law is to maintain social peace, and the goal of SWM is to maintain personal peace. Without SWM in most people in a society, this society is bound to experience unrest, including but not limited to terrorism, lies, hidden robbery of high officials in government and companies, corruption, and cheating to get financial advance.

In other words, the goal of carnal law cannot be achieved without SWM working in most people in a society. As illustrated in the graph about a degenerated society breeding more serial killers, the average mentality and contagious power of a society accounts more than social scholars realize. Not having any spiritual education in school is like letting the animal nature of humans take its course. It results in inundation and flood of disasters from time to time.

Consequently, like animal kingdoms often plagued with power struggle, conflict and war among humans have become inevitable. World War II was a lesson for mankind, and the peace lasted about half a century, but with no spiritual education that grave lesson has slowly faded from people's minds. The ranting and raving between nations have greatly increased over the last few decades, and the elected officials are increasingly feisty, such as leaders of the United States, Russia, and the Philippines.

Carnal law becomes the pivot of people's attention instead of individual SWM. As a result, the internal conflicts of many countries have also increased. A nation purely governed by carnal law is like attempting to build a wall between atoms: it will never work. A solid material such as copper or iron has natural attraction between its similar atoms and does not need to be restrained like the building of jail walls. The affinity of humanity between people is enough to build a nation; too many carnal laws only get in the way of unity.

Though inside people and invisible, individual reflection of SWM can literally be more powerful than carnal law. Lao-Tzu, the founder of Daoism, pointed out that it was not good nor beautiful if all people recognize the same goodness and beauty. Carnal law may be deemed more useful than SWM in the western world, but eastern culture has long abandoned this inferior concept about strict law and order. The West may have some distance to catch up.

When individual SWM loses power to cardinal law, the superficial social peace cannot last. A clean and beautiful street with contaminated trash hiding underneath will create problems later. Writing excessive carnal law is like building a house on a trash dump; sickness and disease are nearly inevitable. With the modern prevalence of school, returning to the use of religion as the primary spiritual teaching tool for a society is impossible. The only way is to go forward to start spiritual education in school.

With the advance of DNA science and forensics, many have been exonerated and freed from years of incarceration, but many innocents perished since the establishment of carnal law many thousands of years ago. We are not saying that carnal law is totally unneeded in a society; figuring out ways to simplify and reduce it is difficult but not impossible, like gradually cleaning up a hoarder's lair. It will take a lot of time and patience.

One of the main purposes of the sacrifice of Jesus Christ was probably to protest the increased prevalence of carnal law. When Jesus criticized and kicked down the marketplace set up in a temple, his intended lecture for the inappropriate mixture of sacred and dirty likely was a protest against people's loss of individual SWM too. The purpose of most religious teachings is to eliminate and to guard against individual SWM.

There can be no true justice without true repentance from individual SWM. Many innocent who were jailed for years were probably not completely innocent after all if the domain of SWM was taken into account. The area of justice in carnal law is smaller than the area of individual SWM. A sad yet very true axiom says that carnal law has nothing to do with justice. True justice must start from individual SWM.

Many working together can realize spiritual education in public school and reduce carnal law in society. The collective strength of the majority of citizens can be formidable that even Congress cannot stop it. Chapter 13 will outline some suggested ways to collect majority power from citizens.

The Sin

As defined at the beginning of this chapter, a sin is the purposeful transgression of a believed good principle in one's spirit. The most common sin is the murder of another human, which violates the Ren principle in the spirit as discussed in chapter 5. The spirit of each person is like a hidden police department and courthouse that sees and judges everything said and done. One may escape from being seen or sentenced for guilty deeds in a real courthouse, but not the police and courthouse inside one's own spirit.

This judgment is automatic and without error, like a computer that rarely errs. What kind of sentence is suitable for a particular sin is also not likely to be mistaken. Unlike a sentenced criminal being put into a jail right away, the spirit may delay a sentence for various reasons. One reason may be to give the mind a second chance to correct itself. Or other sins may later be conjugated to be sentenced together. Yet another possibility is to postpone time for others' benefit like taking care of a sick family member.

Again, probably no accident is truly accidental. They are likely caused by spirit of victim to redeem accumulated sins. This internal judgment deserves even more fear than those by real police department and real courthouse. It is often unseen, unknown, and unpreventable.

Whether an act of causing another's death is a sin, a wrong, or a mistake determines the severity of the sentence handed down by the spirit. A sin is punished more severely than a wrong, and a wrong is punished more than a mistake. As discussed earlier, a serial killer murdering seventeen people may have only committed a wrong, while a murder of only one by another might be a sin. It depends on what principles are written in that spirit. Though the guilty feeling of causing a ship to sink should be the same as that of a Nazi officer in order to promote the checking of one's own SWM, their spiritual levels at the time of death were entirely different.

One may ask about the killing situations in a war relating to individual SWM. The judgment of this killing is subtler. A soldier killing a superior due to resentment certainly constitutes a sin. One ordering to unjustly kill may only have a wrong, but one killing a civilian unnecessarily or out of revenge may have sinned. Some Vietnam War criminal trials resembled this judgment. When a human acting like an animal kills indiscriminately, it is a sin.

Whether an abortion is a sin, a wrong, a mistake, or none of the above is even more intricate. It depends on the circumstance. An abortion done due to the mother's lack of Ren is a sin. One that is done due to an inability to feed or to provide for it may be a wrong, a mistake, or none of the above. A spontaneous abortion may be none of the above. Though prolife is generally right, a woman's right to abort at a warranted situation cannot be overlooked either.

Before agreeing to an abortion, a woman should look deeply into her own soul and spirit for what the spirit truly believes. A decision against one's own spirit is bound to cause a sin and a later regret. Often it is better safe than sorry by not signing on to an abortion if a woman is unsure of the belief of her own spirit. Not advocating prolife or prochoice, we simply attempt to scientifically analyze an abortion to determine whether it causes a sin.

Not only killing another person can cause sin, hurting others can too. Drunk driving itself can be a sin even if nobody is hurt in the process. Addiction to anything often signals the degeneration of a spirit, which can already be a sin by itself. Clouding a mind with alcohol immobilizes the mind and closes any chance of manifesting the spirit. This is virtually the same as killing a spirit at the moment. Blocking spiritual expression or practice on earth is a big sin because it is little different from murdering one's own spirit. If someone is hurt by drunk driving, the sin multiplies.

Not only physically hurting others can be a sin, emotionally hurting others can be too. Abusing a wife or a husband either physically or emotionally demonstrates that a person has worse spiritual quality than some animals. Some people like to abuse their own bodies to enjoy the pain and suffering. This abuse may carry the same weight as abusing others because one should respect and care for a spirit, whether it is another's or one's own. Even the risk of hurting one's own body should be avoided to avoid the risk of sin.

Raping another to satisfy lust is undoubtedly a sin, but raping a spouse may be questionable. A rape may not be punished due to insufficient evidence, but all evidence has been collected by the spiritual judge, who can punish any time. Coveting a neighbor's wife may be a sin due to violation of appropriate principle in spirit. If for no or wrong reason, wantonly disrespecting authority, the poor, parents, or even a stranger can be a sin too. The idea of karma conveys a similar concept about this spiritual judge.

A true Robin Hood may be innocent that he does justice based on spiritual belief, but most robbers and thieves commit some sin. Some corrupt people do deserve to be robbed. If one steals from those who deserve it, it may not be counted as any sin, but it is difficult to judge whether one deserves it or not. The worst stealing is at the moment when one becomes addicted to stealing; no reason exists in that person anymore.

Do not misconceive that stealing or robbing small amounts or trivial materials is innocent. When a spirit judges, it looks more at the nature of a behavior than at the stolen quantity. A pen is treated the same as ten dollars from a spiritual point of view on stealing. Excuses, such as just borrowing, cannot pass the sharp eyes of a spirit.

Lies themselves are not necessarily a sin, but an unrighteous lie to gain personal benefit is. Being selfish is against Ren and righteousness of spirit. When betraying a close family member or a friend, the person violates the merit of consistency. Another possible sin is not deciding wisely and making choices without any consideration. Any serious violation of the five merits commits a sin.

An important note is in order here. After people acquire more spiritual knowledge, they will likely commit more sin, not less. A wrong, not a sin, is often done by one not totally understanding spiritual principles. Punishing a lawyer for a crime is more severe due to the gained knowledge. A priest is more likely to sin than a follower who understands less about sin. People knowing more than others should do better; otherwise, one's own spirit likely punishes one more severely.

The Wrong

As defined in the beginning of this chapter, a wrong is committed when one does a thing but does not know its principle, or when one applies a wrong principle to do it. Right principles exist for doing each thing on earth; the collection of all the right principles is called Tao. High spirits learned these principles well, and they follow them faithfully, or are walking on Tao. The knowledge of many principles is lost, so most people do wrong in life without even knowing it.

When people do not know the right principles, they may use wrong principles to do things. For example, many football players in the United States play for the wrong reasons. Some play for money. Some play because of wishes of parents. Some play to attract attention from others or girlfriends. Some play because it is the most popular sports. All these reasons may not be the right reason to play depending on each individual. One right reason may be to play for fun or spiritual and bodily health.

As the zeroth step, reason for doing a thing determines the success of the whole thing. If the zeroth step is wrong, all steps following that is wrong. If the reason for going on a trip is wrong, the whole trip can be wasted. The reason transforms into drive and motivation, which in turn actuates the physical steps.

Career, academic major, friend, companion, travel, outing, meeting, and phone call all should have a valid reason behind them to keep the spirit alive. Some possible reasons for choosing the abovementioned are higher pay when not necessarily needing it, the potential of making more money while not really enjoy it, no other choice but this one, sexual desire, seeing something never before, finding a potential mate, only for routine, and to quench loneliness. Many above reasons can potentially be wrong.

In the example of playing football, we enumerated four reasons. For the nine activities above, we only mention one of the popular and likely wrong reasons, and one can probably write down at least three other potentially wrong reasons for each activity. If ten people write down thoughts, they add up quickly. Possible wrong reasons can be in the neighborhood of hundreds for each of the nine activities above.

The activities above are the most common one for most people. Most persons probably do ten to fifty activities a day, including but not limited to eating, shopping, driving, reading, meeting, thinking, showering, looking, listening, hearing, carrying, tapping, washing, speaking, pushing, and walking.

The task of reading a text message alone may involve plugging into an electric outlet to charge, opening the cell phone, waiting for it to boot, entering a password, selecting the correct button, reading a message, thinking about how to respond, and an actual reply or forward. Here we listed other activities not listed above. When entering a password, one may be distracted by people's conversation nearby; it counts as another task unrelated to reading a cell phone message.

All these activities work together to accomplish a task, and many tasks may serve one purpose, such as the two tasks of reading a text message and opening a computer to plan an Alaska cruise. From the completion of activity, task, and purpose, a life goal can be accomplished. Each activity is like a small component on a railroad that makes the railroad possible. By complying with reason and principle on each activity, one is walking on Tao.

Be aware of the importance of all-encompassing reason and the ultimate purpose. Many people do not set their life goals and simply pass the time day by day. This passive and aimless use of time spells eventual trouble when death comes. Wishing to be a doctor during childhood is not by itself a life goal. A wish to be a doctor and to serve the sick may be a meaningful life goal. A life goal like this will increase one's Ren.

A better life goal yet is to have multiple careers to develop all five merits, but it is unlikely as most people have only one career. With spiritual wisdom, one can think of a goal encompassing the balance growth of all five merits.

Be aware, though, that a life goal that matches Tao is only half of the game. A train cannot ride on a blueprint; each pebble, rail section, and crosstie is equally important in building a sturdy and safe ride home to Tao. To make the rubber meet the road, one must be practical every inch of the way. Rushing or taking shortcuts will likely result in a fiasco. It would be like a greedy contractor not following the blueprint exactly to rob the owner, who happens to be the same person as the five contractors. Five contractors can equal to one.

Occasionally, some details of a blueprint may not be totally feasible. At such time, revise the plan accordingly to resolve the inconsistency. However, do not deviate from the ultimate goal of a safe and sturdy ride. A train may come to pass at any moment, so do complete the goal early or on time to be ready for the big event.

If the ultimate life goal or reasoning is wrong, millions of wrongs can be committed in a lifetime. A train heading to a wrong destination is bound to make all the wrong turns on its course. One with a wrong life goal is likely to base all doings on wrong principles. Each wrong principle and reason can drive a person to further deviate from Tao. A good life goal and right reasons and principles should be established prior to teenage years.

Most people have never been instructed on how to establish a life principle before their teen years. Some pass time day to day without a definitive goal or purpose in life. Some end up following the routes most others have traveled, a situation where the blind leads another blind. The crucial time to formulate life principles is probably the first ten to fifteen years of a life.

One cannot serve spirit and evil, or God and devil, at the same time. The establishment of a life principle determines whether one will serve spirit or evil, and whether spirituality or the devil. Even though evil and the devil both originate from the mind, this origination has its root during the time of formatting life principle. One wrong can make all others wrong along the way till one's death. This one wrong can also affect whether one will suffer or enjoy life after a physical death.

The Mistake

Though the spiritual punishment for a mistake is comparably less than a sin or a wrong, do not be mistaken that committing a mistake is less significant than the other two. The consequence of a mistake can be deadly or at least cause serious delay. A person may misidentify an unwitting trespasser as an intentional intruder and kill him or her. This mistake likely has a mentality root of overly protecting one's own property.

When writing this book on a laptop computer, we usually have a bag of ice underneath to cool it down and to prolong the run time in a sitting. Usually, three layers of plastic bags are used to ensure that no leak occurs. One time, we were not carefully watching and failed to notice a leak until some water had run out of the bags. Some water seeped into the laptop to cause a slight malfunction, and the USB drives no longer worked.

We were dismayed that the laptop might be damaged and needed to be replaced. Buying another laptop would be essential to finish this book as the library computer time was limited. After a divination showing no need to buy, we scarily waited for a day to let the laptop completely dry out. Sure enough, the laptop was back to normal after its insides completely dried out.

One should always be careful when handling a task at hand. In addition, one needs to keep an eye on the immediate surroundings which can potentially ruin the task. Many accidents can be prevented by simply watching out, particularly an attack by other people. Murders and robberies often happen at the moment when one's attention lapses. Besides noticing one's surroundings, observing mental disturbance of a roommate or a spouse can be vital as well.

The span of one's attention is limited to one task and its surroundings. Multitasking should be done only on related tasks, not those totally unrelated. Texting on a cell phone and driving a car do not mix. Unlike watching out for pedestrians, texting is a completely unrelated task. Another unrelated task is speeding excessively. At excessive speed, the safety of driver, passenger, and surrounding people are all at high risk.

While driving, one of the authors used to speed a lot and was cited repeatedly. Not perceiving the hidden danger of excessive speed, he did not realize that high spirits might be attempting to teach him an important lesson. A citation may not be pleasant, but it can potentially save lives. The initial emotion when getting a citation may be justified; one must later sit down and ponder the possible reasons and principles behind it. Introspection for a mistake can be worth a lot more than the fine for a citation.

Dating two people at a time has a similar effect as performing two tasks at the same time. The main reason that a lie detector works most of the time is that most people are faithful to their own bodies. A body frequently reacts to every thought faithfully; it adequately reacts to every thought not conforming to what happened if that memory is vivid. As Dr. Masaru Emoto demonstrated with rice and water experiments, one's thoughts literally affect physical matters more than most realize. A thought process can be detected by others if their senses are keen enough.

Even a wrong attempt to date someone or to finish a pending task can be detrimental. A week before we tried to finalize the writing of this book, one of the authors wanted to date a female at a clinical trial. She was also interested, and they agreed to meet soon after the clinical trial. At the Sunday, she did not show up as promised. That author ended up wasting one week of his time planning an empty relationship. Our book project was hence delayed.

No difference from performing any task, understanding another person takes time and effort. The time and effort can take away what should be available for another important task. A reason why many just involving in a relationship suddenly find their time to be a rare commodity is due to both the amount of time and effort needed in a relationship. Prior to the clinical trial, he already got word from divination that dating should have been temporarily suspended; apparently it did not sink into his mind. It ended up costing him some time and energy before joining us for this book.

Intentionally, many do not want a goal or purpose in life. Missing a life goal can especially spell doom when other supporting props are missing. One example of the props is one's job or career. When people retire, many lose their direction and sense of purpose, despite how a job or career is not a real-life goal by itself. Banking on a job or a family as a prop is not only risky, but may be downright rotten. A job or family is there to support one's life goal, not the other way around.

Some people soon become ill and die after they retire from a job of decades. They do not know that their illnesses began in childhood when no life goal or purpose was determined. They have been mistaken throughout life regarding a job or career alone as a life goal. A mistake of not deciding a life goal at childhood is like letting others decide one's own life goal; it often ends up like a mismatched jigsaw puzzle not resembling anything.

Except in school, a person should always have a goal or purpose in life. While in school, the sole purpose is to graduate. When working full-time, people can easily fall into the trap of believing in routine and regular income. Unlike the alternating days and nights cycling people to live a lively and dynamic life forward, an unchanged routine for years or decades fools people into thinking that a routine will last forever.

Beware of following false targets others set up, especially in a society which does not have any spiritual course in school. A mistake can be easily made by following others blindly without any checking by self. This mistake may seem to be insignificant, but it can have many serious effects and adverse consequences. Lao-Tzu said in his book that if a beauty is recognized by most, it is no longer a beauty, and if a good deed is commended by most, the deed is not good anymore. A mistake in following other's judgment is like a wrong turn for a life goal, it can be eternally deadly.

Some good examples of this kind of collective falsehood are Germany and Japan in WWII. The faith of the populace in their countries was all mistaken to the point of being willing to sacrifice themselves for a mistakenly wrong cause. When most people are going in one direction, it may not always be the right one for all individuals.

A small mistake in the mind can cause a lot of wrong and sin when the mistake manifests. When aiming a rifle at a target, one-sixteenth of an inch difference in aiming can result in feet or yards difference at the target. Do be careful at all time and do not overlook any tiny mistake that can cause disasters in the future.

SWM the Key to Spiritual Realization

Constantly checking SWM is the key to spiritual realization. Realizing spirit is the awakening of spirit to the point of enlightenment. Due to the large disparity of SWM among people, we cannot possibly elaborate on all the methods of eliminating every individual SWM besides giving the method of divination and the concept of SWM. It is up to each individual to discover his or her own SWMs and to get rid of them.

The authors are mundane spiritual practitioners who are not even qualified to check into spirits of others. However, we know the importance of mind in playing the key role of igniting nearly all SWM. Particularly, the seeds of a mind hidden in the subconscious can sprout any time if it has not been cleaned out regularly. We elaborated on these hidden mental seeds extensively in our last book.

The diverse ways of eliminating each seed also differ from one person to the next, similar to the diverse ways of quitting smoking. Some like to swamp themselves with excessive smoke each day to be sick and tired about it; others may prefer the help of patch and medicine. Whatever the methods are, the end goal is the same: to eradicate personal SWM. It is not an easy goal to achieve; nearly all saints still have SWM from time to time.

The major difference between the SWM of a saint and those of a commoner is that a saint often perceives his or her own SWM right away while a commoner is seldom aware of his or her own SWM. A small difference in heart often amounts to a huge difference in end result. The delicate nature of this keen sense of one's own SWM is like the delicate food prepared by a top chef. One dish alone often suffices to show the years of training and experience, which are totally unique to each top chef.

A top chef follows spiritual instinct from years of education and experience equally; a very top spiritual practitioner resorts to knowledge of Tao and personal experience equally. Knowing only the concept of SWM is gravely insufficient in reaching enlightenment. A practitioner must be constantly vigilant and watch out for where his or her own mind is heading and any potential seeds in the mind.

As mentioned in our last book, many authors have had some experience with this extreme joy of enlightenment. Besides the joy, the immediate knowledge of all the reasons behind each sentence of a spiritual teaching is not found in any mental level. Though a mind has a better reasoning ability than the spirit, the spirit innately knows all the logic and reasons without thinking. A computer is faster than people because the speed of electricity is comparable to spirituality. Do not be arrogant on the thought that the mind can outperform the spirit.

Ultimately, heaven and hell exist in the mind. A spirit is inherently free and rich; the mind needs to learn from the spirit to experience the enormous wisdom and joy. Nowadays most people have their spirits trapped by the mind. Taken over by the unnecessarily smart and active mind, a spirit falls asleep. One of the best ways to squash this overactive and excessively smart mind is to reduce it to nothing.

Do not be afraid that mind will become inactive after learning from spirit. A space ship travels at more than the speed of sound, but people inside do not feel its movement. A bicycle going at twenty miles an hour already takes the wind and heat very hard. After learning from a spirit, the mind is quieter than before but can accomplish a lot more than before.

Spiritual practice must be 24/7 to make it function well. One may ask how a mind can practice while sleeping at night. The preparation when a person is going to bed is the most important time for practicing at night. The moment of waking up is similar to that of going to sleep; one usually has a spiritual feeling about what will happen during the day. The spiritual preparation is at work at the beginning of a day or a night. During times of wakefulness, not a second should be left to chance in order to solidify Tao practice; it also helps to carry the practice into the night.

During every second in a twenty-four-hour period, intensive attention on practice of Tao takes precedent over all other tasks during the day or the night. A focused mind can connect with spirit and body to work out disagreement. This attention connects to spirit to keep it awake, just like the twin computer example discussed in chapter 4. A small area of the mind ought to be constantly connected to the spirit to keep it awake.

Always keeping an eye on one's own mind and behavior is not selfish; rather, it is a righteous thing to do. A sick person cannot possibly help others; a person with disarray of mind or spirit inside is literally sick and deviates from Tao. Such a person cannot possibly teach others Tao or help others to promote Tao.

In today's world, way too many attractions and distractions exist in the environment that additional pull of personal attention is not warranted. When a fire breaks out, fire alarms automatically detect it and alert people to leave. When a commotion breaks out, police is on the scene within a few minutes. Unneeded worry or attention to outside world sucks one's spiritual practice to bare bones. For a person to live, flesh and blood are also needed besides bones. Resting the mind is not easy, but it is doable.

If mostly free of SWM, one can help reduce others' SWM. A person who still smokes is not suited for helping others to quit. The success of eliminating one's own SWM is sufficient to advise others on how to reduce individual SWM. Not much instruction is needed for cleaning a house, but experience counts, such as different ways of cleaning up oil.

For a person not mostly free of SWM to teach SWM is like the blind leading another blind. The lecture of a molesting priest is likely skewed by the addition of abusing young boys. Obsession and addiction are like magnets displacing an iron from its original righteous position. All down streams are wrong thereafter.

A spirit is often compared to a tree. Making a tree grow upright, ropes and wooden supports are needed before the tree trunk is settled into an upright position. Others' advices and troubles in life are such ropes and vises. Repairing a broken soul is painful, but it is necessary if one wishes to return to spiritual homeland. Getting rid of most SWM may be uncomfortable or painful to a mind, but no pain no gain in spirituality.

CHAPTER TWELVE

Tao (the Way, the Truth, the Life)

Before we explain what Tao is, let us use recent news to illustrate it since the concept of Tao is even more abstract than that of spirituality. Karen Klein, forty-six, was the mother of a ten-year-old son and the wife of Eric. They rented a car in Las Vegas to visit the North Rim of the Grand Canyon. Their GPS misguided to detour them to a service road when a main road was closed. When they tried to turn around, their car got stuck in mud at a place with no cell phone signal.

Eric Klein had injured his back earlier in a car accident, so Karen decided to search for help by foot at 2:30 p.m. on December 22, 2016, banking on her past stamina as a triathlete and on survival training. Walking twenty-six miles in thirty hours straight, she had consumed the little food she carried and had subsisted on some pine twig and urine. Her foot was injured, and one of the feet no longer fit into her shoes. Nearly exhausted and badly injured, she walked ten feet, collapsed, picked herself up, and collapsed again.

For the last nine hours and last few miles, she literally moved her legs forward with her hands before finding a guard shack with blanket inside. Totally exhausted due to the walk and no sleep for forty-five hours, she still managed to stay awake for yet another six hours before a rescue team finally arrived to find her barely conscious. Some of her toes were later amputated due to frostbite.

Just like most news have portrayed, the moral of this news was inspiring. She was determined, strongly willed, persistent, and courageous to look for help for her son and husband. Refusing to let her mother bury her or to leave her son without a mother, she kept herself awake in the last six hours. Nevertheless, we see some lessons about Tao and spirituality that they probably should have learned in their childhood or youth.

The first lesson is that they never consulted high spirits or God before deciding to embark on the Grand Canyon journey. Being able to afford the money and time does not mean they should spend it at will, especially for a long journey away from home. In our last book, another mother died during a long family vacation from San Diego to Florida. Karen was lucky to be alive. If not for her extreme survival determination, she would have died if she fell asleep or was injured more severely. Divination is about consulting the Tao in high spirits or God, not just anybody.

Every time before preparing to visit a new place or start a new relationship, one ought to always ask high spirits or God. This consultation is not superstition; it is about the unknown place or people. Only high spirits or God can judge people and places in depth, not most humans. At most, we judge from the surface, which can be misleading. The potential danger of the encounters can be deadly. The fine powder used for stage effect at a block party in Taiwan caught fire and killed many. Most humans could not foresee this kind of potential danger.

The fact that Karen and Eric trusted the GPS but not spiritual direction was ironic. This lack of faith in spirituality is quite common nowadays, even for some who know divination. Due to past wrong answers, a brother of one of the authors criticized that author for believing in it. As discussed in our books, most errors are either correctable by common sense or intended to test the will of a person. Persistence can uphold the faith.

If Karen and Eric had consulted God for the trip, the calamity would be a test of Karen's will to survive. Though it saved her, her determination actually nearly killed her. Her choice of continuing to march farther from husband and son a few hours into her journey was caused by the mental linearity we discussed in chapter 9. Unlike spiritual wisdom of knowing to go back when needed, this linearity knows only going forward. Also, she could have consulted the spirits a few hours into her walking on whether to continue the walk or not.

Whether to believe in a particular answer of a divination must heavily depend on the reason of the person asking. If Karen, using her spiritual wisdom, felt that she probably had walked too far after seeing no potential help in sight, she should have started to walk back. It is also why we keep stressing that divination can never be 100 percent accurate. Spiritual reasoning is the way, not being linear and blindly pushing forward.

A car trapped in mud probably was not deadly, but the decisions to hike and to continue the aimless hike probably could have been. The nearly fatal decisions came from faulty reasoning of the mind, not the spirit. With no prior spiritual training, they tended to reason with flaw, which was the direct result of an education with no spiritual component. Karen's survival training probably pushed her to make the faulty decision too by giving her overconfidence.

Out of desperation with no help in sight, Eric climbed to high ground to summon help with his cell phone. Karen was stuck for another half day after Eric and the son were rescued. Eric should have thought about walking to high ground first before agreeing to Karen's walk to find rescue. At least, he should have instructed Karen to walk back before going too far without seeing any help.

This nearly fatal visit to Grand Canyon and Eric's car accident earlier were more likely related to the faulty reasoning of Eric than of Karen. A husband is often the pillar of a family, especially in the sense of spiritual reasoning. Like a ballroom dance where a female follows the lead of the male, this reasoning philosophy is contagious to the wife. Whether a choice is conforming to Tao or not depends on the reason behind it. The wrong choice of looking for help likely spun out of Eric's faulty reasoning or nonconformance with Tao for years.

With a wrong supporting reason or principle, a will to survive can cause a death which the will tried to prevent. Karen's will to physically survive simultaneously clouded her judgment about whether to push forward or to turn back in the first few hours of her walk. Without setting a life goal, people work on a career for the sole reason of physical survival. This aimless move forward is likely to hit a wall or an accident eventually. These hidden erroneous reasons are not easy to detect without a keen insight.

Karen might have learned a lesson of being prepared from the ordeal, but her faulty reasoning will probably march on to cause more calamities in their lives. Survival training does not teach people proper reasoning ability. Her will to survive for her son and her mother may not be enough to rescue her the next time. Only a spiritual education can correct her faulty reasoning. (Ref 23)

One of the authors joined the National Guard part-time as a medic in a forward MASH in Arizona after the approval of high spirits or God. During the first Gulf War, that author and his mother were scared when his unit was notified to prepare for mobilization. However, the war ended before the unit was mobilized due to the light casualties of the first Gulf War on the US side. That author was truly blessed by the divination.

A blessing is not just a wish or some words. It carries real power to change events on earth. Many people have seen the movie *Bruce Almighty* and probably think that the power of God happens only in a movie. As mentioned in our last book, the power of God and high spirits often hides from public view to preserve humbleness and to prevent coveting of the power. This work in the background nevertheless is usually as powerful as, or more so, than a full display of the power.

Explanation of Tao, Yin, Yang, and Cycle

The word *Tao* has two basic meanings in Chinese. The first one means an avenue or a pathway. Originating before Confucius's time, the second one means the original principle, life, or way through which the whole universe begins, progresses, or ends. This second meaning was first written in a book called *Tao Te Ching* by Lao-Tzu. It has no corresponding word in English, so translating as Tao is appropriate.

In the book *Tao Te Ching*, Tao is said to be indescribable by words. Once Tao is described, its essence of existing before and after the existence of the universe is lost. Such a profound definition captivated the attentions of scholars both foreign and domestic. Even most commoners in China have difficulty grasping its essential meaning. We can only do our best to try to write what we know, which may or not be totally accurate. After all, Tao is not describable.

A good way to visualize Tao is as a train track. Not riding on a track, a train derails and is unable to go anywhere. A person who does things against Tao is like a train not riding on a track and will be stopped soon. One who does things according to Tao will likely prosper, like a train going forward on a track smoothly.

Jesus Christ described Tao as the way, the truth, and the life. The life aspect is the spirituality; the truth aspect is the principle. The way is exactly the same term used in ancient China. With the large time and distance apart, it was amazing how Jesus Christ made the same description about Tao as Lao-Tzu and Confucius. Buddha described Tao as nothingness, which could create lives of all variety. All religions point to the same origin of theory about Tao.

Spirituality is part of Tao, namely the life part. The truth and principle part of Tao manifests in spirituality too, but it is not obvious. When people reason or deduct, they use the inner side of spirit. On the other hand, Tao is the force behind the movement of all stars and planets. Though lifeless, Tao exists on earth and the sun, so they can create lives on earth. Without Tao, life on earth is impossible.

Other names for Tao are nonpolar and infinite, or absence of pole and boundless. Tao can create one, or unipolar, which then create yin and yang, or two-polar, which create all others. Most lives or materials created have two poles, such as male and female, or positive and negative. All creation starts with Tao, and all termination starts with Tao.

Yang is the positive side or the one facing up or outside. Earth's surface facing the sun is yang. On the other hand, yin is the negative side or the one facing down or inside. Earth's surface which does not face the sun is yin. Some high spirits say that a yin and a yang constitute Tao. Without alternating days and nights, life would be impossible. Only days or only nights would be either too hot or too cold and unsuitable for life.

In other words, yin is hidden and yang is obvious. What is unknown is yin, and what is known is yang. Knowledge or those already humanly known is yang, and an unknown like the existence of dark energy is yin. Yet another one is that humans live in the world of yang while ghosts live in the world of yin.

Tao includes both yin and yang, so if a person wishes to return to Tao Heaven, he or she must balance yin and yang to achieve it. Only the proper proportion between yin and yang within the mind, body, and spirit can the person achieve Tao and return to the true heaven. Too much yin or too much yang is like missing one of the supporting rails causing the train to stop moving or become dead stuck at the same place.

The intent, wish, thought, mentality, attitude, personality, and psychology are yin, or the inside hidden in a person. Without speaking or writing, this yin is invisible to others. The expressed word, wink, smile, deed, exercise, and other movements are yang, or the obvious outside others can see. The expressed and the hidden interact constantly to create all effects on earth. Such a complicated interaction is the consummation of Tao.

As an example of building a house, an architect must first walk up to a piece of land to inspect its soil property, environment, and weather. Later, he or she must sit down to calculate, to plan, and to draw on paper or computer. When the house is being built, the architect must check to ensure all aspects of the house is down according to the blueprint. If not feasible, the blueprint must be modified to accommodate.

Above interactions between yin and yang make Tao possible, like a train track must consist of two steel bars on each side. The left-hand side is yang, and the right-hand side is yin. The left brain of yang is more logical, analytical, and objective; the right brain of yin is more intuitive, creative, and subjective. The yin and yang of the brain must complement each other to make the mind work seamlessly.

As illustrated on the South Korean flag, yin and yang are not absolute by themselves. Each has a little bit of the other residing within. A yin has a little yang, and a yang has a little yin. This mix and blend brings more harmony. The nighttime has the moon and star lights, so are the lights during dawn and sunset. The daytime has cloud cover at times or mountain shadows. One pure yin or one pure yang would not consummate a Tao.

If a male is too strong, too abrupt, or too straightforward, he risks being broken or being ground by others or life events. If a female is too weak, too flexible, or too compromising, she is at risk of being washed away or dispersed by others or happenings in life. Lives from heaven are called spiritual propensity; enacting and following this propensity is called Tao. The return or repair of Tao is called religious or spiritual teaching.

Though male is yang and female is yin, Tao does not mean a female must always be paired with a male, neither vice versa. Differing from animal, a human can return to Tao by making up what is lacking in each gender. Female can concoct male qualities such as being strong, outgoing, and precise. Male can formulate female qualities like being soft, tranquil, and approximate. Not only one should possess balanced female and male qualities, the regular interchange between the opposite qualities ensure spiritual completeness.

Day and night cycle with each other to make lives on earth possible. Yin and yang should also cycle to conform to Tao. An immobile car on a road will soon be shuffled aside for passing traffic. An idle person is bound to be squashed by the moving earth and other people eventually. The momentum of cycles creates life; without following this cycle, life dies.

This interchange of yin and yang moves all things forward in the universe. To thrive, a person must learn and perform this very basic principle of the universe. With a very strong will, one can stay awake up to eight days, but hallucination, slurred speech, short attention span, and paranoia set in after a few days. Lying in bed every day might be good for depressed patients, but beyond a limit can cause bed sores, muscle and tendon pain, headache, drowsy, loss of focus, and maybe feeling even more depressed.

The cycle of mind can be analogized to the cycle between rich and poor. Being poor, one often sharpens the mind to diligently study in school and to work hard in a job. The dedication and focus on making money often enriches one to millionaire or even billionaire status. After becoming rich, one often wants to enjoy the wealth and soon foregoes the concentration and diligence. The loss of these qualities makes one poor again; hence, the cycle continues.

The cycle of a spirit embodying between human, ghost, and low angel repeats itself in a similar way. Being rich or poor is not related to having a low or high spirit. When one with low spirit gives up the physical body, he or she cannot change the way of thinking, so the soul stays near earth as either a ghost or a low angel. After feeling tired of being a ghost or a low angel, one reincarnates as a human or an animal. Without the learning and practice of spirituality, this cycle never ends.

On the other hand, a high spirit knows how to cycle his or her own internal yin and yang according to Tao learned during a lifetime. Their minds and spirits can escape from being repeatedly cycled by Tao of the universe. Scientists have learned that the sun, earth, and the solar system will vanish someday when the internal fuel of sun is used up. Long before this total destruction, the earth will not be habitable by any life. At that time, no spiritual learning will be possible.

A mind is purely yin, and a spirit is purely yang. Common knowledge among most adults in Taiwan and China is that males belong to yang and females belong to yin. One can match the properties of yin to being quiet, introverted, and having a hidden way of thinking to the qualities of a lot of females. One can also fit the properties of yang being active, extroverted, and having clear, concise thought processes to most males. One may deduct that the male on average has better spirituality than the female because spirit is purely yang.

Wrong. Do not feel bad if you guessed wrong because some authors also did. The average spiritual level of the female is likely higher than that of the male, according to our divination. We surmise that the qualities of spirit are closer to those of female than to those of male. Loving peace and showing compassion to animals and others are a couple of similar qualities. All males should learn from their female counterparts to absorb those good feminine qualities to learn spirituality better.

Heaven and Hell

Some discussions about heaven and hell were in chapter 9; let us elaborate more here. Some say that heaven and hell are in the mind. It is true considering that the pain and suffering in hell and the joy and comfort in heaven are in the minds of those living there. On earth, the sometimes unbearable poverty suffered by the poor and the luxury often enjoyed by the rich virtually paint a similar picture as hell and heaven. Without a mind or body to perceive, no pain or comfort is possible.

Even if sent to the real Tao Heaven by mistake, one who is not prepared enough likely will not last. As told in the story of the Tao practitioner in chapter 10, a single unjust look at a lady transgressed heavenly law. A coveting look at the gold used to build Tao Heaven may also be a sin. If having the propensity of looking at beautiful women, one should ask oneself whether one is able to resist looking when a beauty walks by. Also one should ask oneself whether one is willing to stop searching for additional wealth. If not, one may not be ready to go to Tao Heaven.

Though heavenly law on personal behaviors is stricter than earthly law, people in Tao Heaven have a lot more freedom than all countries on earth. No visa or passport is needed to travel to most parts of the universe. One can love anybody in anywhere as long as two mutually agree. Staying up all night for several nights if one needs to. Sleep all day for few weeks or years if one likes. Less restriction and more freedom are in Tao Heaven than earth.

Some Tao practitioner said that if Tao is a foot tall, the devil is one yard tall. It indicates the large potential of a mind to take over its spirit. Being as humble as one can be is the key to avoiding this takeover. Humbling to the point of owning nothing is the ultimate humbleness. Devils do not oppose all Tao practitioners on purpose, but they test to see their true heart.

If one can be as humble as Tao; then the devil has no place to grow in. Tao is zero or nothingness. The devil grows on the seeds of wickedness in the minds of people. Vanishing one's own mind and body, one is safe from the devil.

The roughly situated heavenly law sees the whole picture of a person instead of the detail of a person with clearly written earthly law. An example is the use of pornography. If one looks at a nude picture to satisfy lust at the wrong moment and wrong time, this look violates Tao and the person is not worthy to be in Tao Heaven. If one looks at the same picture but does not use it for any purpose at all, no transgression has occurred.

An act alone does not determine an SWM, but the intention behind the act does. A huge distance between heaven, earth, and hell is often measured in the huge minds of most people; a tiny mind sees little distance. Few can subdue and reduce their minds to very tiny, let alone to nothingness. Most minds make the distance huge, but it is really not.

Permanent and long-lasting habits are particularly troublesome in preventing most people from going to heaven. Tao Heaven does not want them to even sweep floors even if they plead and beg. Like a temple in China where no dusting was ever needed for decades, Tao Heaven likely cleans itself automatically. A perfect spirituality prevents any dust from settling there.

Obsession and SWM often are the reasons for being barred from Tao Heaven. Eliminating all possible obsessions and watching out for all individual

SWM are the keys to heaven. Addictions are the manifestation of heavy-duty obsessions. Keep self versatile in various interests to avoid each potential addiction along a life course as discussed in our last book. A rolling stone gathers no moss. A constant willingness to accept change can ward off laziness and obsession, thus preventing addiction.

Not leaving a loved one or rich possession behind, the very thing that one should mourn or cry at one's own death is an insufficient heavenly deposit to redeem SWM. Most have SWM whether intentional or not; even a soon-to-be saint likely is not immune. Often, people commit an SWM without even realizing it. A heavenly deposit account can probably redeem SWM of this nature, though probably not those done intentionally.

All should reduce obsessions and increase heavenly account as soon as possible. The obsessions include all material possessions such as the one and a half bagels some were reluctant to give out. Emptied people come, and emptied people go. Often, bad karma is conjured by obsessions and depleted heavenly account.

Even if one has done many good deeds, whether the heavenly account is sufficient is unknown until the time of death, but it can be too late then. Do not be complacent as the Falcons in Super Bowl LI. A tiny sin at the end of one's life can wipe out all the heavenly deposit within an hour. Spiritually speaking, the most important time of one's life is the final few years, months, or even days. Deviating from Tao at those crucial time periods can contribute to the loss of a chance to enter Tao Heaven forever.

A consistent faith in Tao till the end of one's life makes one's endgame much easier than without this faith. Prematurely believing in an eventual victory often sabotages this faith as the people's faith in the Falcons did. Loss of faith results in reduced mental and physical strength, which people rarely recover from. This small difference in faith may seem to be small, but its impact can be tremendous.

Three heavens and three hells exist. Below Tao Heaven is Chi Heaven, where angels, gods, and goddesses who do not know spirituality or Tao reside. Earthly heaven refers to those living who have no obsession or SWM. Earthly hell are those mentally bounded by wealth or those with lots of obsessions or SWM. Chi Hell holds the deceased spirits who have many SWM and obsessions, but they still have conscience. Tao Hell, on the other hand, holds the deceased spirits with uncontrollable obsessions, kind of like a mental hospital. The quality of one's own mind determines which heaven or hell one will end up in.

God the Mother and Her Ten Commandments

The Holy Bible is one of the most printed books in the world, God the Father has been well known for millennia. Christianity and its Bible have been especially more popular in the western world than in the eastern world.

Contrarily, God the Mother is not as well-known except in some eastern countries, particularly in some places where the Oneness of Tao is taught. Therefore, we will focus on the book written by God the Mother about a century ago. The book's name is *The Ten Commandments to Lecture Her Children by God the Mother*, which is specifically so named in that book.

The word count of the Holy Bible is over seven hundred thousand, but the book in Chinese by the Mother God has only fifty pages and about one thousand words. Not a short ten sentences of commandments as in the Holy Bible, the book by the Mother God has ten chapters, with each chapter consisting of from thirty-five to fifty poetic sentences. Each sentence consists of two ten-word phrases. Most Chinese poems use five-word or seven-word phrases. In each chapter, the tone of every sentence rhymes the same; the rhyme tone of each chapter differs.

The page disparity between the two books does not determine the potential impact on people. Most of the authors had read both, but we felt more emotional impact from the book by Mother God than by Father God, though we felt an extreme sense of righteousness after reading the Holy Bible in its entirety. The loving tears throughout the Mother God's book moved us in our teens, and still do today.

In the first nine pages, many saints and high spirits were the harbingers before the arrival of God the Mother. Among them were the five saints mentioned in chapter 10. Muhammad said using worship, temple, and Quran alone can hardly escape death. Jesus Christ wrote that the Holy Bible has tons of hidden messages. Lao-Tzu wrote that *Tao Te Ching* is not exhaustive in describing all truth. Buddha wrote that spirituality is truly immaterial but not really empty. Confucius said the true face of a person can be seen by oneself if the mind can be utterly quiet to ponder reasons.

In her prologue after the arrival of Mother God, she explained that Tao is like roads traveled by people. Right road leads to heaven, and wrong roads lead to hell. Numbered in thousands, none of the roads is the right path but the One Tao Mother God was then bestowing. Although many people in China had received lessons of Tao up until then, the vast majority was lax in the practice of Tao, and the Mother God was gravely saddened.

Some high spirits were ordained to shoulder the important work of salvation. All religions will merge into one soon. At that time, she had difficulty picking meritorious leaders to lead the way of propagating Tao due to complacency or lack of determination for Tao. Prior to that time, many high spirits had come down from Tao Heaven to write some lectures but to no avail, so she was extremely saddened to the point of having bloody tears.

The right time to practice Tao is now, whose preciousness is worth thousands of gold. When this time is lost, one will regret it for centuries, so do ponder deeply to push forward for Tao. The book Mother God was writing would be respected and guarded by many high spirits. Any disrespect of the book will result in calamity to that person. Hopefully, all children of God practice Tao solidly to reach enlightenment and eventually to return to Tao Heaven.

The gist of the first commandment or first chapter states the origin of spirits and the beginning of the universe somewhat similar to the Book of Genesis in the Holy Bible. Before coming down to earth, the brotherhood and sisterhood of all spirits in Tao Heaven was strong, and they never left God. The extremely honorable spiritual freedom was not restrained by season cycle or yin and yang. The beautiful scenery in Tao Heaven was free to travel around; when tired, piano or chess was played. Heavenly fruits were extremely delicious; the shoes and clothes on earth do not compare at all to those in heaven.

After the proper time came, the universe was created from Tao. The interchangeability between Tao and principle is hidden in the near nothingness of spirituality. This creative process is like a zero giving birth to one, which gives birth to two, which to three and so on to billions. The secret of creation from nothingness to materials is difficult to completely explain even by high spirits who know Tao.

After the universe was created, earth needed people to govern. Reluctantly, God let children come down. Initially, they went back to Tao Heaven every time they came down. They did not wish to govern earth. Reluctantly using the last resort, God tricked the children into drinking bloody wine and secretly took away their magical shoes and clothes. After they were awake from the wine, God sadly explained why and told the children to go and govern earth and to forget about returning to Tao Heaven for now. Fresh water and tree fruits would provide their livelihood. God also promised to write and save the children at the proper time. After hearing the words, the children were crying about being unable to return Tao Heaven right away.

The separation of God and children was painful, and the suffering of children has been a long sixty thousand years. The Mother God felt sorry and uneasy about the pain of her children. The time has come to fulfill the original promise of salvation. Therefore, Tao was bestowed on earth. The painful tears of the Mother God for greatly missing the children forced her to stop at the moment and to cut short this chapter.

The second chapter is about how God the Mother initiated to propagate Tao for the very first time in history. It began about one hundred years ago in China several decades before the Communists started to govern. God the Mother ordered all spirits living in Tao Heaven to come to earth and preach and to save as many as possible, including ghosts, gods, and goddesses in Chi Heaven. The order of God the Mother has the highest priority over all others in the universe.

The three treasures of the One Tao are symbolic for proper credential and for propagating to all. The receivers of Tao are guaranteed to return to Tao Heaven. The proof is in their dead bodies, which stayed soft and fresh for a long time. The tradition of Tao has been on earth since ancient times from Lao-Tzu to Confucius, to his disciples, to Buddha in India, and back to China again, to name only a few prominent examples. This tradition of Tao has never been broken.

Knowledge and practice confined to a selected few before, Tao was popularized for the first time to all who wished to learn and practice. This One Tao from God the Mother has no duplicate in the universe. High spirits and humans needs to help each other to propagate Tao. At the dawn of Tao, a real leader is hard to find; hence, this book of Ten Commandments was written. Preaching Tao to others is unavoidable when practicing it; being as patient as a mother's heart to remind others repeatedly is needed to convince Tao to others.

Practicing on self is the first step before preaching to others. No vanity or a fake Tao mask can cheat. Partial heart or half diligence toward Tao results in the spirit being pressed by a mountain for millennia. Even for those who achieved high Tao before, returning to Tao Heaven would be impossible if they have no real achievement on Tao or with insufficient goodness inside.

Leaders of Tao have particularly heavy responsibility in teaching and directing. Ponder deeply on methods to save others. Let the mind change like clouds, and intention like river water, by following the up or down, the square or circle, and being flexible to extend or retract. But do not compromise the principle, against which is a big wrong. Get rid of greed, obsession, and sticky love to keep the spiritual body clean and tranquil.

Be particularly more careful at a higher position; the physical law on the severity of a fall injury applies to leaders of Tao. Be careful 24/7. Be afraid of wishes and thoughts, and match behaviors with words. Comply with all virtues and moral values to stay on the safe side. Follow spiritual lectures faithfully to reach Tao Heaven; otherwise, wantonly following one's own will ends up putting self in hell.

The third chapter explains how material and nothingness are from the same Tao origin, and how Tao could create millions of diverse organisms. Not only creating the universe and earth, Tao made heavens and hells too. Humans do not know their own Tao inside, so they are bound by their own life and death. Many reasons for being lost on earth are alcohol, sexual desire, wealth, fame, greed, vanity, emotions, lack of love and affection, and others.

The fourth chapter expounds on the short-term nature of life and various methods of practicing Tao. No matter how good, all house, clothing, food, children, and spouse do not last; a whole family spiritually awake and practicing Tao is the best. The insatiable desire to pursue fame and wealth never ends, and one ends up in front of the mirror to expose the ugliness shortly after death. The bitterness of hell is extremely saddening and difficult to talk about and causes Mother God to have a lot of tears. One's direct ancestors living in the spirit cycle of heaven, hell, and earth are looking forward to the offspring's avid practice of Tao to save them.

The fifth chapter talks about the coming of disasters conjured by human karma. Propagation of Tao and disasters happen now close to the end of human time; both were decreed by God and induced by sixty thousand years of human wrongs and sins. Appropriate order in government, company, family, and friends has been gravely disturbed. All occupations are greedy and try to legally con others; even people of religiosity study and practice on surface only. One ought to be terrified by these impending disasters and walk on Tao soon to avoid them.

The sixth chapter advises on the importance of wishes and thoughts while practicing Tao. Like a child should listen to parents, adults should listen to words in the Ten Commandments of Mother God. Helping to propagate Tao and consummating others will help oneself. One should be diligent in Tao practice to include rich or poor, male or female, and not discriminate. Even those returned to Tao Heaven have suffered greatly; do not doubt the truth of Tao and spirituality due to a little pain and suffering. Dawn of Tao is the best time to practice to be included in the one hundred and forty-four thousand.

The seventh chapter urges people to search and practice Tao to avoid disasters. A Tao teaching is worth one's own life and shall be remembered for a lifetime. One against Tao teacher summons retribution. Exhaust appropriateness relating to parent, sibling, friend, wife, and government in one's practice as well as all spiritual merits. Leaders should tolerate and be inclusive; women, men, and followers should respect and harmonize to help promote Tao.

Heavenly deposit account does not redeem any sin after the time of deposit. Suffering from being tired, injustice, disdain of others, exposure to weather, and other pains, practicing Tao is not easy but a whole lot easier now than in antiquity. These sufferings are to settle the mind and propensity of an individual. Joy and happiness are only at the end of pain and suffering.

The eighth chapter points to the selection and election of Tao pioneers. The false happiness of daily life and the real suffering of daily drudge distract Tao practice. The hidden Tao exams are real to test true heart and soul. Sufferings of many saints in the old days are used as examples, including that of Confucius.

A beautiful lady used hot oil to destroy her face in order to prevent beauty attraction and to facilitate her practice of Tao. In comparison, practicing Tao today is a whole lot easier than the old days. Worried about her lost children, God the Mother ponders ways to save them so hard that her heart is broken into pieces.

The ninth chapter counsels on the proper ways of practicing Tao and spirituality. Mind is not a mirror, and spiritual propensity is not the opening blossom of a plum tree in snow. Spiritual light appears when not a single dust drops on mind. Many unrighteous religions flourish to confuse people about Tao. The Tao conferred by God is one and only that the same as Tai Chi created by Tao, no others are right.

The teaching of righteous religions merges into this One Tao. The common ground between different religions is expounded upon. The poor get Tao before the rich and before the official. Do not be confounded by wicked spiritual power such as a ride on clouds or the movement of mountain and sea. They will lose power one day when God orders them to cease. The rich will worship the poor. The five merits and Tao will unite the world.

The tenth chapter talks about the endgame and revelation. The students of Tao will be in the thousands. Practice of Tao based on reason and principle is the best, followed by chi practice, in which chi movement is used to motivate spirits. It is then followed by material practices like reciting sutra, physical worship, or repeat singing.

Some revelations matching the last chapter of the Holy Bible are disclosed in hidden meaning text as the Bible did. The ideal Tao world is opened up on earth, and no more animals will be killed. The blessed signs from heaven are abundant, and the Tao pioneers are honored. With Tao, the dead will return to Tao Heaven to enjoy freedom and richness forever. Only at the time of Tao consummation will God the Mother stop worrying.

The epilogue of fifteen poetic sentences reminds and urges all practitioners to work hard for Tao enthusiastically and with vigilant mind. Some words in the book were mistaken and in need of correction. Do popularize this book to spread and to save people. With big reluctance to leave beloved children, she went back and returned many times while crying.

Whew, our translation of its gist had not been easy as trying to match the meanings as much as we could. Some authors were enormously moved by the motherly love to all spirits by Mother God. Having a chance to read a complete Chinese version, one likely will be moved too, maybe also to the point of heavy tears. We are not aware of an English print. If one wishes to translate and publish an English version, we will be more than happy to help. Contact us on the email address in chapter 1.

Divination More Art Than Science

Conversing with high spirits or God is more of an art than a science. Sometimes in art, a counter expression is used to sarcastically disagree with an irony. In conversation, one may say, "Yeah, right" to pretend agreement, but the tone of voice has declared the disagreement. Similarly in divination, a high spirit likely uses a sarcastic reply as needed, particularly if one asks a question out of line of one's level of Tao practice.

One time, some authors were discontent with the injustice of a traffic ticket. Those authors asked high spirits whether they could skip on paying and the answer was positive. Years later, they suffered by paying more than twice of the original fine amount. They came to realize how stupid it was to ask the question of whether to pay a citation or not. The extra money paid was a good lesson worthwhile to learn about sarcasm in divination.

Sarcasm in divination is harder to recognize than one in conversation due to no tone of voice or facial expression accompanying a divination answer. Over the years, many of the authors have learned to recognize that several negative words of the thirty-two words used in divination often point to potential sarcasm. A sarcastic answer may indicate that the question should not be asked or that one needs to have faith in one's own reasoning or judgment.

When in doubt of a sarcastic answer, an additional question of yes or no should be inquired to determine whether it is actually sarcastic. When a lot of sarcastic answers occur in a short period of time, do not panic as it may be a good sign that one has spiritually grown. Now, some of which the divine used to answer should be known from asking oneself.

A bad prediction being indicated as good is more difficult to judge than a good one being indicated as bad. So far, the authors have only one experience in the first category but many in the second. Our future divination experience may help us to be more capable of recognizing the first category of sarcasm. However, an experience of something bad shown as good is not necessarily bad. From that bad thing shown as good divination, that author met a good friend he had lost contact with for twenty years.

Besides making sure that one's questions conform to Tao, other prerequisites should be checked before a divination takes place. The foremost on a checklist is whether one is totally unsure about the answer to a question. For example, a person has high interest in art but not so high in engineering despite an extensive ability. That person should focus on asking all the areas in art such as photography, oil painting, color painting, sculpture, fashion clothing, advertising, or other artistic areas.

Divination based on purely profiting purpose can be disastrous down the road. If the person also asks many majors such as medicine or pharmacology, she or he may be in big trouble if the two are shown as better than all the artistic areas. After graduation, the real trial begins, such as seeing nasty diseases or being forced to deal with disgruntled customers. Many doctors and lawyers are disciplined by government for greedy acts toward patients and clients. Earning money without any joy dries up one's own spirituality.

Uncertainty is the first perquisite; one cannot ask for the sake of asking, especially attempting to test divination accuracy. Though true that a question requires little effort on the part of inquirer, honor of high spirits cannot be abused. Judging the truth of divination takes few years at the minimum, but a doubt only takes few weeks to ferment and to give up on it. If not fully believing, one should not ask to test the truth of high spirits; it may backfire. An uncertainty is about the question to be asked; a doubt is regarding high spirits or God. The two are totally different. Believe prior to asking, not the other way around.

A kind of uncertainty involves potential risk on the road. Before asking about a trip to Florida during summertime, think twice about the risk of hurricane. Before planning to visit a slum downtown, check the danger of gangs there. Before going even near a semi-active volcano, balance the potential benefit and the possibility of sudden eruption. Do not blame GPS error, the planning is likely wrong at the start already.

Going to a rundown area such as a slum in a city downtown carries the potential liability to Tao and spirituality. For example, an area with roughly half of the houses unoccupied is rundown. One or two houses out of twenty may not be bad, but ten to twelve is likely rundown. Prior to complete Tao, a person who dies prematurely sabotages his or her own spiritual potential and may affect Tao achievement in the world.

The third prerequisite is being mentally prepared to balance reasoning with faith in divination. The two must be fully balanced for divination to function properly. Leaning too much to faith in divination may result in possible superstition and in blocking Tao forward. Inclining too much toward reasoning, doubts can soon hurt faith. This art of balancing act may take few years to achieve. Without equilibrating faith and reason, recognizing sarcasm in divination is nearly impossible.

A well-known Confucian quote states that the heavenly directive is called spiritual propensity, acting out this directive is called Tao, and the repair or return to Tao is called spiritual learning or religiosity. Each one already has this hidden directive inside to enable discerning right from wrong. This spiritual directive can be further developed to wisdom.

To forgo this heavenly directive is the same as abandoning divination, both of which violate Tao. An even combination of reason and faith in divination matches Tao better than an uneven blend. As Mother God says, high spirits and humans need to work closely together to propagate Tao forward. Too much faith in high spirits is not always good for the overall Tao because all people already possess the potential of Tao inside.

The fourth prerequisite is to eliminate personal bias and stubbornness as much as possible. They hinder proper interpretation of divination answers. For example, one addicted to nude pictures of the opposite gender is biased toward the possession of those pictures. This bias can become stubbornness, which prevents one from unsticking from the addiction.

This stubborn bias steers a person away from getting closer to Tao as what divination is trying to do. One can stubbornly hold on to an addition such as cigarette smoking or being excessively clean, not to mention drugs and alcohol. A divination answer of quitting smoking can be interpreted as sarcasm by a stubborn person while it is not.

A decade of regular divination is like a steady relationship with high spirits or God. Though the two never meet in person, the same goal of Tao is enough to strongly unite them. A recognizable face is not needed as displayed in some temples; the goal of striving toward Tao is the strongest bond in between. In fact, not seeing one another is probably better than seeing.

Most people tend to judge others based on an outside look, which may or may not match the internal spirit. Immaterial and transparent, the spirit who does divination for a person is better not to be seen to better represent Tao and to increase faith. After all, Tao is invisible; seeing a high spirit who represents Tao does not mean one sees Tao. After Tao enters one's own mind, one has no need to see it, maybe only to feel it.

The more truthfully a person treats a relationship, the more likely it will last. Being sincere is the fifth prerequisite of divination. Faith is a long-term belief; on the other hand, sincerity differs from one moment to the next. One may have faith but no sincerity at the moment, or one may have sincerity now or then but no faith in a lifetime.

Both faith and sincerity are important in achieving short-term and long-term goals. Not being sincere at all times often blemishes a marital relationship by causing dissatisfaction. Within either party, lacking faith toward another can end in divorce soon. Being sincere at the moment can affect the accuracy of that divination. Without faith, divination can be affected to the point of becoming totally inaccurate.

A relationship between husband and wife is dynamic and can change depending on their interactions. A relationship between a person and the high spirits is also dynamic and subject to change. Not just during the moment of divination, one's regular thoughts count too as high spirits can readily read them. High spirits do not need to follow a person around to read their mind because one's thoughts are faithfully recorded in the spiritual level.

Signs and symptoms always exist in a wife or a husband who cheats or only intends to. If an average person can perceive them, high spirits no doubt can too. To make a relationship steady, one should commit and be consistent on all fronts. Manifesting one's own spirituality needs to be in sync with one's spiritual growth in order to inch closer to Tao. Perception and wisdom will increase slowly but surely with the guidance of divination.

Asking too many or too few questions does not conform to Tao. In the beginning when faith is shaky, fewer questions are expected. However, as time accumulates, the number of questions asked should increase to the point of daily divination. Most people make hundreds of decisions daily; it would be weird to have no questions asked a whole day unless one is sick mentally or physically. Even during a vacation, decision making is nonstop, such as the food to eat or the clothing to wear.

A small decision can constitute a small correction toward or away from Tao. The accumulation of corrections can amount to being on or missing the target. Asking too few questions may conjure a disaster such as the couple stuck in snowy Grand Canyon or the couple traveling to Florida in our last book. Most people today do not ask spiritual questions at all. They try to hold on to their individuality to decide all things by themselves, but what they hold on to is actually their own personalities, not their spiritual individuality.

On the other hand, asking too many questions is not good either. A wild mind often wants to do a lot of things in life, so most asked questions deviate from Tao. Those unnecessary questions may cause distaste in high spirits to indicate sarcasm instead. An overly frugal mind may also ask too many questions, such as the one asked by one author about paying citations. Fighting an injustice with total silence does not conform to Tao.

The best use of divination is to find SWM and to correct them, not those for daily chores. In this use to correct SWM, yes or no answers based on two objects instead of five is appropriate. Both positive and both negative means no; a positive and a negative means yes.

The five objects represent thirty-two words as the number two raised to the fifth power equals thirty-two. As wise as Confucius was, knowing the Book of Change, or I Ching, one can utilize six objects instead of five like he did. Although twice as clear as the thirty-two-word version, I Ching is more difficult to understand. The version with thirty-two words was later simplified by one who studied I Ching.

We are not aware of any translation of this simplified book with thirty-two words. If any reader wants a copy of this in English, we can mail it with a payment of fifty dollars as we described in our last book. Be sure to email us first before sending a payment. Not all readers who request will qualify as we explained in our last book that we do not wish to cause harm.

With only few pages to summarize what each of the thirty-two words means, we do not translate all pages of the original Chinese book as we are not professional translators. In addition, getting to know too much detail of each word can lose the whole picture of what is right or wrong. One wishing to volunteer the translation of this book is welcome to contact us. Our email address is at the end of chapter 1.

Initially when we wrote the amount above, we wished to reduce the original price of $50 in our last book to $10. High spirits or God denied it. We apologize that our feet are tied to walk on Tao with divination. Our initial intention was to popularize divination to as many as we could with the minimum impact on the wallet of readers. Later we recalled that Confucius earned heavenly directive at the age of fifty. The $50 also covers any email questions about divination.

A word of caution to those who wish to request a commission, which was the term used in our last book. A person can only request to send in $50 once a month. One must wait at least a full month before requesting again via email. The same person using a different email address may anger high spirits. We do not know what could happen from such anger, so do not blame the authors if one purposefully does wrong and ends up in calamity. The person who suffers has only him- or herself to blame.

CHAPTER THIRTEEN

Reform of Government

The injustice of governments in all levels is rampant across the board in nearly every country on earth. Our previous book mentioned some examples; let us give one more. Before our Arizona car registration expired, we filed paperwork with the Arizona Motor Vehicle Division to extend the time as we needed to stay in California to finish some personal affairs. Some months later, some policemen in the City of Brea in California cited us for the expired tag.

The citation was correctable with the signature of a police officer, so the fine could be reduced to ten dollars. Even after submitting a copy of the renewed registration with the tag still adhered to the paperwork, we failed the first level of appeal. Many Phoenix policemen we talked to refused to sign the back of a citation from out of state, and we had to go to a nearby city to have our ticket signed.

At the same time, we wanted to send in the $10 reduced fine and request a hearing, which was the second level of appeal. Later, we discovered that we must pay the full fine of seventy-six dollars before we were allowed to request the hearing. To demand citizens to pay a full fine first then allowing an appeal is simply unjust to the bone. At the time of our rage upon learning this injustice, we cursed the City of Brea to every sort of calamity they would deserve despite their celebration of one hundred years of history and our initial intent to volunteer for the city. We vowed to avoid stepping into Brea, California, in the future whenever possible.

Even though $76 is not a huge amount, the prevalence of similar injustice and people's disgust toward authority in all governments can be deduced. Though most people forget this kind of injustice soon to move on with their lives, this kind of karma accumulates and can often cause future calamity. Similar injustice in state and federal levels can cause even more headache and an unjust amount of money than those in the city level. Many of the internal unrest in lots of countries were likely due to collective dissatisfaction from millions of citizens. The root of injustice is the structure of governments.

One main reason why Donald Trump was elected the president of the United States is people's dissatisfaction with the government. However, electing a different president does not solve the root problem of injustice in the government infrastructure. We highly respect the founding fathers of the United States for establishing a very good democracy in 1776. Who today would drive a century-old car without any repair or improvement? Like a thought or a word, a political system is still a material subject to deterioration.

Collective will is the most important ingredient for collective change. Changing government structure has been talked about for decades, if not centuries, but no change ever occurred in the United States. Only the collective will of the majority of citizens can make it happen today and now. Today's representative system may never garner collective will from most citizens.

The representative democracy in many countries in the world today began in the seventeenth century, though the concept and limited practice existed way back from ancient Greece. Popular education and political participation made representative democracy possible. Women did not have the right to vote until the early twentieth century as they were considered inferior to men. At least 60 percent of the populace was illiterate prior to the eighteenth century; today it is less than 10 percent.

Popularity of representative democracy went hand in hand with popularity of public education. With no prevalent public education, representative democracy might have been impossible. Education really is at the heart of all democracy, representative or direct. A representative democracy cannot function well without literacy in most people; it is even truer for direct democracy.

Nearly all dictionaries define *democracy* as *representative democracy* where the president and Congress are elected by people to govern a country. We prefer to define it as *true democracy* or *direct democracy* where the citizens have the privilege to directly decide crucial affairs now decided only by elected officials. Referendum during the election days is really not considered a direct democracy; it's a tag-along train ride with the election of public officials.

A few countries such as Switzerland practice direct democracy where citizens decide major issues of the nation despite some problems that might have been caused by the lack of spiritual education. This kind of democracy is a step in the right direction, but many other improvements can be done to this democracy. Exactly what kinds of improvements can be done need years of experiment and trial; here we only give some suggestions.

A good way to improve government structure is to designate this job to an independent branch of the government away from the executive branch, which tends to have bias on structure needed. We mentioned this branch in our last book as the Election and Qualifying Branch. This branch looks at a government as a whole to tailor it to fit the needs of the nation.

As mentioned in our last book, many functions of Congress have transgressed the original scope intended by the founding fathers. Though a high percentage of the congressmen and women are law school graduates and qualified to be judges, they are never intentionally elected to be judges as to preside over a congressional hearing to discover the truth. Furthermore, most of them are not trained or educated as investigators or detectives; not doing a good job often is unavoidable. Like a kid wearing adult-sized clothes, these exotic functions performed by the Congress do not fit them well.

The attorney general's office in the executive branch of the United States is also inappropriate as the highest prosecuting office. Justice cannot be asseverated by the executive branch due to the executive nature and potential bias of this branch. Many people are selfish because they do not have an independent mental area to examine themselves regarding their own faults and mistakes. This same reason prompted the founding fathers to separate the judicial branch from the executive branch. The ordering and construction of Air Force One was an example we mentioned in our last book.

The investigative and prosecuting functions in the executive and legislative branches currently performed by the Congress and the president should be reassigned to a unique branch, which for now we will call the Investigation and Prosecuting Branch. Independent from the other four branches, it initiates investigations into the wrongdoings of the president and any Congress members as well as judges. FBI, CIA, NSA, and other investigative departments should be moved to this branch too.

The Quality Branch

The source of most problems and injustices within governments is within their structures or so-called systems. Some people ask: "Do you believe the system?" Our question is: "Would you trust a 241-year-old automobile which has not been substantially improved or repaired?" All machinery on earth must be constantly improved to maintain its functionality; otherwise, they are likely to face cruel elimination like past countless empires and dynasties that never bothered to change their structures.

Does one want to see one's own country be eliminated or does one want to improve the structure of one's own government? This question is for all citizens of all countries on earth.

US President Trump is shaking up the government structure for now to reduce the cost. How about the later presidents? After the next few presidents, we can almost guarantee that the government will grow obese again. At that time, would Americans find another president as crazy or even crazier than Trump? Can the 241-year-old system withstand the test of a person with a Hitler personality? One is encouraged to ponder the nightmare consequence of not changing political structure regularly.

Fundamentally, this branch deals with people and structure qualities, so it can be named Quality Branch instead of the longer name Structure, Election, and Qualifying Branch. The goal of this Quality Branch is to recommend plans for governmental structure improvement to be voted on by qualified citizens, to oversee elections fairly, to qualify public office candidates for upcoming elections, and to qualify volunteers to participate in government decision and policy making. These four major functions of the Quality Brach are to ensure quality of government structure and personnel. In a factory, quality control can be the most important department of a company to ensure its success.

This branch monitors the functionality of each branch and department and recommends structure improvement if needed. Department of Homeland Security was created only after the terrorist attack of 2001, which was way too late after the extremely costly disaster. Not only new departments should be added to catch up with political, social, economic, and other changes, obsolete departments should be eliminated as soon as they become so. The function of adding or eliminating a department should not be the job of the president, who is gone every four or eight years.

Another function is to handle all elections fairly. No future runoff elections should ever be voted by judges again as happened at the turn of this century. Judges are not presidential electors. A simple change on election procedure can prevent this grave injustice to the whole nation as well as to the candidates. We conjecture that one main reason for the terrorist attack on September 11, 2001, was due to this grave injustice in the United States. The presidential election was literally stolen, yet the people could not do anything but accept it. What a pity for the system.

Yet another function is to qualify all public office candidates. Before being a candidate, one should be scrutinized carefully to eliminate liars, cheaters, and unethical persons. When spiritual education and research become popular, this will be easier when one's spiritual practice record is reviewed to reveal trustworthiness. The brain scan history and the spiritual level of a potential candidate should also be investigated.

The general public simply does not have enough time, money, or resources to do an investigation on all the candidates. The media may investigate some candidates, but not all; also, the media is often biased toward certain candidates. The money and time to investigate potential candidates is well spent just contemplating the immense mental trauma in the general public caused by various past US presidents such as President Nixon.

Likely the most important function of this branch is to qualify volunteering citizens to help government to make good decisions. These volunteers can also do topic research or discussion to find a solution for a problem. It will also greatly boost the accountability of departments and branches as some citizens are always monitoring each of them.

One primary function of this branch is to transform representative democracy to true democracy and to improve government infrastructure in all levels and all branches of governments. In a direct democracy, all citizens should have the privilege of participating in the daily decision-making process of all levels of a government. The Quality Branch needs to sift through and pass qualified citizens to participate in all decision and discussion processes to realize a true democracy.

Retired or not, chief executive officers and other top-level officers of major companies are likely interested in participating in the decision-making process of economic policy of government. They can be qualified by the Quality Branch to become volunteers in helping to shape economic policy of the nation. PhDs in economics or other financial related fields can also be qualified. Lay people who are versed in or knowledgeable about this particular field can pass the same standard examination designed by the Quality Branch to qualify.

After being established, the Quality Branch is likely to become the pillar of a government. People constitute governments; quality people constitute quality governments. A similar adage has been proven to be true in the business world. Election alone can occasionally produce inferior public officials as political history has proven it. This is why nearly all public company top-level executives are seldom elected by general shareholders, rather they are chosen by the board members who know the candidates in person.

Likewise, hand-picking alone can at times produce inferior officers. Though Tim Cook is doing a good job taking over for Steve Jobs, the innovational edge may have been largely lost within Apple Inc. As the pillar of a government, all workers at the Quality Branch ought to possess certain qualities to warrant the quality of a whole government. The chief of the Quality Branch should also be popularly elected like the president is.

Their very first quality is not to be affiliated with any political party. Joining a party means one agrees with all or most principles of that party. This agreement can produce biases which may or may not be the original opinion of that person. Most party joiners are biased at least to an extent with their own party and principles. Other qualities of workers in this branch may be fairness, integrity, high ethics, good communication and people skills, faithfulness, and being well versed in the fields of organizational efficiency, budgeting, surveying methods, and election law and procedure, to name only some basics.

The personal quality of the chief of the Quality Branch should be extremely ethical, possessing great organizing skill of a company, shrewd in budgeting process, deep realization of human nature and spirituality, life-tested uncompromising character, and familiar with the ethics and process of all elections. Initially, the chief can be hand-picked by the president to set up this branch due to the transitional period and the needed cooperation with the president. After people become familiar with this new branch, the chief should be elected publicly.

The Structure-Improving Function of the Quality Branch

Even though we agree with the philosophy of the Republican Party that government should be small to conserve national revenue, we do not agree with their philosophy of saving money by cutting programs with substantial future benefits. The benefit of environmental programs might not be seen right away in the next few years, but the money spent has a lot of future payback. Just look at the serious smog problem of the People's Republic of China; the smog sprawled into other neighboring countries, including the Republic of China, a.k.a. Taiwan. The human cost of curing lung cancer can greatly exceed the cost of environmental protection.

Large governmental spending sometimes is necessary to prevent future disasters. Without the spending on mentally ill people, there would probably be more incidents of mass murders like those who went postal. Weapon access control for the mentally ill only resolves part of the problem, a lot of people are not even aware of their mental illness, let alone seeking psychiatric help. One of the authors stated that he did not even understand mental illness at the early stage of his onset.

The structure-improving function should not rest on the president of a country because of the inevitable rotation between presidents. Experts in organizational efficiency like some CEOs of major companies can be hired to take on this specialized job. Good department heads should not be restricted to be citizens of a country; ability of a person should be the only key to choose. The United States grants work visas for technical workers, why not for department heads.

The functions of budgeting and qualifying department heads should also be removed to the Quality Branch due to the nature of the executive and legislative branches. Letting the president decide the budget for each department is like letting a twelve-year-old child manage a candy store; no one can prevent the child from eating the candy. The reduced environmental budget in the Trump government fully illustrates this point, so is the example in our last book regarding the budgeting for and construction of the president's airplanes.

Irregular budgeting for each department is analogous to the vastly inconsistent quantity of meals that can cause stomach disorder which is likely to induce other future illness such as indigestion or ulcer. The Quality Branch can gradually reduce the budget if the need is no longer warranted, such as the department of education. After spiritual education is popularized, supervision for education should be greatly reduced after self-learning takes priority over teaching. After some time, the department of education may be combined into another department.

After the Quality Branch figures out the proper budget for each branch and department, it should be approved by qualified volunteer citizens. More eyes reduce injustice. Budget cuts in a department can cause some to unjustly lose their jobs especially if this cut is unjustified. Similar to that the president should not have the power to hire or to dismiss federal employees of nondepartment heads, the budgeting department should not have that power either.

Volunteering citizens concerned about the environment would certainly object to a cut at the Environmental Protection Agency. Qualified citizen voters who care about national defense would not approve a reduction in the defense budget. With diversified volunteers placed in all budgeting areas, they can approve budgets such as the wall with Mexico, infrastructure construction, public radio and television, emergency, Science Foundation, and so on. Whether a budget ought to be majority approved or by two-thirds may be left to the discretion of Quality Branch policy, which can be approved by volunteering voters who oversee the Quality Branch.

The number of volunteers monitoring each branch and department depends on the amount of public interest. The defense budget probably would attract more enthusiasm than that for education; food safety is likely to retain more people than Park Services. A limit should not be set for the number of volunteering participants. The more the merrier, the government should be happy with the extra free help and reduced responsibility if problems occur. No hairs of future presidents should turn grey prematurely.

With thousands or even millions of volunteering voters and overseers, physical participation is not possible. Strong passwords coupled with remote iris scanning and fingerprint checks may be implemented to boost Internet security. Other security measures may also be recommended by FBI or other security experts.

Monitoring government is a constant task, not once every few years. Busy at passing law, Congress is grossly unable to monitor the executive branch. Approving government regulation and law should happen every few weeks or months and provide ample time for consideration. Many bills passed by Congress have holes that even they do not realize.

Citizens who volunteer to participate in policy or law approval should be expected to do some research, not just reading what each department publishes. It takes time and effort for people to help the government, but it is worth it for both sides. A volunteer might be limited to five to ten departments to join to avoid stressing out on personal life.

The number of people employed by each department in a government should be controlled by the Quality Branch, not the president. Stable use of budget reduces national debt and saves the government from constant cycle between slim and fat. Private donation to government should be allowed and encouraged. But citizens will be willing to do so only after they can approve the budget and monitor government.

All supervisors and managers should be elected by each department except the department heads. Middle and lower level management are used to coordinate bottom workers, not to boss them around or to do little. Electing supervisors and managers would ensure basic workers proper dignity and reduced discrimination.

Limiting service time of a supervisor or manager can ensure a chance for other basic workers to experience the position. A supervisor or manager who comes from the basic level is more likely to understand difficulty and hardship of basic workers than those who have never worked in the basic level. Working as a supervisor or manager too long also has the effect of totally forgetting the difficulty and hardship of basic workers. Department heads need to work with presidents, so they can be hand-picked and approved by volunteering voters.

The Qualifying and Surveying Functions of the Quality Branch

All candidates for public office and representatives should be qualified first before being put on a ballot. Written examination probably is not the most suitable to qualify applicants. Extensive background check and oral examination may also be needed. Reputation and previous lawsuits may also be looked into. We are not sure if President Nixon would pass this rigorous qualifying process to be put on the ballot of a presidential election.

People who wish to participate in government decision making should also be qualified as well. Knowledge alone cannot determine qualification; integrity, honesty, reputation, and personal credit history may also be checked. A person who filed bankruptcy or defrauded others may not be qualified, especially to volunteer in budget approval. Participating in policy making and law approval is not a right, but a privilege.

In addition, qualification of jurors should also be done in this department. Many jurors are not willing to participate in deciding a criminal or civil case. Some may prefer a criminal case over a civil one; while others may be the opposite. Forcing a person to sit on jury duty which one dislikes is against humanity and Tao.

The main reason why some do not like to do jury duty is their lack of time. The physically or mentally challenged likely have more time than others who work full-time. Supervisors, managers, and top-level management probably have more time than the basic workers. People who are recuperating from an illness or disease also might be available.

Being able to participate electronically as a juror can save time. The O.J. Simpson trial had demonstrated exactly this feasibility. Closed circuit television and secret voting would ensure minimum influence from other jurors. The increased number of jurors from twelve to hundreds or thousands of jurors would eliminate any problems of hung jury or deadlock. Simple majority, two-thirds, or three-quarters can decide a case.

Besides qualifying candidates for election and for volunteering in government decision making, the Quality Branch should conduct regular surveys to yardstick the performance of government and citizen satisfaction.

Like a company wanting to earn business from as many customers as possible, a government needs to earn the heart of most citizens. Survey is one of the best tools to do so. A government also can improve its structure based on survey.

Needs of citizens are likely to reflect on a survey. When parts of a body feel painful, that person knows to find a first aid kit, so should a government. Without survey, governments are flying blind and basing their governing way only on what they think, instead of people's needs. A big city government often tries to eliminate the homeless problem, but it fails to consult citizens on their opinions before doing it.

Without this feedback loop from surveys, government would not know how to modify itself, like a person trying to look at his or her own dress without a mirror. Surveys conducted by private organizations may be biased, as the survey of the 2016 presidential election had shown. Majority of the surveys reported totally different results than the real votes. Official survey should be kept confidential so that those who express dissatisfaction do not have to worry about retribution.

Above two functions correlate to the function of improving government infrastructure. Without quality people, a quality government is not possible. Without quality opinions, many quality performances are not possible. The Quality Branch ensures a government has both good people working inside by the people and good performance output for the people.

The Investigation and Prosecution Branch

As we mentioned in our last book and earlier in this book, investigation and prosecution of any crime or wrongdoing in the government should be separated from the executive branch to ensure fairness and freedom from interference. The threatening behavior of President Trump toward people attempting to investigate him fully demonstrate our point. Furthermore, like the Quality Branch, all workers in this branch should not have any party affiliation to ensure impartiality.

The problem of the FBI director investigating Hillary Clinton should not have happened if the director were nonpartisan and free of party involvement. A phenomenon in the United States is that most people are independent, but all presidents are either Democrats or Republicans. A candidate from the independent pool probably should be recommended to represent people who are independent.

In fact, three of the five branches of government should require their employees to totally not be involved with any party. Without a doubt, the judges and jurors in the judicial branch need to be as impartial as they can be, so any party affiliation should not be allowed for them. A big folly in the US is that the presidents pick those judges aligning with their party ideology to be Supreme Court justices. All justices should be publicly voted in instead of being hand-picked by a person. A wrong mix of the executive branch and the judicial branch has created this folly for centuries.

The Quality Branch needs to be impartial to ensure that the processes of qualifying candidates or volunteers are not tainted by party affiliation. The Investigation and Prosecution Branch works closely with the judicial branch, so all workers there should also be independent. FBI, CIA, NSA, Justice Department, and other investigative and prosecuting departments should be moved to this branch to ensure the impartiality of looking into government wrongdoing. In addition, this branch should initiate investigations on its own for any injustice that happened, even when nobody reports it.

The contamination of ground water at Hinkly, California, investigated by Erin Brockovich, as we mentioned in our last book, should have been investigated and prosecuted by this branch for the sake of asserting justice. Any injustice in a nation hurts the integrity of this nation; injustice can spread to other places similar to uncontrolled gangs. The money spent on the investigation and prosecution of injustice will pay the nation back in the long run.

The chief of this branch probably should also be elected just like the president. A suitable person for this job should have personal qualities of uncompromising sense of justice and a track record of fighting for injustice. Integrity and honesty are a must. Other qualities should be comparable to a branch head such as the president.

Reforms of Legislative Branch

The arrogance and high salary of Congress need to be taken away by the Quality Branch. Each representative can be substituted with many volunteer participants in that district. People who live in a particular district for at least some time can be qualified to vote and to count for that seat of representative. This localized vote count would preserve the locality of each representative from a district. This new representative system is similar to the Electoral College system that keeps locality of voters.

The majority of vote count from a particular district determines the vote of this representative. Or it should be called a pseudo representative because not a real person is present on Capitol Hill to be paid more money than most citizens. The most waste of taxpayer's money likely is not on government projects, but on the unnecessary people government hires.

The Legislative Branch may need a chief to be elected by popular vote too. The special qualities of this chief are good communication skill and good understanding of the plight of the general populace. Empathy and compassion are superb qualities to have for taking care of the poor and the suffering. Special talent in forming good argument may be a plus to convince and align different opinions from various locality voters.

Reforms of Judicial Branch

As we mentioned earlier, all Supreme Court justices should be directly elected by popular vote. Or each justice can be elected by one of nine roughly equal areas of the nation. The chief justice probably should be elected as well by all nine justices, and the serving time of the chief justice should be limited to allow other justices a chance to be the chief. Like other judges, justices should not have any party affiliation to ensure impartiality.

Also as mentioned earlier, jurors should be randomly selected from a pool of willing people who have been qualified by the Quality Branch. Likely, jurors were limited to twelve due to limited means of transportation, and electronic communication did not even exist. Nowadays, the number of jurors should be much larger than twelve as the age of electronic communication is here to stay. Number of jurors in the hundreds is possible. If more jurors participate in a case, the justice of that case will more likely be asserted as the various biases of jurors can be evened out.

The judicial proceedings should be greatly simplified to facilitate the turnover rate of cases. An elimination of judges suggested in our last book may be too extreme, but the key role of judges today should be reduced substantially; after all, jury makes the judgment, not the judges, who should be more like advisers than judges. Jury should also sentence criminals as many judges are either too lenient or too strict in the number of years sentenced.

Small claims should be free or with nominal deposit. Many municipal court judges are not fair in deciding traffic citation appeals. Electronic juries should be used to decide small claims cases and traffic citation appeals. Uncomplicated judicial processes facilitate quick return of justice and fast retribution of injustice. Often waiting for months or years to get a result, the court system of today does not keep pace with population and technology growth.

Reforms of Executive Branch

The Executive Branch should be a lot smaller after many of the departments are moved to other branches. Congress has been trying to subdue the power of the president for decades; now they do not have to. The update of infrastructure would itself limit the power of the president except in emergency or disasters of national scale. As we mentioned above, all departments should have first-line supervisors and managers elected by basic government employees to serve a limited amount of time each term.

The new Brazilian president moved out of the palace because a ghost was found inside the palace. A president of a country probably should not be forced to live at a fixed and designated location where all the past presidents live. With the distributed power from the president to a large number of qualified citizen voters and counselors, the president would become less important except in an unforeseen emergency. The freedom of the president cannot be too restricted in order to attract highly qualified candidates.

For the additional freedom of being president and department heads, they should not be paid at all like President Trump, who refuses to take the money. They, however, should be required to own a minimum number of treasury bonds before being qualified as candidates. The credit of the treasury bonds rests on the shoulders of the president and department heads. If they are not doing a good job for the country, they should be the first to suffer financially.

The chiefs for other four branches should also not be paid and be required to own the same minimum number of treasury bonds as the president. The nine justices of the Supreme Court, the senators, and the department heads in other branches should also follow suit, though the number of treasury bonds they should own can be reduced. Their perks like entertainment, meals, and lodging have compensated them enough. From the bottom of their hearts, they should serve based on their pure enthusiasm and passion for the country, not based on the amount of their salary.

CHAPTER FOURTEEN

Reforms of Public Companies

Recently by chance, we read the article "The Age of Rudeness" in the *New York Times* magazine. Ms. Rachel Cusk explained how she had discovered others' many rudeness in her daily life as well as sensed her own rudeness. We agreed how this generation is rude in general and progressively so. The rudeness likely has existed for a few generations now. (Ref 24)

Before the industrial revolution, the slow pace of horse carriage and walking by foot did not bother most people. At that time, most could take it easy during an afternoon tea. After the revolution, the notion that time equals money has become more and more prominent in people's minds. People's mentality has been driven into watching the time spent on each task.

On one hand, it is good that people waste less time in doing chores; on the other, the tendency to rush and finish tasks gradually became a trend in many societies. Readily, a social psychologist can point out the contagiousness of a widespread fashion in a society. He or she can affirm the contagiousness of being rude too.

On the outside, the self-motivated rush is better for a company, an economy, and the material gain of that person. On the inside, this rush has created a distortion in general mentality. This distortion twists the priority of time efficiency beyond personal quality. In fact, personal quality education in public school has seriously declined particularly in the past few decades. Education has moved on to emphasize the importance of science over all other fields, including personal quality. How sad it is, and it is gravely against Tao.

This constant push for time efficiency has downgraded people's mental quality to look only at short-term profit, not long-term benefit. Money and time are elevated to the highest importance; they trump safety, kindness, respect, prudence, or doing the right thing. The *Challenger* disaster of NASA in 1986 was a prime example where the management sacrificed tiny safety concerns to time efficiency.

The general mentality of rudeness is the disrespect toward others caused by the philosophy of time efficiency. This philosophy has been further revved up by heavy commercialization in the last few decades. The increased fierce competition between countries on productivity, GDP, and economic growth are a few examples. The increased conflicts between nations follow the same mentality of disrespect toward others.

Respect is a moral value in the mind and a spiritual quality. The increase of road rage cases a few decades ago was a sign of the increase of this disrespect. The erosion of moral values due to reduced faith in religion and the lack of a substantial spiritual education in school combine to cause wars around the globe and the use of chemical weapons. As global leaders, many developed countries are responsible for not slowing down or steering away the world locomotive of mentality away from this disrespect.

Increasingly regulating public companies is probably the most effective way of slowing down this mental locomotive of rudeness. For governments to respect individual freedom is the right direction, but letting public companies weather public mentality at will via commercialization is a huge mistake of governments. A parent is wrong to let the children do whatever they wish without any teaching against rudeness.

The companies of the West tend to treat their workers less humanely than those of the East do. Employee monitoring methods are often more intimidating in the West than in the East. In the West, seldom is a worker allowed to go home early even if all work has been done well that day. Most companies pay by the hours and often demand labor at all hours with few breaks. It is like a parsimonious person wanting to squeeze the last drop out of a lemon.

Accountability is often used as a disguised reason for the unwarranted stinginess by the western companies. They often find more tasks for those who have done their work more efficiently than others. This unrighteous and lack-of-Ren frugalness may seem like a small quality, but the steering of a huge locomotive to another track requires precisely this kind of attention to detail. The supervisors and managers, on the other hand, often take off to play golf on company time. The enormous irony is that they are paid twice or even more.

One root cause of this animalistic treatment of basic workers is the animalistic education of the West as a tradition. All children are forced to attend school with no exception. This forced education of not asking student interest and the attitude of disregarding what students like create an animalistic education. The forced educational attitude spills into the culture in politics and economy. It downgrades the whole culture to be animalistic.

Responsibilities of Governments to Regulate Companies

The duty of regulating companies no doubt rests on the shoulders of governments. Companies whose shares are publicly traded in the stock market should be the main focus in the beginning. Once mentality and culture of public companies change, other private companies and publicly owned companies likely will follow the good model.

The current regulations on public companies are certainly not enough. As we stressed in our last book, for a company to bear the connotation of being public, it must be regulated to resemble the nature of being publicly owned. In essence, a publicly traded company is owned by the public, and a government can do whatever it wishes to achieve public control. Nowadays, nearly all the governments in the world are semi-public, meaning they belong to elected officials, so those semi-public governments should not regulate public companies.

After a government becomes truly publicly owned as described in the last chapter with many volunteer voters to monitor each department, that public government can start to regulate public companies heavily. Therefore, we disagree with the idea of the Republican Party that companies should be left alone. Companies are not individuals who need freedom and room to develop intellectually. Upon joining such a company, the fully intelligent and grown adults do not need freedom anymore. The public responsibilities of the company preoccupy and precede individual freedom.

Of course, a government which does not have its supervisors and managers elected by the basic workers in each department cannot possibly write regulations to unreasonably demand from public companies. The government must fix itself first to become a model before regulating companies. Demanding children not to smoke cigarettes by a smoking parent often only conjures hidden disdain and defiance.

The current practice of conferring more power to people with more shares of stocks does not conform to Tao. Do rich people like Donald Trump, Barack Obama, and Hillary Clinton cast more than one vote during election? When a country goes down, all citizens within it are affected, so the wealthy do not have the privilege of depositing more than one vote in an election. Likewise, all shareholders should have an equal vote in company affairs.

When a company loses money, all shareholders lose money, so no one should have more privilege than others. Profit or loss of stocks results from the choice of owning the stocks, not the amount invested. Today's extra privilege discriminates against those with fewer stock shares. Using the number of hold shares to qualify higher position applicants in the company is justified because higher positions can better determine whether the company will lose or profit.

A millionaire or billionaire does not necessarily have a better idea of managing the whole country. Likewise, a high-percentage shareholder does not always have a better method of increasing profit for a company. The quality of a shareholder should be the only consideration for whether that person can participate in company decision making, not the quantity of shares one holds.

In addition, a high-percentage shareholder can have bias knowingly or unknowingly. This bias is comparable to that of a king or emperor who may decide based on a selfish reason such as lust on females or hatred toward other races. The first emperor of China and Hitler are some examples. Most of what they decided was not based on the best interest of their nations, maybe only at the beginning or in small portion. Only popular votes can potentially even out the various biases among diverse people.

Most companies have a six-month probationary period for new hires. During this period, a new employee can be dismissed for no reason. This period also gives the new employee a chance to quit with no large impact to the company. Within this period, one should not be allowed to vote because one is unfamiliar with company people and culture. After this time, an employee should be required to purchase a minimum number of company shares to ensure loyalty to the job and the company. The dividend also works as a reward for this exchange of faith.

When a government mandates public companies to require basic workers to hold a minimum number of company stock, it should also stipulate that candidates of high positions hold more shares than basic workers before a department elects its supervisor or manager. The more shares held than basic workers remind them that every decision they make can cost them more than basic workers.

The increased dividend from the higher percentage shareholding of people in high positions also rewards their good decision making. As a result of their share dividend, no higher wage should be allowed for people in higher positions of the company. Today's system of clearly delineating investment from employment functions against the company like a double-edged sword: the loyalty of workers from top to bottom cannot be guaranteed, and the investors lose money not due to their decisions.

As discussed in our last book, all positions higher than the basic workers' should be paid equal or less than that of the basic workers due to the lighter work load of higher positions. The ability to make better decisions should be the qualification of the position or the election criteria, not a yard stick to decide the amount of pay. In fact, the very top positions of a company probably should not be paid as they are already paid enough from their shares held.

The owner of a private company earns what is left after balancing between the income and the expense. Likewise, top management should also only benefit from the amount of shares held, which can be a profit or a loss like a private company owner. The absurdity of CEO, CFO, and other top management being paid huge amounts should be completely outlawed for the justice of company basic workers and shareholders, as well as for the justice of the country.

Like the presidents, government department heads, governors, and mayors not being paid, CEO and other top-level company management should not be paid a salary. The profit or loss of the shares held is their income. Election may not always produce the best quality people for the key policy makers of a company. Sometimes, the best suited person for a top management job may not be popular enough to be elected.

The top-level positions may be chosen by the board, as the board members likely would know the candidates personally better than thousands of workers. An alternative is for basic workers to elect from the chosen candidates by the board, similar to the in-depth qualifying process of a presidential candidate by the Quality Branch of a government.

All governing board members of a company should be elected by the whole company one at a time, stead of depending on the number of shares held. A large shareholder may not be interested in sitting on the board to monitor company operation, or does not have enough ability to do so. The scandals of bad policy and fraudulent account creation at Wells Fargo Bank and the bad decisions at Bank of America some years earlier was at least partly due to the ineptness of the governing board.

Without proper personal experience in watching company operation within each board member, the top management can do pretty much whatever they want like a boy managing a candy store and rewarding himself heavily. When such a scandal happens, all basic employees of the company are seriously impacted, so excluding them from electing each board member is not just.

As an insider, a worker of a company knows the best about any discrimination, management style, law violation, and company culture. Board members alone may not have enough eyes to watch over what happens at the basic level of a company. The government should hire at least one employee per one thousand company workers to work side by side with the basic workers.

From day-to-day contact, a governmental monitor working at a company can report anything out of the ordinary to the government before the company deviates away from the right way too much. It is beneficial both for the wellbeing of the basic workers and for the integrity of the company. A healthy public company also benefits the country as a whole.

Top management decides the direction and speed of a company. The overall tone and policy should be approved by the whole company and shareholders, not just the governing board. A train locomotive leads all the carts following it, and all the carts need to know where they are heading to prevent a fall into a broken bridge or some other disaster, which also affects the carts. The government has the power to endow the eyes for those who follow the top management.

With a limited number of workers in a company, there likely are not enough basic workers to monitor each company department like a country's citizens monitoring the government. But approval right of company policy set by top management should be granted to basic workers to prevent potential company scandals such as what happened to Bank of America and Wells Fargo Bank.

Encouraging High Company Quality with Incentives

After Steve Jobs passed away, Tim Cook took over Apple Inc. and dropped the culture of innovation established by Steve Jobs. This kind of innovative spirit not only can make a lot of profit for Apple, it helps the whole country financially as well. The country and its government has a vested interest in the prosperity of companies inside its borders. Giving proper incentives to encourage similar thriving company cultures like the past innovative edge of Apple can boost the economy of the country.

These incentives do not necessarily have to be in the form of monetary reward. Public praise or something else can be an incentive too. A well-managed company may have qualities such as taking good care of its workers or letting the workers decide their own hours. Deciding one's own working hours is highly feasible and likely; after all, the basic workers own the company stocks. The owners of a company likely will be concerned about its survival and will do their best jobs for the company, which is the same as doing it for themselves.

In the military, the most important reason for soldiers to reenlist is the comradeship. Similarly, when workers know each other and establish good relations, they are likely to stay and be loyal. The harmonious and intimate working relations foster quality company culture and boost dedication. Building a culture takes a long time.

Currently, most company cultures form from the weathering of top management on down to the lower managers and supervisors, then to the basic workers. This approach of top to bottom does not last long and is unnatural that not majority of workers can agree or accept. With an approach of bottom to top, a whole company can be more synchronized and cooperative. It also conforms to Tao. With the wrong way of doing things, it often takes more effort and gets less result.

Other qualities making a company great include but are not limited to not putting money or time as the highest priority, organizational efficiency, investing in the future, going the extra mile to care for customers, and improving quality of workers through training and education. Like the practice of Tao has no upper limit, a company's melioration toward high quality is boundless.

Watching the bottom line too closely often constrains the endless potential of a company, as demonstrated by numerous failed public companies in history. Their failures were largely due to the lack of innovation, holding on to the old way of doing business, or inferior quality of employees or management. For the decay of a company to happen, it must first die internally. Innovation and raising quality keep a company alive like the constant breath needed by a person.

Upgrading company cultures in a country can be achieved by strict governmental regulation and close monitoring. The elevation of all company cultures promotes the change of people's habit of rushing through all tasks to save time and money. In turn, with the peel off of rushing tendency, people brush away their need to be rude to others. Consequently, the age of rudeness can end. Otherwise, the rudeness escalates as it is happening now all over the world. With deteriorating cultures, everybody suffers.

CHAPTER FIFTEEN

Reforms of Education from the Root

Discussed first, the reforms of government and public company have the fastest and the widest effects on most populace. Nonetheless, those reforms cannot take root and will not last forever without educational reform. It takes longer to see the effects of educational reforms because reforms of the mind take time. Reforms of government and public companies mostly fix the outside structure, not inside the minds.

Education in essence is to increase the quality of people. In our last book, we compared today's education to boxes like the classrooms which strongly hold the teachers and students alike. Mass produced, rigid, inflexible, and not tailored to each individual characterize education, which is perfect to teach animals which are unable to utilize spirituality. For humans, such an education kills spirituality of almost all graduates and transforms them to not much better than animals.

Education as it is today does not enhance people's quality and instead downgrades them by several degrees. Science, literature, and mathematics are tools used by one with motivation and drive. Without revving up the person first and shoving tools into that person is like loading up a truck full of building materials without even checking whether it has an engine inside or not. A full truckload of materials is useless unless at the construction site.

Without knowing the main essence of education as increasing people quality, today's education produces mediocre quality graduates albeit with substantial knowledge. It is by no accident that many leaders of countries today do not have high quality, an inevitable result that the education has focused only on science, literature, and mathematics. Not advocating today's education being abolished, we wish to instill quality education, or including the teaching of spirituality.

Learning knowledge without learning spirituality enables some people to do more crimes than if without. For example, with increased knowledge, electronic scammers are able to create elaborate schemes to rake in millions of unrighteous money from unscrupulous general populace. With no spiritual education to ensure integrity before teaching computer software, malicious hackers likely will escalate as it is happening now. Illegal stock trades can only happen to those with insider information of knowing how.

Sometimes legally, some smart top company officers scam their companies of millions of dollars before paying the shareholders. Some accountants know the practice well to hide assets from taxation and rob the country. All with high financial knowledge, some greedy Wells Fargo employees and its imprudent management caused empty account creation to earn bonus. Without spiritual education, the knowledge acquired may serve to increase the capacity of some people to do bad things to others or organizations.

Learning Methods More Important Than Teaching Methods

One main reason why video games are so popular among children is that they can enjoy the individuality not found in family or school. Teaching involves at least two people: one teacher and one student, but learning involves only one. From elementary school to university, all educational formats today have teaching precede learning. This setting of placing learning as passive and teaching as active is totally wrong, especially after elementary school. Learning should always be played as the most active role.

A major pitfall of today's education is to emphasize excessively on teaching and not enough on self-learning. At a very young age, when learning methods have not grown in the concept, children truly need to be taught by teachers instead of learning by themselves. The teaching of learning methods should begin at early age, and increased practice on learning by self should be gradually introduced. At the end of elementary school, most should have learned to self-study with basic methods learned in language, mathematics, chemistry, and physics, provided the text books are clear enough and the tool books are available.

The increased use of learning methods may not work without first discovering the true interest and passion of each student. The interest can be discovered through observation, interview, or questionnaire. Interests of people change over time, especially during growth. A pupil may like mathematics at a young age and gradually like literature in their teenage years, or vice versa. No one is likely to be interested in all disciplines all at the same time.

The combination of discovering interest and emphasizing self-learning likely will lead to a lot more learning and less teaching. With a dictionary and other research tools, no words should ever be taught on a blackboard except maybe in the first year. With the key learning strategy of practice, practice, and practice, mathematics may become as fun as video games that some may become addicted to it. Each discipline of knowledge has some very good learning methods, but some may not be so good; trial and error will inform each student. The key is to clearly tell the students how to learn those learning methods and to try them all.

Though not all learning methods are suitable to a particular student, the student can try and find out the best one suitable to retain. For example, many well-known memorization methods are in various books and are available for choosing. Exactly which method will work on which student is totally unknown until after one tries it. Trying them out one by one is the only way to find out for the student. Maybe only one works well, or maybe a few of them works. Those that work well will do wonders for that student.

Above principle of putting interests and learning method before teaching method is consistent with individual spirituality. Spiritual wisdom emphasizes individuality and looking at the whole picture. Modern educators wrongly assume that all young people have the same level of interest at the same age. This collective group thinking ignores individuality and interest. The learning of spirituality in elementary school can also help to discover a person's interests.

Another major pitfall of today's education, as pointed out in our last book, is the lack of hands-on experience. Seeing is one thing; doing is yet another. Interested in anatomy in books, a student can be completely turned off by animal dissection. Another pupil not interested in the book may be interested in operating on animals alive. Like trying out memorization methods, no one can be sure until after one tries.

We entirely agree that children should not be exploited by forcing them to labor continuously full-time without any chance of learning knowledge. However, forbidding children to work on their interests and what has been learned surpasses the original concern for children's welfare. In fact, this overstepping forbiddance hurts children's chance for real experience, which may not arrive again later in life with the level of interest. All learning should soon be followed up with real work experience to solidify the acquired knowledge or they are soon forgotten or become unfamiliar.

Not only work experience should accompany learning while being a student, but also learning should continue while being a worker. Many companies provide educational incentive while on the job, but most focus only on what is related to the job assignment using personal spare time. Only after work and learning go hand in hand is learning till old age possible.

The motivation behind learning and work should be personal interest. Being compelled to work due to the need to survive may not differ much from animals which survive from one meal to the next. Personal spirituality also thrives on the expansion of personal interests in a lifetime.

Most entrepreneurs need to be versatile in many unrelated fields. Starting a business is easy, but mastering all fields of a business is not. Registering a business name with the city, paying taxes, and hiring quality workers are all aspects of a business unrelated to the core business. The organization and prioritization skills of spiritual wisdom can be used to deal with the many aspects of a business.

Blending experience with learning is the best way to memorize; it seeps into the root of the spirit instantly. A balanced diet with proteins, carbohydrates, water, minerals, and fiber is easier to digest than an insipid diet of only one ingredient, like today's form of education. Learning from mistakes is also important in learning.

Too eager to produce perfect students, today's education does not emphasize the significant use of learning from mistakes or wrongdoing. Though sin, wrong, and mistakes can cause trouble or at least a headache or loss of material, this loss has its value in improving the future. Not existing in other animals, this important attribute empowers humans to explore their spirituality. Not teaching the importance of SWM fails the education.

Hopefully, our dream and vision of shipping thousands of students to a foreign country to learn another language can become reality in the future. Long cruise travel should not be reserved for the seniors or retirees whose energy and interests have somewhat waned compared to the youth. Practical learning and learning on the job touch the soul and spirit like fresh and cold mountain water; it feels so good.

The Right to Choose a Teacher

One problem that nearly no one sees in today's education is the designation of teachers instead of being chosen by the student. Recalling all elementary and high school teachers, one often does not like all of the teachers. Everyone prefers some teachers and dislikes others. The degree of like and dislike varies. This preference also differs from one student to the next. Likely, no two students have the same preference for all the teachers.

Most people probably had the experience that they learn better with a liked teacher. This has been studied by psychology. Conversely, a student often does not do well with a disliked teacher. The affinity between a teacher and a student depends on both personality and spirituality. Oftentimes, people cannot explain why they like or dislike a particular teacher or student.

Most students would wish that a liked teacher continues to teach the next semester. Changing teachers constantly for a student is another problem. The rollercoaster ride between teachers can wreak havoc on a student's mental stability and learning consistency. Finding a good teacher who can teach for all twelve years of basic school would be better than changing teachers all the time.

Forcing one to stay with a student-chosen teacher for all twelve years would be wrong. When a student grows up, the preference may change. The student-teacher relationship may turn stale or sour at some future time. If needed, a student can initiate to change the teacher, but a teacher probably should not initiate the change. Fundamentally, a student plays the key role of this educational arrangement.

After a student has practiced basic learning methods, a teacher can gradually turn into a mentor. The role of a mentor would replace the role of a teacher as the student's learning methods become mature. This private arrangement of a teacher or a mentor for each student will not cost more than the educational system today. The time needed to spend as a teacher is substantially more than a mentor.

Ten minutes of teaching or mentoring by a preferred teacher or mentor is likely more effective than hundreds of lecture hours in a classroom by a disliked teacher. Also, a classroom full of other students can often distract the attention of each student. In essence, studying and learning is an individual affair, not a collective one.

Like government and public company employees who can elect their own supervisors and managers, students should be able to select their own teachers. Before a choice, students need to be taught on the wisdom of choosing people. Adults often underestimate children's ability of choosing good people because they wrongly assume that good people choice must be based on knowledge, which children do not have a lot of.

Children often possess better people judging ability than most adults probably due to their stronger spiritual strength before being overloaded with knowledge. The criteria of choosing a teacher used to teach a student can be numerous. Here, we only list some as examples. Though fully judging a person based on appearance is shallow, appearance can be a good starting point. A child just needs to be reminded that outside looks do not represent everything inside.

Another judging criterion is affinity between a student and a teacher. When a child dislikes or likes an adult, the reason may be mental or spiritual. No matter what the exact reason is, a child probably is not capable of articulating the exact reason. Therefore, an adult needs to be patient and respect a child's decision for the time being.

A third criterion is the teacher's patience, quality, and personality. Patience probably exists in today's most elementary school teachers because they know the slow process of children's mental development. An outgoing personality is not necessarily good if the quality of paying attention to detail is affected due to the personality.

Personal qualities may include flexibility, adaptability, creativity, positive attitude, commitment, honesty, and communicational skill. While the adult is present, a child can learn to interview a teacher to sense these qualities via observation and child-designed questions. While interviewing a teacher, a child can also learn to judge people more accurately than using spiritual intuition.

Although the depth of knowledge of a teacher likely cannot be judged by very young children, teenagers can usually know it during an interview. Judging people through their spirituality is likely the specialty of children and teenagers; the adults only need to guide them a little bit. Methodology of teaching cannot be judged easily except during a trial period. A six-month trial period should be sufficient to discover whether the methodology of a teacher matches a child.

Some people may argue that this private teacher and mentor system would cost an arm and a leg to the taxpayer. In fact, the cost likely will be reduced due to the decreased hours needed to teach. Nowadays, students go to school five days a week. With the match of learning with interest and teacher with student, pupils do not need to go to school every weekday. Library and study room are available for students to study and research. A student would love to spend more than eight hours a day on a topic he or she is interested in.

Even in school, a teacher can monitor and tutor many students at the same time. Spending ten minutes with a liked tutor is more effective than hours with a disliked one. The attention of a teacher can be rotated to several students in a one-hour period. A student's self-studying habit is the key for enabling this kind of rotation. This habit of studying by self should be gradually fostered from the first or second grade.

At the beginning stage of learning, more private teachers should be hired to implement the self-study method of education. After students become accustomed to self-study, university and high school will not need that many classrooms to teach. The savings at higher education should be returned to compensate the cost of hiring more private teachers in the beginning.

Differences between Knowledge Education and Spiritual Education

Knowledge and spiritual education enhance one another. With only knowledge education, the quality of people and their lives is substantially reduced, as is happening today. With only spiritual education, the spiritual learning suffers without scientific approach or technological advantage such as a potential brain scan to gauge one's spirituality. Universal understanding of Tao also suffers. Knowing the differences between knowledge education and spiritual education helps to further understand both kinds of education.

One major difference is that a student can be substantially better than the teacher in spiritual education. Knowledge is material data stored in the brain. As nonmaterial, spiritual practice and its knowledge do not register inside the brain; in other words, this ability can be innate from birth hidden in one's spirit. A word or sentence can come into one's mind from nowhere or one's spirit. Hence, a teacher is not necessarily better than a student who has a lot of innate spirituality.

In spirituality, spiritual practice is more important than spiritual knowledge. A teacher may know more than a student, but knowing more does not mean practicing better. Contrarily, a teacher in mathematics often knows better than a student about mathematics; the same thing is largely true for other scientific fields. In spiritual learning, the tangible knowledge and the intangible practice must complement each other to advance both into spirituality.

The abstract nature of spirituality also drastically differs from the concrete nature of knowledge. Visible and touchable, knowledge is easier to reason and relate than spirituality. Invisible, the spiritual truth must be mentally imagined and linked to create connections. Initially, using visible knowledge is faster than utilizing invisible spirituality, but later when a person's spirituality grows to a substantial level, the invisible spirit becomes much faster than concrete mental manipulation.

Think of the difference between a computer and a Chinese abacus, or *suanpan*. After training, some people can imagine an abacus inside the mind to do calculation. If doing it successfully, this invisible abacus is much faster than a real abacus. When one's spiritual practice surpasses a satisfactory level, the power of a spirit can outperform that of material knowledge.

Another difference is the timing of pursuing the reason behind knowledge; knowledge education put it as the last stage, but spiritual education put it as the first stage. Young children often ask questions of why, but their curiosity soon diminishes after being swamped with a vast amount of knowledge to memorize. Perhaps the only place in today's education where pursuing underlying reason becomes required is in PhD programs.

Without understanding the reason behind knowledge before memorizing it is like a person not hungry but being forced to eat. Vomiting out the swallowed memory is inevitable as is happening in many high school dropouts. The reason for learning a particular field is hidden in the interests expressed by students.

All students possess different spiritual qualities, which generate different interests toward various fields of knowledge. The characteristic of interest is like the property of a material as hardness of iron and softness of cotton. Pursuit of reasons on all things should begin in early stage, not later. Quality of knowledge considerably outweighs quantity of knowledge, so jamming knowledge into children only produces the opposite effects of vomiting and malnutrition.

Learning knowledge before knowing the reason behind it is aimless and dangerous. Knowing the reason why is more important than learning itself. Reason drives motivation, which drives interest. Ego often is the byproduct of learning without first knowing why one needs to learn. The possessed knowledge is gone at death, but the ego remains. This wrong is common among some scholars full of knowledge but without spirituality.

The reason for a physical body is its spirit. No other reason is needed to explain why children ask why all the time.

When Jesus Christ said that he was the way, the truth, and the life, he really meant that the spirit had those qualities. Truth is the reason or principle behind all lives. Without touching the reason behind a life, the way is impassably blocked. If Jesus Christ had any ego, he would not have volunteered to die on the cross. The reason for ego is materialism, not spirituality.

When the physical body of Jesus Christ died on the cross, his spiritual body lived on and later showed itself with the disciples. No longer having a brain to perceive pain, this showing differed from his physical body. A spirit may be invisible to the human who possesses it, but at the moment of seriously tapping the power, the spirit is vastly stronger than the physical body, just as the amount of dark energy is much more than visible energy.

Before becoming one, all saints suffered physically or emotionally. Not that ordeals or torments are enjoyable, but they greatly enhance the adherence of spirituality to one's soul. If all humans learn the reasons of all knowledge before learning it, this suffering may be fully avoided.

The Teaching of Sin, Wrong, and Mistake (SWM)

Probably no one has perfect spirituality on earth, not even saints when they lived on earth. A rare spiritual condition is that a living person's spirit can leave his or her body at will. This spirit off may not be aided by other spirits. However, being able to leave the body at will is not a sure indicator of perfect spirituality; the five merits of this spirit may not be perfect.

On the other end of spectrum, a perfect spirit may not be able to leave its physical body at will, or one may not wish to. The reason why we want to stress this is that having a perfect spirit or not should not be the reason behind whether one reflects on one's own SWM. Such reflection should come as second nature for high spirits after years of Tao practice.

In chapter 11, we extensively explained SWM. To review a little bit, sin happens when a person purposely does what is against his or her five merits in the spirit. Wrong happens when one should know or ask but fails to do so. Mistake happens when a person carelessly or riskily performs a task even though it confirms to spirituality. Killing a good person is a sin. Killing a serious abuser is a wrong. Driving into a tree trunk and killing a passenger while doing a good deed is a mistake.

The most serious sin is probably to forgo introspection of one's own SWM. A farmland with all crops being stopped is full of weeds and not producing any harvest. If a person stops repenting, it is the exact moment of spiritual death prior to a physical death. Giving up on one's own spirituality is like damaging one's own life boat that no other vessels will come to rescue. After one learns to check one's own SWM, be aware of this complete stoppage of the engine. Only constant checking of one's own SWM provides the power to reach Tao or the other bank of the river.

Learning past mistakes should be a major lesson for all children. The *Challenger* disaster of 1986, the awakening of German people after WWII, and the rise and fall of Bill O'Reilly can be good lessons. Most people learn from their own mistakes; others' SWMs can be good lecture materials to teach how to reflect on one's own SWM.

The Teaching of Avoiding and Conquering Addiction

In our last book, we covered extensively the danger of addiction. The teaching of ways to avoid and to conquer addiction is very important at a young age to prevent and to cure all potential addictions later in life. Being prepared to avoid or to deal with a lifelong problem, one creates a mentality of moving all the time to prevent being stuck. With so many possible different kinds of addictions, it is impossible to have a method which will cure all addictions, but some commonly used mental techniques should be taught.

The first lesson is to avoid any trap if at all possible. A truck driving on a muddy road is expected to have one of its tires stuck in mud most of the time. A hiking trip to an area where few trees are present is expected to cause sunburn. Avoiding a potentially risky situation prevents a possible addiction. Prevention is better than cure.

An addiction is kind of like a wheel stuck in mud so that the vehicle is going nowhere except the spinning its wheels at the same location. Fostering the habit of constantly changing one's interests is a wonderful way of keeping self from being bogged down by addiction. Rolling stones gather no moss. Versatile interests keep the mind occupied without being stuck at one interest only.

The third lesson is on understanding where an addiction occurs in mind. Knowledge of addiction is in the conscious level, but addiction is hidden in the subconscious. The distance between the two levels means that knowledge alone is hardly sufficient to cure an addiction. Regularly and carefully checking the subconscious mind may prevent addiction but probably not suited for active people or young children. Habit is another name for addiction, though it causes less harm. Habit can be changed, so is an addiction; it just takes more time and effort.

Determination and strong will are the most important weapons in conquering addiction. For each kind of addiction, different specialized lessons may exist. Those who have been through a particular kind of addiction know the best way to beat this kind of addiction. One hundred people who quit cigarette smoking successfully may provide the exact advice a person stuck in smoking needs. The same principle applies to alcohol or drug addiction.

The Teaching of Divination

The teaching of divination is scientific because no magical power is involved, at least not seeable to the one who asks. The reasoning capacity of an inquirer must be at least half of the game to continue; otherwise, one soon loses faith and gives it up. At least 80 percent accuracy rates have been observed by all authors and many readers who asked for years. The sixty-two words in the *Book of Change*, or the simplified thirty-two words version later, are similar to languages among humans. Each unique word has a specific meaning designated by saints thousands of years ago. Though Confucius disliked magical power or too much worship, he used it too.

Divination can probably be taught during teenage years when they face a surge of choices in life, though a younger age is also a possibility if one is highly spiritual and not prone to superstition. The prerequisites discussed in chapter 12 such as uncertainty, sarcasm, and one's own reasoning are good precautions to teach before the actual teaching of divination. A good reasoning ability is especially important to counter any potential superstition after learning and practicing divination.

Teaching children to have appropriate attitude toward the spiritual world is very important. With too much or too little respect, a child may give up divination years or decades later. Faith in one's own spirituality should first be established before commencing to teach divination. A tendency to pursue extreme accuracy is a sign of not being mentally ready. Recording every divination answers by children and checked by adults is a good way to ensure that their questions are appropriate and with right attitude. Keep an open mind if they ask question about sexuality.

Before one decides to teach a child divination, a divination by the adult is probably the best tie breaker in the final decision before starting a divination lesson. The adult may be overestimating a child's readiness through the filtering lens of either too loving or not loving enough. One may also underestimate a child's readiness from being too cautious or being biased against the child. Parents or guardians may not understand their children as well as high spirits do; otherwise, a lot of family conflicts between generations would not have existed.

The Teaching of Astrology and Zodiac

Though mysterious, astrology and zodiac can help people to understand Tao later in life. Many have the experience of comparing the accuracy of astrology within their own family. Some likely already found it to be true for themselves and a few family members or friends. Most science disciplines today cannot explain 100 percent of world phenomena. Psychology and sociology are not exact sciences either. Astrology and zodiac should be taught in elementary school with some precautions before its teaching.

All elementary school students should be informed about the limited ability of science to explain all things on earth and the universe, such as some magical events. Some potential causes of inaccuracy in astrology and zodiac should also be taught before the learning. A major cause of astrological inaccuracy is spiritual force of one's own or family members. The spirituality of parents can change astrological accuracy of children. A person who works on SWM avidly is also likely to have its fate altered.

A factor which may influence astrological accuracy is the qualities of friends and family. A parent who uses drugs or alcohol heavily is likely to deteriorate a child's fate. Befriending one who smokes cigarettes can cut short one's life. Befriending a potential drunk driver can result in premature death at a young age. Another factor is the will and determination of a person. One diligently pursuing a life goal is likely to have a better fate than one who does not.

Yet another factor can change astrological accuracy is the quality of a spouse or child. A spiritual spouse can change their fate if one listens to and follows the spiritual advice of the spouse. A child with high spirituality can change the fate of his or her parents if they do not suppress such spirituality in a child. Over controlling of the parents, especially in many eastern countries, often squash the spirituality in children. Major events in a society, country, or world are factors too. People born during WWII would have much different fate than those who are born today even if their signs are identical.

One main purpose of learning astrology and zodiac is to realize and to correct one's own weakness in the subconscious level. Through this understanding, personal mentality and spirituality can be vastly improved if one pays attention to compensate it. Erroneously, the popularly held opinions about its purpose as to know one's own fate, to match a future mate, or even to manipulate others should be corrected and strongly expunged. Only with the right reason and mentality can one become qualified to learn astrology and zodiac. A strong knowledge in this field combined with wrong attitudes can lead to greed and eventual destruction of self.

The learning of astrology and zodiac should follow the learning of reflecting on one's own SWM, not before it. Trying to find guidance in astrology without reflecting on one's own SWM is like trying to steal from an empty bank vault, one is bound to return empty handed. Only after one learns the importance of repenting to one's own spirituality does one become qualified in finding one's own weakness via astrology. Before becoming versed in examining one's own SWM, one may be wrongly directed into pursuing wrong purpose of this learning. This learning can destroy oneself if not being handled carefully.

A main spiritual practice while learning spirituality is not to harm others unjustly. Using what is learned from astrology and zodiac to harm others or to benefit oneself gravely violates this practice and should be strongly forewarned. Such behavior or even intention itself can often conjure opposition from high spirits, who may impart a calamity or illness to warn the person. Even a death is likely not ruled out.

Astrology and zodiac should also not be used to find a lifetime companion. People change, so is the accuracy of astrology. Referencing it to find a mate has the assumption that neither the seeker nor the sought-after would ever change in a lifetime. The spiritual advance of either partner later in life can result in the separation of such a couple. Divorce often evolves into ugly fight or even sometimes death as illustrated by many domestic disputes or crimes reenacted on television.

The best moment to strengthen a weakness is at the critical or disastrous time of a life. At the time of trial and tribulation, so to speak, is the best period to correct one's own SWM and boost spirituality. Lessons of practicing spirituality are not fully learned until the test period is passed safely. Most saints know this well. One of our recent experiences also demonstrates it.

One day a few months earlier, an apparently homeless person passed our camping site at a parking lot and asked for some bread. We were just preparing to finish the last one and a half bagels we had left in our carbohydrate department. They were delicious and tasty, so we were reluctant to give them away. We had a lot of extra fruit and vegetables, so we offered a banana and tomato to him. After he refused the offer and walked away with nothing, we realized that we might have done a sin by not giving him the remaining bagels. To our great consternation later, our sin of this was confirmed by high spirits that we failed the test.

Most tests are done at the moment of leisure and relaxation to guarantee the accuracy and depth of an unannounced quiz, which can count much more than a big written examination. A word uttered or a spontaneous behavior betrays one's deep subconscious mind much more than a three-hundred-page PhD dissertation. Watching one's each tiny word or behavior and correcting it counts more than writing a salvation book for the world. To one's own spirit and spirituality, no others is as important as correcting one's own SWM, especially only knowledge of astrology.

The Teaching of Symbolic, Prioritizing, and Organizational skills

Our previous book advocates the teaching of symbols before that of formal languages. The main purpose of our advocacy was to inspire the growth of spirit, whose main tool of communication is symbols, not languages. Like primitive symbols, naturally uncomplicated spirits prefer straightforward expressions, not like a carousel roundabout stating the same point repeatedly. An inspiring art often describes an intuitive feeling or concept with some simple expression.

The simplicity of nature corresponds to the simplicity of spirituality. The intelligence of human often blocks the way of spiritual expression. A main reason why ancient humans could discover and invent was their spirituality, likely inspired by their simple and uncomplicated lives.

In addition, symbolically representing real world, abstract symbols facilitate the grasp of one's own spirit and spirituality, which are also abstract. A picture is worth a thousand words, so there is no need to bother with excessive pages if a few drawings can fully express it. A good example is that Buddha plucked a flower to show his disciples to indicate the importance of one's own spirit and spirituality surpassing all his dharma.

As quoted earlier in a teaching of Confucius that the ability to prioritize reveals the near arrival of one's Tao. A spirit prefers its own prioritizing skill over the amount of money earned each year or the degree of comfort acquired. Especially, prioritizing one's life goals counts much more than a university degree received from any university. Prioritizing lesson is a must for spiritual study, particularly the practicing ability of this skill.

Majority of life's miseries are due to a reversed order of life goals. Putting money first is probably the most common sin caused by wrong prioritization. The success of personal spirituality should always be the number one life goal. A failed spirituality cannot even be avoided by trillions of dollars and with no repentance of one's own SWM. Value wise, guarding one's individual spirituality is worth much more than the time used for physical survival.

Only with a totally straight life goal of conforming to Tao can other attached goals like marriage or career be straight. If the center pillar of a house is erected wrong, the finished house is bound to be crooked or unsafe. Many run into accidents without even knowing why; some accidentally die but not even know any life purpose or goal. The lesson of prioritization needs to start from prioritizing daily chores. One should learn to focus the available time in a day to the intended goals for that day; also, one should ensure those daily goals align with the life goal of Tao.

Organizational skill is yet another key lesson to learn Tao and spirituality. As mentioned above, spirit prefers simple things. Having nothing is the easiest to organize; sustaining a physical life makes many things complicated. Without any food in a kitchen cabinet means no organization needed. Fasting for three days not only lets the digesting system rest easy but also gets rid of body waste. The best way to travel is not to carry any luggage if one can afford to.

More difficult to organize than zero, one is the next easiest thing to organize. One luggage is better than two. One computer is easier to work with than multiple ones due to the needed collaboration of data flow in between. One pair of shoes requires no choosing in the morning. One exclusive department handling economy is easier to manage than several economy-related departments. Many of what was mentioned may be intuitive, but most people lose sight due to external influencing factors or internal excessive desires.

Organizational skill is the door to concentration, focus, communication, achievement, and many others. The best organizational skill is probably the ability to reduce many things to one or even to zero. It is nearly impossible for many people who routinely carry more than three large sets of luggage, and often they find many of the prepared never being used on the trip. Word reduction to a few is difficult for people who often talk redundantly. A facial expression often speaks more than a thousand words.

Organization needs time and constant effort, but such time and effort are well worth it. A closet full of clothes can become a mess again within a few days after being organized. Returning this closet to the original order is likely to take much more time and effort than a regular upkeep. A kitchen not being cleaned up daily will demand laborious scrubbing of oil residue weeks later. A disorganized office or living quarters can often affect one's concentration on the task at hand.

Growth Ultimately Important

Not only a world trend, individuality jives with the spiritual development of the world. Spiritual growth needs to be done individually, not by group like taking care of a pine farm. After all, a class of more than thirty students is like a wild forest with many vastly diverse species. Do not expect them to all learn well from one teacher with the same lecture. All future learning should be individualized.

Only an individualized lesson plan can foster individual growth, not a mass-produced lecture inside a box packaged class. The latter teaches all students with the same material at the same time. Especially, an individual progress differs from others. With the introduction of variety of learning methods, the educational cost in the later stages likely will drastically reduce. Hopefully, the high cost of attending university will be a phenomenon of the past in the near future. The cost for early stages may increase due to the large number of individualized instructors needed.

When the focus of education is placed on group growth, some students in the group are bound to wither due to indigestion of the lesson plan designed for the whole group. If many plants grow closely together, the nutrition in the earth is not sufficient to sustain all the plants. Putting a plant on each pot would ensure the nutrition and water not being shared with others. Thus, the growth of each individual can be certain, and the group as a whole grows better too.

Spiritual growth needs more individualized attention than mental growth. Memorizing what is read grows the mind; understanding the reason of why it should be memorized grows the spirit. One can often master the understanding of Tao and spirituality through reasoning extensively on knowledge of spiritual nature. A good example of this extensive reasoning is the writing of our two books.

Despite possessing advanced college degrees, all the authors do not fully know spirituality or Tao despite our initial knowledge from an early age. Through the writing of these two books, our mental and spiritual growth was enormous. Even with advanced degrees, knowledge of Tao and spirituality alone cannot automatically provide reasons behind it. Besides reflecting on one's own SWM, one must ponder deeply to totally conjugate the hidden reasons before starting to realize Tao and spirituality.

The growth of spiritual knowledge itself merely adds weight to a belly and a brain. A spiritual growth digests the food into energy and creating neuron connections. All nutrients supplement each other to grow a person spiritually. A spiritual growth and a tight fit between one yin and one yang create Tao and move it forward.

Improving the reasoning skill is the main reason why our first book encourages writing of a book at teenage years. The writing would likely benefit the student more than reading Shakespeare ten times. In teaching, quantity is more important than quality. In learning, quantity does not always digest into quality, especially in spiritual learning. Spiritual quality is what matters most when a person tries to utilize the acquired knowledge of Tao and spirituality.

Chapter Sixteen

Revelation

About two years prior to the publishing of this book, the authors had received instruction through divination that this book should be published by June 2017. Largely due to procrastination of the authors, majority of this book was written within a one-month period from the tenth of April to the eleventh of May in 2017. Roughly one-third of this book was written in the previous five months. Considering the approaching deadline, we thought about omitting this chapter entirely.

Another reason why we would prefer not to write this chapter is that we do not wish to steal the thunder of the Bible by naming this last chapter the same as in the Holy Bible. The last book of the New Testament in the Holy Bible is also named Revelation. The name Revelation in the last chapter of our last book was thought to be a one-time deal because we took a more mystic route to write that book.

To be consistent with our last book, the title of this chapter Revelation was decided before we started to write this book. However, after starting to write, we realized that we probably should portray this book as scientifically as possible to fit our assertion that spiritual education can be a scientific discipline. To strengthen the scientific appearance of this book and to increase the chance of spirituality being scientifically included were our third and fourth reasons for trying to omit this chapter.

Unfortunately for the authors and fortunately for the readers, high spirits or God squashed our intention to omit this chapter when we finally asked. No matter how many reasons a person can enumerate, they may not be conforming to Tao or the right way for a person or country to do things. From the divination, we have sinned in our procrastination. We repent and shall do our best to change this bad habit.

The Book of Rites was written before Confucius's time and was used in the Zhou Dynasty, which governed China from 256 BC to 1046 BC. One of the chapters, "Datong," describes an ideal world where people are largely the same. They love and help each other and do not fight with each other anymore. On the surface, the two Chinese words *Datong* means generally the same with small difference. The chapter of Datong begins with the sentence: "When the big Tao is practiced around the world."

The chapter Datong continues to describe a world where the whole world belongs to the general public. In this world, merited and capable people are elected. Being spiritually consistent and harmonic, people care also for others' parents and children. Therefore, the near-death are taken care of, the strong are engaged in full-time duty, the children are brought up well, and those who lose their companion and become lonely or the disabled are properly fed.

The second half of the chapter describes that the male follows spiritual appropriateness and do not covet females who do not belong to them. -The female has a family to return to. Money or usable goods are hated to be wasted, and those who possess extra money or such goods do not hold it when others need it. Most favor being self-sufficient by using their own labor, but they unselfishly help others when others need it. The above results in no evil thoughts surface in mind, and no one wishes to be a thief or robber. So door locks are unnecessary; all above is called Datong.

A reality check with Datong ideal, nearly all countries belong to the elected officials and representatives. Often the rich and famous are elected, and many are not spiritually consistent or harmonic. There is loneliness when a parent or a child dies; not many are willing to be a foster parent. Hospices and social security care for most, but many able bodies do not have a full-time duty. Most children and disabled are cared for, but their loneliness is prevalent.

Also, school does not teach spirituality, so many males have not learned appropriateness and have been coveting females via inappropriate looks. Lust is appropriate in a bedroom with the one whom one belongs to, but not so at the wrong place or wrong time. Most females have a family to return to, but many do not. Waste is popular in many developed nations, especially in some governments.

In addition, most wealthy are selfish and do not donate a large proportion of their wealth to benefit the public. All people growing their own food in their backyard may not be a good idea, but at least it helps the growers to exercise without using the gym. Most young adults are willing to help when asked. Thieves and robbers are still national headaches as most schools have no spiritual education.

Many of the ideas in the Datong chapter have been implemented since World War II, but many have not, likely due to the lack of understanding in Tao and spirituality. Without understanding it, it could not be taught. Only through the teaching of Tao and spirituality can the world achieve Datong without letting it be a dream or imagination like a utopia.

Abstract and immaterial, most spirits have similar qualities such as loving peace and tranquility, being balanced, and possessing the five merits. On the other hand, most minds are overactive, not knowing Tao, naive about the impermanence of physical body, and ignorant about the existence of their own spirits. Spiritual and Tao education likely is the only salvation to most populace and to reach Datong.

Converse with One Earthly – Beyond Magic, Half Answer, Match Leftright

Ch 1 The Book Title and Etcetera (34)
Title and high spirits defined and their power for the good X5 **(20)**
High spirits refers to those who did good on earth, dead or alive X2
Low spirits like to sabotage others for pleasure or for no reason X2
Earthly means unselfish love and propagation. Authors' names differ, the love the same X4
Readers' criticism and our corrections X2
Laborious divination each paragraph and even to sentence level X5

Differences between This Book and the Last (14)
Read important chapter 1ˢᵗ, suggested 2 4 10 11 12 16, can read this book 1ˢᵗ then last X3
Last book and this written in differ stages of spiritual awareness X2
Qualities vary chapter to chapter, even paragraph to paragraph X1
A book can be inconsistent, which show consistency of truth of spiritual improvement X1
Reasons for outlines appended to this book, all textbooks should X2
Outlines not totally match main text, # of paragraphs, in () total, abbreviate, no grammar X2
Tense, verb, noun, adjective interchangeable, preposition omitted where clear X2
Critics, Questions, and Comments Welcome X1

Ch 2 Testimonies of Readers and Others (38)
Despite accuracy described below, errors always exist X1

Health and Food (9)
Vinegar can hurt rheumatoid arthritis X2
Rice contains trace of arson X1
Sweet addiction and too much body fat can lead to diabetes and heart disease X3
Excessive desire for fried chicken caused diarrhea X2
A St. Louis man: Why strawberry was seldom approved X1

Addictions (6)
Porn caused back-to-back traffic stops X1
Too much desire for many things tips toward materialism and hurts the spirit X2
High spirits and God protect believers by shielding the eyes of potential dangerous people X2
Do not be discouraged by errors in consultation with high spirits or God X1

Magical Events (11)
Mysterious eight words appeared on hand at night with no scientific explanation X6
Amazingly match the eight words with a poem of four sentences from a temple X5

Complacency Hurts (11)
Clinical trial at Ventura, California X6
Homeless water spray and nails sabotage X5

Ch 3 Rise and Wane of a Person or a Nation (7)
Rise and fall of a person or a nation X7

Ch 4 Spirituality as a Scientific Study (216)
The blindfolds of science lead to many educational and social problems X2 **(10)**
Trace of spirituality in many scientific fields and science incomplete without full spirituality X2
Why study of spirituality can and should be part of scientific field X6

Prerequisites for Science to Recognize Spirituality (17)
Admit unknown fully and not pretend almighty, especially regard to invisible X4
Admit weakness in aspects related to humans and their spirituality X3
Admitting existence of subconscious key to resolve addictions and beyond X2
Assume maximum profits and efficiency not necessarily suitable for human and spirit X2
The unseeable manifestation of spiritual world readily be seen X6

Spirit Mind and Body Connected closely and Learn from Each Other (22)
How spirit, mind, and body are connected X3
When they connect, they work wonders. When don't, diseases and disasters X1
Proper distance between mind-spirit promotes mental growth X3
Best way to tame mind is through correct education of spirit, not too tight nor too loose X4
Without the study of spirituality, psychology and psychiatry never truly take off X3
Confucius: "one of three must be the teacher," mind learn from body decay and spirit X8

Differences between Spirit and Mind (52)
Characteristics of spirit, abstract, personality root, prefer bland and quiet, like change, but no inconsistency, five merits, control epigenome, mice experiment as proof X9
Characteristics of mind, subconscious and un defined, dream = un + subconscious X15
Inward vs. outward, intruding thoughts, mind imbalance without spirit, terrorist attack X8
Three dimensional vs. one point, spirit can infinite dimensions, best to touch 3D body X4
Abstract recording vs. bits of information etched on brain X3
Unbiased vs. views from one's own personality X5
Spirit and mind can clash, Hawaii robbed by a same-age male, ECG purposely failed X5
Spirit knows everything but not know why without think, X2
Mind know why not know everything X1

Spirits Often Fall to Sleep (16)
Mentally awake not mean spiritually awake, about 95%–98% people spirits asleep constantly X3
Little inward focus and small distraction keep spirit awake, crooked mind not fully focused X7
Keep calm and peaceful another crucial piece of puzzle to keep spirit awake X1
Even avid spiritual practitioners not have spirits awoken at all time, even try best daily X1
Spiritual abstractness like empty bottle, can be filled, imagine physical body as one X1
Spiritual wisdom key to keep spirit awake X2
Asleep actually more like half awake, trance, morning body not fully awake X1

Spirit, Spirituality, and Other Terms Defined (31)
Spirits defined and the kinds of spirits: hi and lo, incarnated or not X5
Broken spirit = materialistic, attached, agitated, unresolved spirit X3

High spirit = purer spirit, no hierarchy, authority, free-spirited, no sex difference X1

Minimized sex role lower rape/sexual abuse, drive of porn, better mental health X3

Spirituality defined—1. An ideal spirit with or without a physical body X1

2. The scientific study of an ideal spirit X2

3. A partially ideal spirit who strives toward total ideal X1

Spiritual—1. The quality of an ideal spirit

2. Describe a person who strives to achieve spirituality X2

A spiritually healthy person—1. Devoting some time to spirituality each day

2. Open minded to all potential spiritual experience

3. Appreciate all inconvenience and sorrows, which inspire and boost personal spirituality

4. Treat others as one would treat self

5. Trust one's own spirituality and believe in a higher spirit

6. Find joy in the gradual advance of life meaning and spirituality

7. Find joy in helping others' spirituality

8. Sincerely wish and hope to increase spirituality

9. Close half of eyes and ears toward the deterioration and corruption of this world X9

Getting all terminology straight—1. Free of religious influence 2. Unbiased scientifically

Terms like religious studies and pneumatology are religion-specific and non-scientific

Some authors' disappointed at college religious study courses

Pneumatology focus on studying the Holy Spirit, not including human's spirits

Theology, now a word only for Christianity, or expand to encompass major religions X4

Spiritual Study in University and Public School (32)

Future: PhDs versed in all world major religions and write a thesis on one aspect of love

Comparing love in Buddhism, Christianity, Islam, Taoism, and ancient philosophers

Comparing righteousness in above, Comparing faith in above

Comparing respect and courtesy in above, Jesus vs. Confucius

Comparing creation theories, Comparing effectiveness of practicing methods in above X2

The differences of PhD program in spiritual study compared to other PhDs X4

The on and off paper examinations of PhD candidates X7

Prioritization, self-motivation, and organization X2

Readiness to die required of PhD candidates X2

Reduced Achilles' heel by PhD candidates X4

Revelation of personal weakness to PhD advisers X3

Qualifications to graduate with a PhD in Spirituality X1
The humbling quality of PhD in Spirituality X2
The vision of future spiritual education on all levels X5

Spirituality Is the Root of Psychology and Others (20)
Mind body spirit connected, so psychology X5
The experiences on psychology and psychiatry of one of the authors X3
Video games, addictive medicine, other medical fields X4
Education and learning, wise learning > smart teaching X2
Sociology, economics, business administration, archaeology X2
Crime and law enforcement, waste and environment conservation, people factor X2
Art, sports, even scientific fields astronomy and others X2

Mentally Prepared to Study Spirituality (16)
Foreign language 3mo an example X5
Study of spirituality is abstract and the wisdom needed is higher than for materials X5
Inward focus and attention needed to study subconscious and spirituality X6

Ch 5 Ren (Empathy, Kindness, and Love) (81)
Ren 仁 defined, origin of Ren from Confucius to China and Taiwan X4 **(18)**
Empathy, kindness, love, true or false on later two, combined to Ren and then Tao. X5
Love helps humans expand and succeed on earth
Spiritual love is enormous, rarely seeable, and it stimulates growth X2
Difference between growth by love and physical life
Without love edu, most people's love dies soon in life
Example: Serial killers and graphs to demo bad and good love edu X3
Romance = true love? If not, what is?

Love of parent-child basic and instinctive **(14)**
Parent-child conflicts due to repeat interactions and memory X3
Would-be parents must learn to love and respect children and their psychology X3
Parenting lessons for children have multiple advantages X2
Adults' embarrassment as a major hurdle and its solutions X5

Love of couples (14)
Mostly unique in humans, high divorce due to public edu X3
Sameness is one problem of couples, and its solution X2
The invisibility of spirits helps couples dealing with material problems X3

Need more work than parent-child, understand and accept are the keys X2
Spiritual link, not mental or body link, most vital. Respect second. X3
No formula, just love and respect, and understand interaction and power levels

Love of siblings (7)
Has the root in blood, trust, and friendship X2
Trouble time more appreciative of siblings, heed their advice and respect boundary X3
The ones take care you at the end of life. Friend's love similar. X2

Love of stranger ultimate (11)
Distinct humanistic and make towns, other animals non X2
Love-respect-trust-law a series of event and strangers' love ultimately build big cites X3
Strangers' love lessons and food abundance in place, the rest is personal choice X3
Government sets the biggest example of selfishness, so fix government first X2
After an exemplary unselfish government, love toward strangers can be done X1

Spiritual Education of Love begins at basics and ends at love toward strangers (9)
Stories, movies, real-life documentary, drama, play give the whole picture of love X4 Writing books tools to solidify spiritual love, real-life practice furthers it X3
Intrinsically higher study and research needed to answer the easily questionable X2
Love not described but only perceived and practiced. Only in context, not taught. X1 (8)
At the start, love sets humans apart. In the end, love consummates humans at the doom's day X3
Suffering, sacrifice, and reconciliation, clay to make love, create love and feedback X1
The movie *The Miracle Worker* as good example, *24 Days* as a counter example X3

Ch 6 Appropriateness (Respect, Courtesy, and Others) (92)
Merit defined, relationship needs it to maintain, Syria chemical weapon as example X4 (14)
Each spirit differs and is unique similar to one's DNA, so respect self and others X3
Via respecting one's own spirit, one shines one's own spiritual light uniquely and individually X3
The zero in the spirit creates all richness and beauty, so humble and respect all spirits a must X4

Respect Uniquely Human's (9)
Human's traits and characteristics of respect X3
Wearing clothes, worshipping, and ceremonies to show respect X2
Respect existed in nearly all human societies before travel between cultures did X2
The danger of the tool become the master X2

Being Humble the First Step to achieve 100% respect and self-esteem X3 **(8)**
Ego acquired through growing up, competition, and learning X2
Ego can be eliminated via unloading the mental burdens X3

Respect High Spirits and God and learn their great goal, actions, and endurance X3 **(8)**
Endurance and strength are deep within one's spirit and heart X3
Not truly authority on earth, they guide the world to better place X2
Do not try to teach them if not asked to. If they do, teach politely

Respect peers like a double-edged sword X3 **(5)**
Learn their good spirit, help them if needed, but do not rely, keep a distance early X2

Respect mean spirits and keep a long distance from their appearances X2 **(6)**
Mean spirits have potential of being great, have certain rights and dignity X2
Sympathize the darkness inside mean spirits and lend a hand when needed X2

Respect The Weak and Poor Like the Authority and show mercy X2 **(7)**
Only after accepting one's weakness, one can see and correct it X3
Through respect, one can become stronger in spirit X2

Respect and Love complement each other X2 **(9)**
Each one alone has less power toward others, or social power X3
Extend the courtesy even to your enemies X2
Donald Trump as an example of love complementing respect X2

Teaching Spiritual Respect and the reasons behind it important for life success X3 **(15)**
Best way to teach is through good personal example X2
Thanks, sorry, and please most often used words in a world of respect X2
Habit of respectfulness is contagious, so watch every move X1
Movies not good tool to teach, only literal practice receive the impact of ceremonies X2

Observing how one behaves and looks around can tell the depth of spiritual resect X2

Repeat practice and humbling the only ways to practice. X3

Dangers of Overly Appropriate and Respect (11)
Grunt for seeing touching private parts by a person nearby X4
Flatus causes laughter and disgust, differ East and West X3
Over respect toward an authority, Nazi government, Japanese Emperor X1
Respect and appropriate toward the mind and spirit of a person, not title, President Trump X1
Not to respect authority over favorite movie or music stars, over siblings, over parents, over high spirits X2

Ch 7 Consistency (Faith, Trust, Credit, and Others) (103)

Consistency defined, concept of synchronization under spiritual consistency X2 **(36)**
Two Gulf wars as examples to illustrate synchronization X5
Faith, trust, credit, and others, two Gods and human history modification as example X6
Inconsistency between spirit and mind can wreak havoc, caution to spiritual PhD students X3
So many choices of belief, which one is truest? Science? X3
Trust science but know its limitation on subjectivity, materialism, and atheist nature X4
What happens when belief not taught? → Believe in money, power, law, system, heresy X1
Believe in money → materialism, earthy, and nearsighted X3
"power → egotistic, aloof, lost touch w/ reality (Hitler) X2
"law → endless laws. "system → used for 300+ years, procrastinate to change X3
"heresy → scientology, religious cult, terrorist recruiting X4

Subjectivity and Nonlogics of Spiritual Faith (11)
Subjective psychology X5
Belief is a choice, no logic or reason needed or wanted X3
Faith begets logic, efficiency, and power X3

Signs and Symptoms of Lacking Faith within a person X1 **(11)**
Hunch over, unkempt, easily frustrated X3
Easily addicted, no personal opinions, empty headed X3
Relying on others, complacent, prone to digestive illness, depression, anxiety X4

Food and Exercise for Healthy Faith (17)
To inflate ball, to become solid metals X1

Read spirituality related books, especially to boost righteousness X3
Before consulting high spirits or God, ask one's own spirit first X2
Putting one's own spirit at the highest priority, do it subconsciously X4
Reflect addicted, close eyes often, quiet moment by self, or flood it X4
Phy exercise to spur spirit, believe upper limit, challenge to higher not wider X3

Defend Faith with Reasons like Country Boundary (13)

OK to doubt all including high spirit, but not one's own spirit X3
Not just draw a line or put down a landmark, daily work to expand territory X3
Tug of war back and forth, important = keep up pressure, slowly not rush, and sub mind X3
Many aspects: nothing opposite = real, absolute reason to absolute faith X3
More of it, easier to draw strength, establish faith before trusting anyone X1

Belief as Foundation of Faith and Trust (9)

Inside and Outside: trust align Ren and respect; faith align righteousness and wisdom X2
Trust book, people, spirits with reservation; over trust = less faith, not politicians X4
Bible, sutras, this book (inanimate, dead); self-spirit alive X1
Why faith > trust a must? Impossible to constant communicate, to know reasons behind X2

Teaching Spiritual Consistency, Faith, and Trust (6)

With solid faith, mind can and should change like running water, but not principle or promise X3
Faith ideally strongest in one's own spirit → social leaders; today's edu → lost soul, no meaning X3

Ch 8 Righteousness (52)

Definition of righteousness doing the right thing, what is right thing, hard to judge X2 (2)

Learning right and wrong (11)

Conform to spirituality right, not conform wrong, Kill, hurt others, rape, abuse, steal X4
Moral values not cover all, must search answers in spirit, beyond refrain of not do bad X2
Must be fully ready to do right at all time, transcend materialism a must X2
Learning right and wrong laborious and time consuming, divination helps X3

Spiritually Righteous Much Harder Than Mentally Righteous (14)

To be righteous, the spirit must be awake, focus, right principles, each breath X4

Inject the spirit with righteousness at all times X3
Doing is key, watch environment in and people contacted, no unrighteous X4
Thoughts is ultimate practice, especially beginning of a thought X3

Methods of Practicing Righteousness (6)
Watch one's own deeds 24/7, and fill them with it, especially small ones X2
Watch thoughts 24/7, and fill them with it, especially small thought X3
To the point of natural habit X1

The End Goal (17)
Feeling righteous at all time, doing every small task according to this righteousness X2
Having every thought based on this righteousness, experiment of thoughts injected in water X12
Influence others to be righteous X3

Suggested Research Topics (3)
The relationship between posture and righteousness X2
why Ren and righteousness most emphasized in most religions X1

Ch 9 The Spiritual Wisdom (111)
Originated from spirit, not brain or mind, spiritual awake a must X2 (6)
See through truth, can give up learned or possessed; US, Soviet, Hollywood examples X4

Differences between Spiritual Wisdom and Mental Smartness (17)
Street smart vs. academic smart, always sharp vs. sharp and dull depends, medication X4
Shrewd all time vs. depends, good memory never forget vs. OK to release X6
Wish good last and bad ends totally wrong, realize all end eventually X2
Linear vs. whole picture 3D, reasoning and logic vs. root cause and principles X5

See through One's Own Death (29)
Show real size of a fertilized egg to compare and realize eventual return to earth X1
Learn anatomy and composition of physical body, dissect animals, corpses X3
See decay process of corpses, smells, burial process, and tomb X2
Writing a will, assume never see family again, joy of seeing or hearing them again each day X2
Through the realization of one's own eventual bodily death to appreciate one's own spirit X2
Mourn one's own death before others to know what it is like X5
Impossible to go all places and do all things X1

Understand physical death not = spiritual death, water alive and thought experiments X6

Inability to mourn one's own death a marker of unable to expect one's own death deep in heart

Such ability only achieved by months or years of practices X4

Some spirits weak and may never return to Tao, Reasoning Heaven, recycles of spirits X3

Prioritization (10)

Improving self before criticizing, easier, effective, unselfishly give to others X4

Prioritize purchase, house, car, grocery, clothing, shoes, car, house, and computer X2

Things done align with life goal, goal setting, limited time of life, Consolidate chores X2

Recreational activities important, when a goal reached, set another of casual X2

Organization (9)

Starts from organizing toys to personal room, X1

Starts from words to sentences to articles, from outlining to writing X3

Starts from visible to abstract, reduce redundant to one or zero X2

To facilitate life goals, to write and read well, to impress on spirituality X2

Less is more, easier to organize X1

Big Picture and Decision Making (18)

Training of big picture from first grade, see consequences to learn X5

Always step way back first to see big picture before decide, small can impact big X2

Have a divination tool to help choose at teenage years X2

All made at zero point, not to follow another decision or other people, root cause X3

Following fashion or others blindly can be big wrong, or even major sin X4

Traffic light or 3D cross road as an example X2

Be Versatile, Not Just One Interest (15)

Mind linear in nature so stick to one only, spirit 3D in nature so versatile X3

Education theory well rounded program balanced, but wrongly assume one major X1

Principle of consistency applies internally, not externally X3

Conflicts of personality among multiple spouses real problem, not the versatility X1

Entrepreneurs, CEO, presidents must be versatile to deal with various problems X4

Being versatile human nature, candy stores and candies spiritual nature, like sex and food X3

Nothing Is Sure Until Finished (7)

Linear nature of smartness often looks too far ahead, 2017 Super Bowl, other sports X2

Life goals, do not bank on time available, finish early X1

Keep on the toes and do the best all the time except at leisure X1

Life is not limitless or guaranteed for reaching old age X3

Ch 10 Coordinate, Balance, Submerge, and Unify (96)

Five merits to act as one, heavenly deposit vs. five merits X9 (9)

The Absolute Nature of the Five Merits (15)

Eternal truth and lies not opposite, *Time Magazine* article an example X6

Why nearly opposite of merits not good, place of exerting forces matters X4

Not to change self or others, but to repair and return to original shape of spirit X5

The Meaning of Life (15)

No general life meaning, only individual, depend on individual choice X3

Every tiny life met impacts choice of meaning, edu of improve meaning, not $$$ X2

Divination instills meaning before spirit strong enough, push and pull, like guide and whip X5

High spirit experienced know life meaning, Ex: write this book, originally goal $$$ X3

Writing of books -> increase of authors' meaning -> increase readers' meaning X2

The Five Saints and the Two Almighty Gods (62)

Forewords about our ultimate respect to them and purpose of criticism X2

Appropriateness of Mohammad and Islam, too appropriate to be fully righteous X8

Consistency in Jesus Christ and Christianity, too much faith insufficient wisdom X8

Righteous Father the God and emotional Mother the God, may overly so X8

Righteousness of Lao-Tzu and Taoism, abundant righteous to nearly dormant X8

Wisdom of Buddha and Buddhism, high wisdom tiny inappropriate X8

Ren of Confucius and his teaching, lots of Ren not enough faith X8

Being superbly extremely perfect in act or performance not really Tao on earth X2

Slight imperfection expected and justified, lust, nudism, sexual education in early age X10

Ch 11 Sin, Wrong, and Mistake (SWM) (92)

General definitions: What are sins, wrongs, and mistakes, or SWM? X3 (9)

Sin: principle right but purposely against it X2

Wrong: principle wrong or unaware of the wrong principle X2

Mistake: Principle right but err or fault in executing the principle X2

Comparing SWM and carnal laws (24)

Generally correlate to each other X2

Purpose: Carnal laws to maintain social order; SWM to maintain personal spiritual order X4

Domain: Carnal laws exterior focus and may extend to interior; SWM interior focus and . . . X3

Substance: Carnal laws behavioral focus; SWM mental focus; edu defined X5

Goal: Carnal laws social peace < SWM spiritual peace X2

Conflicts: increased tensions in countries; SWM lose to twisted laws X4

Examples: carnal laws jailed many innocent, Jesus as example X2

Justice: SWM > Carnal laws X2

The Sin (14)

Killing another person, even in wartime, judged and sentenced by spirit X5

Abortion may be a sin recorded in the soul, if one spiritually believes X2

Drunk driving, abuse, self-hurting to the point of abandoning one's own spirit, risk X2

Rape to satisfy lust, even a spouse, lust and covet neighbor's wife

Disrespect of authority or the poor, dishonor parents, inappropriate X1

Stealing and robbing unrighteous goods, even small amount or trivial materials X2

Unrighteously lie to others for selfish purposes, unfaithful to close people

Not deciding or choosing wisely, any serious violation of five merits often is sin X1

More spiritual knowledge -> more likely sin X1

The Wrong (15)

Not thinking right principles of doing things, let lust or unrighteous desires lead X1

Ex: playing football for wrong reasons, the ultimate reasoning counts the most X2

Career, academic major, friend, companion, travel, outing, meeting, and phone call X5

Beware of all encompass reason and ultimate purpose, especially life goal and purpose X4

If the ultimate goal of life or reasoning is wrong, millions of wrongs in a lifetime X2

One cannot serve spirit and evil, or God and devil, at the same time X1

The Mistake (15)

Negligence can cause others' death, killing a trespasser X1

Focus and attention on all matters at hand, water seep into laptop as example X3

Do not text and drive at the same time, speed kills X2

Dating two potential mates at the same time akin to task at once X3

Purposely not have a goal in life for each period, retirement a mistake, lead to illness X2

Always have a vision and goal in mind at each moment of life, unless in school X1

Falsehood: A beauty recognized by all is not a true beauty; neither is a goodness X1

Japan, German examples; Russia and China exists for good reasons X2

SWM Key to Spiritual Realization (15)

Each individual drastically differs in SWM and method to eliminate X5

Eventually to real heaven inside the mind, ultimate joy and relief X3

Practice must be 24/7, not a second lapse, mindful and focused attention the key X2

Always watch self, not others or the outer distractions and attractions X2

When SWM mostly free can truly help and teach others spirituality, or blind leads blind X3

Ch 12 Tao (Way, Principle, and Life) (113)

Pennsylvania woman walk 26 miles in 30 hours on snow X3 (**16**)

Though inspirational, lessons of not doing divination a huge one X2

New place or people potentially dangerous, trust in GPS but not divination an irony X2

What seemed to help to survive might cause her near death, modern common sickness X2

Stuck in mud not deadly, decision of hiking was, survival training adversely helped, climbed to high ground, right way for help X2

Tao of Eric and Karen probably wrong for years, what they should have learned X3

Join NG blessed x die in war, power of Tao hidden X2

Explanation of Tao, Yin, Yang, and Cycles (22)

The way, truth, life of words of Jesus analyzed, not just spirituality, how related X6

Yin and yang from Tao, both must be harmonic to return to Tao X3

Thoughts, ideas, wishes inside yin; speaking, behaviors, deeds, moves outside yang X3

Yin and yang not absolute, both have a little of the other inside, must cycle X5

Cycles of mind and low spirits unending; high spirits cycle self no end or beginning X3

Mind pure yin, spirit pure yang, female on average higher spirit than male X2

Heaven and Hell (14)

All in mind, heaven not permanent if violate, loose and restrictive law (see a lady unjust) exists X3

Tao 1 foot Devil 1 yard, Devil not oppose but tests, humble as Tao no devil X2

Laws of Truth Heaven: roughly vs. precisely, whole pic v Tree, on pornography X2
Permanent one, sweep floors afraid not even want, due to obsessions and SWM X2
Deposit may < SWM, what people should be afraid of or cry, not leave loved ones or this world X1
Enough heavenly deposits starts today and now, the bagel story of some author X1
Done many good deeds on earth still not sure, faith to the last minute vital X2
Tao heaven, chi heaven, physical heaven, physical hell, chi hell, Tao hell X1

God the Mother and Her Ten Commandments (31)
Some forewords and prologue, Size differ Holy Bible and 10 commandments of God Mother X6
Yang lots words explicit, yin few words implicit, no less powerful X1
Gist of the Ten Commandments of Mother God, first chapter X4
Second chapter X6, 3th to 6th X4, 7th to 10th X8
Epilogue and the thoughts of authors X2

Divination More Art Than Science (30)
Recognize opposite word of sarcasm, no facial expression to read or tone of voice to hint X4
Bad indicate as good harder to recognize than reverse X1
Pre-conditions to exist before asking, must be really uncertain after reasoning X5
Must try to match indications with one's own reasoning to decide error or opposite word X1
Heavenly life = spiritual property, act out = Tao, reason and divination half and half X2
Personal biases or stubborn can cause wrong interpretation, addiction to porn X2
Mutual interaction, like relationship, define truthfulness of results. More sincere better results X4
Such relationship dynamic and changing over time, must make it steady X2
Ask too many or too few not conform to Tao, just right amount X3
Most beneficial use = reflect SWM, simple better, 64 words in Book of Change X4
Why $50 stayed, maybe divine orders included, not apply again within 1 month X2

Ch 13 Reform of Governments (71)
Injustice of government rampant, examples, good president not solution X5 **(14)**
Only good education and true democracy collect enough willpower to change governments X3
Democracy bases on education. Direct democracy defined and examples X3

Many functions of the current three branches of the governments inappropriate X3

The Quality Branch (15)
Reasons for this branch X3
Goal: government structure improvement, fair and just elections, qualifying people, survey X1
Functions of this branch X7
Personnel requirements for this branch X4

The Structure-Improving Function of Quality Branch (14)
Budgeting and department head qualifying functions should be moved to this Quality Branch X4
All government budgets and policies must be approved by volunteering citizens X3
Secure Internet connection with volunteering citizens crucial X2
Frequency of vote should be few weeks to few months, not few years like now X1
Expect to do research, decision process need time and effort, limit # of departments X1
Number of hires in each department controlled, private donation should be allowed X1
Supervisors and managers elected by workers, department heads hand-picked and approved X2

The Qualifying and Surveying Functions of Quality Branch (9)
The qualifying function of candidates, volunteers to vote, or jury duty X5
The surveying function of measuring satisfaction and performance X3
Functions correlated X1

The Investigation and Prosecution Branch (6)
Monitoring and investigation branch must be independent, no party affiliation X3
Initiate investigation to assert justice X2
Chief of this branch elected& X1

Reforms of Legislative Branch (3)
Votes of representatives can be replaced by pool volunteers X1
Locality of votes can be preserved X1
Chief of this branch elected separately X1

Reforms of Judicial Branch (4)
Supreme Court justices no party affiliation allowed, same as judges X1
Jury randomly selected from such pool of volunteers, let who doesn't like jury or law be X1
Simplified and free justice for small claims X2

Reforms of Executive Branch (4)
Presidential power sharply reduced through infrastructural change X1
Brazil's president moved out because of "ghosts," residence should not be restricted X1
President, chiefs, and department heads not paid, treasury bonds required X2

Ch 14 The Reform of Companies (40)
Article on *New York Times* magazine about rudeness world trend, its origin X3 **(11)**
Rushing to save time and money cause mental rudeness and disrespect X3
Erosion of moral values, how regulating public companies can fix root of rudeness X2
Compare treatment of workers between East and West X3

Responsibilities of Governments to Regulate Companies (21)
Gov do first then regulate public companies, private company and others will follow X4
No 1 share 1 vote, should be 1 shareholder 1 vote, national election no rich > votes
Rich may not better idea or methodology on mgmt., biased known or selfish
Join < six months probably no vote, required to buy shares after such timeframe X5
Supervisors and managers elected, position qualified as # of shares holding X2
Equal or less pay due to less real work, more dividends make up difference X2
CEO and other top-level officials may be elected, chosen by the board, or combo X2
All board members and governing body elected each, not # share hold, WF BA examples X2
At least 1 gov employee /1000 workers, watch discrimination, violation of law and policy X2
Decisions participation as governments, should be mandatory X2

High Company Qualities Encouraged with Incentives (7)
Innovation of company structure, Apple example of innovation first priority X1
Take good care of workers and let them decide their own hours, good quality X1
Use company culture, friendship among workers, and inspiration to draw wills X3
If all implemented, sufficient to turn tide of money and time first X2

Ch 15 Reforms of Public Education (86)
Reform of government and public companies can't root until education take root X1 **(6)**
Not knowing the why of education produces mediocre country heads X3
More edu → more capacity to do bad, some examples, Wells Fargo fraud X2
Industrialization and individuality good but not totally compatible X

Learning methods > important > teaching methods (14)
Learning methods to be introduced at early age and gradually take over X2
Discovery of interests important to match introduction of learning methods X4
Work = Learning → working meaningful, otherwise animals or robots of countries X4
Entrepreneur learning from mistakes, learning by doing X4

The Right to Choose a Teacher (15)
Problems of designated teachers, only need 1 good, can last 12 years
mentor, 10 minutes of guidance > effective than hours of lecture X6
Each student can choose their own teacher like company workers elect a boss X1
Depending on many factors to choose: affinity, quality, knowledge, spirituality, personality, appearance, patience, methodology X5
The cost of private teacher/tutor/mentor might not exceed today's educational system X3

Differences of knowledge edu ↔ spiritual edu (13)
Students can be better than teachers, abstract vs. concrete X5
Knowledge edu only → most failure, because knowledge highest priority, not meaning X3 Learning why > important than learning itself, the reasoning drives motivation X2
All saints suffered phy or emo, not just Jesus, the reason of suffer is the spirit behind X3

The Teaching of Sin Wrong and Mistake (5)
Few is saints on earth, not even previous saints reincarnated X3
Nobody is guilty, but forgo SWM = guilty X1
Learning of past mistakes, what works what does not, *Challenger* disaster X1
The Teaching of Avoiding and Conquering Addictions (5)

Prevention the very first lesson, diverse interest the second X3
Locations of knowledge and addiction differ X1
Determination and people who succeeded important X1

The Teaching of Divination (4)
Some prerequisites and proper attitudes required, divination help to decide X4

The Learning of Zodiac and Astrology (11)
Reason behind learning and accuracy problems should be disclosed before learning X4
Main purpose is to learn one's own weakness X2
Not to use others' weakness against others, not to find a mate X2
Make up one's own weakness at the right and critical moment, the bagel incident X3

Simplicity, Prioritization, and Organizational are Keys (10)
Symbols are simpler and more abstract to facilitate understanding of spirituality X3
Prioritization is the key to separate the importance from the less so, life goal X3
Easiest to organize = nothing, and the next easiest is one X2
Organization is the key to concentration, focus, communication, achieve, others X2

Growth ultimately important, otherwise die off **(7)**
Focus on individual in the right direction, but one step further needed = individual growth
Only individual lesson plans can foster individual growth, not class lessons
Focus on group growth → Some regress, Focus on individual growth → all grow
Spiritual growth not achieved by mere memorizing, but the reason of memorizing
Writing of this book helps readers to grow, but also the authors

Ch 16 Revelation (12)
Reasons of try to omit this chapter: time constraint, not to steal thunder of Bible, to appear scientific, and to boost the chance of being included as a science field, disapproved X4
The world of Datong envisioned before Confucius's time and further explained X3
The comparison of modern world with the ideal, way to reach it X5

REFERENCES

1. New fruit tops "Dirty Dozen" list of most contaminated produce. By Ashley Welch. CBS News, April 12, 2016, 3:48 PM. http://www. cbsnews.com/news/new-fruit-tops-dirty-dozen-list-of-most-contami nated-produce/.
2. EWG's 2017 Shopper's Guide to Pesticides in Produce. Accessed 5/11/2017. https://www.ewg.org/foodnews/summary.php.
3. Tai chi master studied for power to control body. By Krista Conger. Stanford Report, May 7, 2008. Accessed 3/29/2017. http://news.stan ford.edu/news/2008/may7/med-taichi-050708.html.
4. Rehab Success Rates and Statistics. American Addiction Centers. Ac cessed 5/13/2017 http://americanaddictioncenters.org/rehab-guide/ success-rates-and-statistics/.
5. The Emergence of Individuality in Genetically Identical Mice. May 13, 2013. Accessed 5/13/2017. http://www.kurzweilai.net/the-emer gence-of-individuality-in-genetically-identical-mice.
6. How Can Identical Twins Turn Out So Different? Jon Hamilton. NPR: All Things Considered. May 9, 20134:19 PM ET. http://www.npr.org/ sections/health-shots/2013/05/14/182633402/how-can-identical-twins-turn-out-so-different 4/24/2017.
7. First Peoples. PBS. Aired: 2015-06-24 04:00. http://www.pbs.org/first-peoples/home/ 3/29/2017.
8. Top 3 Factors Influencing Personality Development. Article Shared by Aishwarya Sinha. Accessed 4/24/2017. http://www.psychologydiscus sion.net/personality-development-2/top-3-factors-influencing-person ality-development/1934.
9. Environment in Personality. Mee Young Jeong. Accessed 5/15/2017. https://www.citelighter.com/science/psychology/knowledgecards/ environment-in-personality.
10. Let Sleeping Bears Lie: Even When Hibernating, They Are Primed to Fend Off a Sudden Attack. By Richard Hartley-parkinson. Updated: 04:23 EDT, 17 August 2011. http://www.dailymail.co.uk/sciencetech/ article-2026862/Let-sleeping-bears-lie-Even-hibernating-sense-pres ence-humans.html.
11. Spiritual but Not Religious. Wikipedia. Accessed 5/19/2017 https:// en.wikipedia.org/wiki/Spiritual_but_not_religious.

12. Spiritual but Not Religious—The vital interplay between submission and freedom. Amy Hollywood. Home/Winter/Spring 2010. Vol. 38, Nos. 1 and 2. Accessed 5/19/2017 https://bulletin.hds.harvard.edu/ articles/winterspring2010/spiritual-not-religious.

13. Spiritual but Not Religious. Wikipedia. Accessed 4/5/2017. Definition paragraph 3, 4. https://en.wikipedia.org/wiki/Spiritual_but_not_re ligious.

14. Waste Generation. Urban development series—knowledge papers. Accessed 5/25/2017 http://siteresources.worldbank.org/INTURBAN DEVELOPMENT/Resources/336387-1334852610766/Chap3.pdf.

15. Great Human Odyssey. PBS. Accessed 4/6/2017 http://www.pbs.org/ wgbh/nova/evolution/great-human-odyssey.html.

16. 11 Animals that Mate for Life. Mother Nature Network. Accessed 5/29/2017. http://www.mnn.com/earth-matters/animals/photos/11-animals-that-mate-for-life/old-faithful.

17. WATER, Thank you, I hate you, You're stupid, and Ignore. Inventor3. YouTube. Rice Consciousness experiment, inspired by Dr. Masaru Emoto. https://www.youtube.com/watch?v=NQDlCfykPx8.

18. Secret of Water—The Movie. Documentary Film. February 23, 2015. Accessed 5/7/2017. http://secretofwaterthemovie.com/

19. Read President Trump's Interview with TIME on Truth and Falsehoods. Published 3/22. Accessed 4/26/2017. http://time.com/4710456/don ald-trump-time-interview-truth-falsehood/

20. I Ching. Wikipedia. Accessed 4/27/2017. https://en.wikipedia.org/ wiki/I_Ching.

21. Milankovitch Cycles and Glaciation. Indiana University Bloomington. Accessed 6/29/2017. http://www.indiana.edu/~geol105/images/ gaia_chapter_4/milankovitch.htm.

22. Milutin Milankovitch. NASA. Accessed 6/29/2017. https://earthobser vatory.nasa.gov/Features/Milankovitch/milankovitch_2.php.

23. Las Vegas Woman Who Walked 26 Miles in Snowy Grand Canyon to Save Family Tells Ordeal. Dec 27 2016, 9:17 am ET. By Emma Margo lin and John Getter. Accessed 4/20/2017. http://www.nbcnews.com/ news/us-news/las-vegas-woman-who-walked-26-miles-snowy-grand-canyon-n700371.

24. The Age of Rudeness. Rachel Cusk. the *New York Times Magazine*. Feb, 15, 2017. p38. Read Feb 19, 2017.

INDEX

Edwards Brothers Inc.
Ann Arbor MI. USA
October 13, 2017